Pour Rebe

Avec mon soutien
amical.

Corinne

Wage and Welfare

New Perspectives on Employment and Social Rights in Europe

P.I.E.-Peter Lang

Bruxelles · Bern · Berlin · Frankfurt/M · New York · Oxford · Wien

This book is the fruit of a collective endeavour, but we owe special thanks to three members of the network for their crucial contributions to making this publication possible: Corinne Gobin, who established contact with the publisher, P.I.E.-Peter Lang; Virginie Vathelet, our network administrative co-ordinator at GREE/CNRS, for her superb assistance and her patient and professional work in preparing the manuscript for publication; and Merle Shore, our translator, whose rigorous approach and valuable comments helped us to clarify our thinking and to bring our work to the English-speaking public.

This project was funded by the European Commission within the framework of the 5th European Research Programme. We are particularly grateful to Fadila Boughanemi of the Research Directorate-General, who has been our network's scientific officer for the past several years, for her strong interest, precious help and constant encouragement.

Qu'il leur soit rendu ici à chacun un vibrant hommage !

Bernadette CLASQUIN, Nathalie MONCEL,
Mark HARVEY & Bernard FRIOT (eds.)

Wage and Welfare

New Perspectives on Employment and Social Rights in Europe

"Work & Society"
No.43

© P.I.E.-Peter Lang S.A.
PRESSES INTERUNIVERSITAIRES EUROPÉENNES
Brussels, 2004
1 avenue Maurice, 1050 Brussels, Belgium
info@peterlang.com; www.peterlang.net

ISSN 1376-0955
ISBN 90-5201-214-8
US ISBN 0-8204-6616-6
D/2004/5678/08
Printed in Germany

Bibliographic information published by "Die Deutsche Bibliothek"

"Die Deutsche Bibliothek" lists this publication in the "Deutsche Nationalbibliografie"; detailed bibliographic data is available in the Internet at <http://dnb.ddb.de>.

*CIP available from the British Library, GB
and the Library of Congress, USA.*

Contents

List of Acronyms

ABM	Arbeitsbeschaffungsmaßnahme – Employment-creating measures
AAH	Allocation Adulte Handicapé – Disabled adults allowance
AAW	Algemene Arbeidsongeschiktheids Wet – General disablement benefits act
AGIRC	Association Générale des Institutions de Retraite des Cadres – Supplementary pension scheme for managers
AOW	Algemene Ouderdoms Wet – General old age pensions act
API	Allocation Parent Isolé – Single parent allowance
ARRCO	Association des Régimes de Retraite Complémentaire – Supplementary pension scheme for non-managerial workers
CEC	Commission of the European Communities
CJEC	Court of Justice of the European Communities
CMU	Couverture Maladie Universelle – Universal health coverage
DARES	Direction de l'Animation de la Recherche des Études et des Statistiques – Directorate for research of the French ministry of labour
DG	Directorate-General
ECSC	European Coal and Steel Community
EEC	European Economic Community
EMU	Economic and Monetary Union
GDP	Gross Domestic Product
JWG	Jeugd Werk Garantie Plan – Youth employment guarantee plan
OECD	Organisation for Economic Co-operation and Development
PARE	Programme d'Aide au Retour à l'Emploi – Back to work plan
RMI	Revenu Minimum d'Insertion – Minimum income benefit
SEA	Single European Act
SMIC	Salaire Minimum Interprofessionnel de Croissance – National growth minimum wage
TEU	Treaty of the European Union
UNICE	Union of Industrial and Employers' Confederations of Europe NBNB
WAJONG	Wet Arbeidsongeschiktheidsvoorziening voor jonggehandicapten – Disablement assistance act for young handicapped persons

WAO	Wet op de Arbeids Ongeschiktheidsverzekering – Disablement benefits act
WAZ	Wet Arbeidsongeschiktheidsverzekering Zelfstandigen – Self-employed persons disablement benefits act
WIW	Wet Inschakeling Werzoekenden – Jobseekers integration act
WVA-SPAK	Wet Vermindering Arbeidskosten – Lowering labour costs act

Wage and Welfare:
Background and Content

Bernadette CLASQUIN and Nathalie MONCEL

While the construction of the European Union is envisaged, first and foremost, in terms of economic integration, the question of the well-being of its working populations remains politically conflictual and is yet to be clearly addressed. Research circles in the social sciences are producing alternative analyses that can prove of use for those committed to furthering the construction of a social Europe. And those of us who seek to achieve that aim by forming an international team find ourselves embarking on a truly collective venture.

The present book represents a progress report on the work undertaken by a network whose line of enquiry centres on the social construction of employment. The aim is not to present research results but to introduce the problematic we are developing in order to contribute to the debate. Our first three years of discussion and reflection, and our concerted effort to grasp national realities, have led us to choose a particular point of entry for our analysis: that of the resources linked to employment and social protection and channelled through the central vehicle of the wage tied to the employment relation. We have sought to develop an original conceptual framework based on the following hypothesis: an analysis of the resources flowing through the wage and the associated rights for the population as a whole enables us to account for significant changes in the spheres of employment and social protection. The key question raised by the chapters in this volume is that of the construction/transformation of social rights over resources.

These problematics have been addressed, although from different angles and with diverse aims, by other researchers whose works have stimulated our thinking and with which we initiate a debate in the chapters that follow. The majority of these works, however, either develop analytical categories that are marked by the social protection systems of the northern European countries, or apply Anglo-Saxon categories to other national systems. A primary objective of our group, which is largely composed of researchers from the Latin countries, has been to propose an alternative approach. Our idea has been to take the construction of employment in France and the southern European countries as starting point and to further develop the resulting analytical methods by integrating data from the British, German and Dutch contexts[1]. The categories used to elaborate our conceptual framework seek to take account of national realities which cannot always be expressed by the accepted Anglo-Saxon terminology. This has entailed a cautious approach to the choice of vocabulary, which is explained in the discussion on terminology that follows this introduction.

A collective process

The present work is the fruit of several years of collective debate and discussion. However, it must be seen as a freeze-frame, a working tool that will be honed by future empirical studies. We have been engaged in a labour of preparation, of establishing a common framework and understanding amongst a transnational team of people, now ready to take the next step towards a new research agenda. The analytical framework and categories that will be presented here, as well as their current limitations, are so closely related to the conditions under which they were developed that the latter warrant a brief explanation.

The "Social Construction of Employment" network was formed in 1997 with the initial aim of examining the relationship between employment dynamics and the causes of social exclusion. The basic hypothesis was that exclusion does not mean exclusion from work but from employment as socially defined by wage forms, working conditions and related social rights. The production of detailed national case studies permitted the network to progressively construct our current line of enquiry by bringing our analysis of employment into relation with an analysis of the wage and social rights.

The network received the support of the European Commission within the framework of the 4th and 5th Research Programmes (Targeted Socio-Economic Research and Improving the Socio-Economic Knowledge Base). The initial group comprised French, Italian, Spanish, Portuguese and British research teams. It was enlarged in 2000 to include participants from two northern European countries (Germany and the Netherlands), as well as researchers from Belgium with a view to addressing issues related to the construction of the European Union.

---

[1] The analysis will, in the future, be extended to take account of other northern European countries which we were unable to include at the time of writing.

The network has now been joined by an Austrian team, and on the basis of the analytical framework presented in this book, is currently working on a research project called "Employees' Resources and Social Rights in Europe" (RESORE)[2].

The countries of origin of the fifteen authors of the present work are, for a large part, continental, which reflects our initial choice to favour the southern European countries. While all are academics, we come from different disciplinary backgrounds, and our trajectories and levels of experience are diverse (about half were just beginning their academic careers or had a precarious professional status at the time of writing). And yet, a true dialogue was established that has enabled us to further develop our problematic. In the essence of what makes an encounter, as Merleau-Ponty (1945: p. 407) observes,

> Il y a en particulier un objet culturel qui va jouer un rôle essentiel dans la perception d'autrui: c'est le langage. Dans l'expérience du dialogue, il se constitue entre autrui et moi un terrain commun, ma pensée et la sienne ne font qu'un seul tissu, mes propos et ceux de l'interlocuteur sont appelés par l'état de la discussion, ils s'insèrent dans une opération commune dont aucun de nous n'est le créateur[3].

Our previous research experiences, whether these were individual or as members of national research teams, were thus expressed through studies and discussions of national realities; it was in this work process that concepts stemming from our national research environments were expressed and exchanged and that we reached beyond our respective ethnocentrisms in order to find transversal categories for the dynamics under study. The issue of language is part of this effort to understand national realities: the process of objectivation requires a rigorous endeavour to name the object without stripping it of its societal connotations, without crushing or dulling its meaning. This endeavour has been one of the major concerns in writing this book even if the different chapters show how much remains to be accomplished in the in-depth debates to come.

Our search for complementarity has led us to draw on four disciplinary fields – sociology, economy, political science and social psychol-

---

[2]   Website address: http://www.univ-nancy2.fr/RECHERCHE/EPS/RESORE.

[3]   There is a particular cultural object that will play an essential role in the perception of the other: language. In the experience of dialogue, a common ground between the other and myself is constituted, my thinking and the other's thinking form a single fabric, my words and those of my interlocutor are brought forth by the state of the discussion, they are part of a common venture of which neither of us is the creator.

ogy – in forms that vary of course according to the academic trajectory and country of origin of each of the authors. This collaboration reflects a clear choice to examine the linkages between employment, resources and rights from different points of view. It has involved developing a form of transdisciplinarity, which according to Dupuis (2002: p. 195), is characterised "by an integrative movement. But it presupposes [...] 'opening up' to the multiplicity of 'causalities' or levels of meaning that are at one and the same time indissociable, irreducible to one another, and complementary". Thus, the construction of our object proceeds from the "recognition of the existence of different levels of reality governed by different types of logic" and "does not strive for mastery of several disciplines but aims to open all disciplines to that which they share and to that which lies beyond them"(Nicolescu, Freitas and Morin, 1994). Our micro-society of researchers is thus engaged in a *co-construction of meaning*, and the conceptual framework presented in the first chapter is the most tangible result of this endeavour. The chapters that follow, in which various facets of the object of our research are introduced, were written by sub-groups formed on the basis of their interest in the themes chosen by the group as a whole. The book is the product of this continual going back and forth between individual members, sub-groups and the group as a whole.

This "opening up" cannot however simply be limited to a conjunction of disciplines; our shared vision has been sustained by a form of collective motivation, for, as Bourdieu (2002: p. 173) so rightly observes, "*l'analyste fait partie du monde qu'il cherche à objectiver et la science qu'il produit n'est qu'une des forces qui s'affrontent dans ce monde*"[4]. By taking the analysis of the resource flows channelled through the wage as the point of entry for an examination of the transformations of employment and social rights, our network aims to contribute to a critical analysis of current reforms. Ultimately, this means both engaging in scientific debate and providing arguments for the social movement.

The originality of our approach

The composition of our group and the topics we deal with clearly place a comparative approach at the centre of the process of scientific production. Our ambition has been to rethink the components of the employment-wage-social protection triptych and their modes of articula-

---

[4]   "Analysts belong to the world they are seeking to objectivate and the science they produce is but one of the forces confronting each other in this world."

tion. Thus, the wage is not examined as a price, cost or income, but as an institution establishing the linkage between the other two components of this triptych. Employment is not simply an input of productive systems or a factor of social integration: we consider it to be the dominant mode of social recognition of work in capitalist societies. And social protection is not viewed as just a matter for the state, but as being an integral part of the wage relation.

Changes in employment and social protection are examined through transformations of the institutional forms governing the circulation of resources. This approach is of interest because it permits to establish a relation between the question of social protection and the more overall question of the total reproduction of labour, on the one hand, and the creation and distribution of the wealth produced by the division of labour, on the other. The nature of the linkages between social protection and production is often a blind spot in analyses of social policy (commonly referred to as "welfare" studies) that examine the respective roles of the market, the state and the family, but do not consider their close interconnections with the productive sphere[5]. In symmetrical fashion, analyses of systems of production and their transformations tend to reduce the sphere of social protection to one of the institutions necessary to the functioning of capitalism, and accompanying its evolution[6].

Our line of questioning thus, to some extent, ties up with current preoccupations concerning a reconfiguration of the European social model. This model has been defined, beyond national specificities, by such characteristics as "more stable jobs; opportunities for reskilling; regular wage increases; regular and shorter working hours; improving working conditions; diversified social protection against various risks; collective bargaining, information and consultation rights."[7]

---

[5] A recent study on the future of social protection systems in Europe states that the question of the institutional design of welfare systems "has to do with how we wish to produce welfare. This means deciding on how responsibilities ought to be divided between markets (purchased welfare) families (the reciprocity of kin) and government (solidarity)" (Esping-Andersen G., Gallie D., Hemerijck A. and Myles J., 2001: p. 13).

[6] As stated by Mishra (1996: p. 320): "What is of interest here is the economistic and functionalist nature of this interpretation of the Keynesian or Fordist welfare state and its successor regime. In equating a particular stage in capitalist production with a functionally appropriate from of state modes of economic and social regulation, this approach tends to devaluate the role of politics and ideology."

[7] Rodrigues, M.J. (2003).

15

It is precisely the national variations of the links between employment, the wage and social protection that fuelled the network's discussions and reflections. In reference to the societal analysis approach (Maurice, 2000), differences between countries are not considered here as particularities to be related to a theoretical model: they constitute givens that need to be explained in terms of the inter-relationships between political, economic and social factors in each country[8]. Thus, comparisons are made between the societal complexes within which each phenomenon is socially situated and constructed (Maurice, 2000). A comparative approach is accordingly an integral part of the development of an analytical framework seeking to account for configurations and their transformations. It is perhaps here, in the analysis of the dynamics of national systems, that the network is best able to contribute new elements.

Our approach, which took as starting point a description of the three basic dimensions of the wage relation (mobilisation, use and reproduction of labour), has led us to distinguish four spheres for the observation of the articulation between the components of the employment-wage-social protection triptych. These are: industrial relations systems, public policy frameworks, employment systems and social hierarchies. Our hypothesis is that it is within these spheres – which we consider decisive but not exhaustive – and in their internal and external tensions that the processes of institutionalisation and transformation of the links between employment, the wage and social protection are to be found.

This book thus proposes to explore how each of these spheres participates in the construction of the triptych in a specific way depending on the country, and to identify the vehicles of change in a range of areas, such as transformations of the forms of employment, the development of labour market policies, pension reforms, the swing to a logic of competencies in vocational training systems, the implementation of social pacts, and last but not least, the processes involved in the construction of the European Union. The comparisons presented in the chapters that follow thus focus more on an identification of the sources of change than on a systematic presentation of societal logics and their transformation.

---

[8] Berthelot, J.M. (2000: p. 90) gives a clear comparison between a standard analytical model and societal analysis: "The same abstract relationship which, logically, exists prior to its development into concrete forms, is no longer conceived of as unfolding within different societal contexts; rather, these societal contexts are now seen as producing specific types of organisation and forms of generality. In other words, there is a shift from model-building to a constructionist perspective."

Contents of the book

The first two chapters lay the basis of the conceptual framework used to analyse the links between employment, the wage and social protection. Chapter 1 develops the instruments for the analysis of the modes of construction of rights over resources and their transformations. Considering the wage as the central institution channelling resource flows linked to employment and financing social protection, it confronts the debates on the limits of and distinctions between social rights and private rights, and market and non-market forms. It seeks to go beyond static oppositions and the bias of an ethnocentric representation of a specific reality, and proposes categories for analysing resource flows, and the conditions of entitlement to and management of these flows, that permit to account for their linkages and the nature of the social rights stemming from them.

The second chapter focuses on employment as a social construction, and addresses the question of the linkages between work and social protection within the framework of the wage relation. It shows how these linkages are often considered from a functionalist perspective whereas they are constituent of employment in wage societies. The identification of the changes in employment brought about by transformations of resource flows sheds fresh light on the impact of public labour market policies and on the emergence of the phenomenon of social exclusion. Thus the link between work and social protection offers a new angle for the analysis of the effects of public policies and opens the way for questions on possible alternative bases for rights to resources.

The following chapters each explore the spheres in which the links between work, wage and social protection are constituted, in an attempt to reveal the forces of change and to evaluate the tensions specific to certain societal spaces.

Chapter 3 is of a particular nature, in that it draws on the results of a prior investigation in order to present a typology of resource regimes and interpret the changes in rights to and over resources that have taken place in three countries. Political debates and modalities of power are examined in order to identify dynamics of change in recent reforms of systems of employment and social protection. Here it is thus the sphere of public action that is being observed, bringing to the fore the question of the evolution of the role of the state in the transformations of the status of the wage-earner and the citizen.

The focus of Chapter 4 is on the sphere of social hierarchies. It develops a particular aspect of the construction of rights to resources through an examination of the role of credentials as mediator between work and wage. This perspective reveals some of the institutional forms serving to determine the wage. The comparison between three systems of vocational training highlights debates on the passage from qualification/credentials to competencies, and reveals how the issues diverge according to the impact of the educational sphere on the determination of rights to resources.

Chapter 5 focuses on the forms of power linked to rights over resources, and in particular, the role played by unions in three countries in recent years. Common trends towards wage moderation, the decentralisation of collective bargaining and the instrumentalisation of European integration are identified, and the role of the unions in these developments is examined by situating the actors within their specific spheres of action and decision-making.

Finally, Chapter 6, addressing the sphere of transnational action, examines the production of norms at EU level, and the consequences in terms of decisions on resources. From a more overall point of view, this raises the question of the impact of European integration on the dynamics of change concerning rights over resources; the entry points for this analysis are the instruments implemented by the EU (employment policies, social agenda, retirement pensions) and union initiatives to organise at the supranational level.

Because this book is the product of a collective endeavour to develop a problematic, and is not a result of field research, the various chapters open avenues of discussion in several fields and develop a broad line of questioning, but the answers remain partial and will of course need a more systematic confrontation with empirical data. But may we ask the reader to bear in mind that it is precisely in the difficult process of writing, especially when this is a collective venture, that the process of objectivation takes form, and that concrete agreement is forged. From this point of view, and beyond the debate we have sought to introduce, we hope to share some of the joys of those encounters and meetings held in our different countries that are essential to any intellectual undertaking, and the awareness that they are rare, and to be savoured.

References

Berthelot, J.M. (2000), "The Implications of 'Societal Analysis' for a Programme of Research", in Maurice M. and Sorge A. (ed.), *Embedding Organizations*, Amsterdam, John Benjamins Publishing Company, pp. 89-99.

Bourdieu, P. (2002), *Science de la science et réflexivité*, lectures at the Collège de France 2000-2001, Paris, Raisons d'Agir.

Dupuis, P.A. (2002), *Anthropologie temporelle des parcours singuliers en éducation et en formation*, Note de synthèse pour l'Habilitation à Diriger des Recherches, Université de Nancy 2.

Esping-Andersen, G., Gallie, D., Hemerijck, A. and Myles, J. (2001), *Why We Need a New Welfare*, Oxford, Oxford University Press.

Maurice, M. (2000), "The Paradoxes of Societal Analysis. A Review of the Past and Prospects for the Future", in M. Maurice and A. Sorge (eds), *Embedding Organizations*, Amsterdam, John Benjamins Publishing Company, pp. 13-36.

Mishra, R. (1996), "The Welfare of Nations", in Boyer R. and D. Drache (eds), *States against Markets – The limits of globalisation*, London, Routledge, pp. 316-333.

Nicolescu, B., Freitas, L. and Morin, E. (editorial committee) (1994), Charter of Transdisciplinarity, adopted at the First World Congress of Transdisciplinarity, Portugal.

Merleau-Ponty, M. (1945), *Phénoménologie de la perception*, Paris, Gallimard.

Rodrigues, M.J. (ed.) (2003), The New Knowledge Economy in Europe: a Strategy for International competitiveness and Social Cohesion, Cheltenham, Edward Elgar.

Questions of Terminology

Merle SHORE

Our choice to publish this book in English has raised some challenging problems that will ring a familiar bell to many research workers engaged in international comparisons or working in transnational groups. Finding a suitable way of expressing one country's national reality in a different country's language is more complicated than simply finding a "corresponding" word, and particular attention must be paid to avoiding the pitfall of using terms which, in the societal context of the chosen language, describe a different reality. In some cases, the ways social institutions are formed can produce quite different meanings of the same words, and alternative solutions have to be found. In the discussion that follows, the essential dialogue is between French and English, since these are the two languages that are used in the network. Our particular concern has been to avoid introducing an Anglo-Saxon bias through the use of the English language. However, we have yet to explore further the problems that may arise from using French terms to describe other national systems, in particular those of the continental countries.

These considerations aside, the attempt to describe very different societal realities in one language – English – has led us to make certain choices in the use of terminology that warrant some explanation. The principal problems encountered can be grouped together, under four main topics:

Welfare and welfare state

Welfare has been established by the Anglo-Saxon literature as the accepted term for what, in the continental countries, is called social protection. The institutional differences underpinning these two expressions are particularly well illustrated by the equally widely accepted notion of *welfare state*. This term, which stems from an Anglo-Saxon representation of social protection, corresponds to the Anglo-Nordic systems that are essentially based on state provision, and as such, contrast sharply with the continental model. We have thus generally preferred the expressions *social protection system* and *welfare system*, and

21

as a rule, have chosen to use the term *social protection* when discussing the continental systems.

The term *tutelary state* has been proposed to characterise certain transformations of the role of the state that are described in Chapter 3. While, due to its novelty, its meaning may not be immediately obvious, it is used to express the discourse on "benevolent" public action (the state stepping in to "protect" target populations) and is not to be confused with the notion of *disciplinary state* which is more often used to describe the transformations of the Anglo-Saxon *welfare state* introduced by workfare measures and disciplinary policies. The use of the word *tutelary* in other expressions (such as *tutelary allowance*) – although undoubtedly awkward in English – has been maintained in order to express the link with the *tutelary state*.

Social contributions and cotisations sociales

Modes of financing social protection systems are historical constructions that are expressed by how they are named. Thus *cotisations sociales* in France and *social insurance contributions* in the UK, for instance, refer to very different societal systems. For want of a better way of expressing these realties, we have adopted *social contributions* as a generic term, but we are fully aware that this tends to mask what we consider to be fundamental differences between modes of sourcing. Since the mechanisms of the *cotisation sociale* have been theorised elsewhere[1], we have chosen to retain this expression when discussing the French case. It should be noted, moreover, that *social contributions* is also the term used by Eurostat (the EU Statistical Office) to present harmonised data. Although the different forms of wage-based contributions and deductions levied on the wage are frequently lumped together under the heading *tax on wages*, this is an expression we obviously contest, given that our approach postulates a differentiation of social rights on the basis of the source of financing.

Qualification and credentials

The word *qualification* exists in both English and French but with different meanings, and in the continental countries conveys a notion that has no direct equivalent in the Anglo-Saxon countries. While in the latter the word, in its formal sense, relates to the accreditation of training, in the continental countries it expresses the articulation between

---

[1] Friot, B. (1998), *Puissances du Salariat : Emploi et Protection Sociale* à la Française, Paris, La Dispute.

credential (certificate, diploma or degree), job and wage. This articulation, which exists to varying degrees, is linked in particular to the existence of *classification grids (grilles de classification)* which are societal realities essential to the functioning of the labour market in these countries. In order to avoid any confusion, for readers from the continental countries and English speakers alike, the term *credential* has been used as a synonym to replace the English *qualification*, and *qualification system* to convey the continental notion.

Collective actors

The term *social actors* has generally, although not always, been preferred to *social partners*, since the latter has an ambiguous connotation: it can imply shared interests as between commercial partners, whereas from our perspective, we are dealing with a context of wage conflict. *Wage conflict* expresses the confrontation between employers and employees over wage-related issues within the framework of the relation between capital and labour.

In the continental countries, there exists a level of legally enforceable collective agreements above the company and sectoral levels, called *interprofessionnel* in France, and which has been translated here by *cross-sectoral* or *multi-branch.*

In some continental countries, the social protection bodies are jointly managed by representatives of employees' and employers' organisations; in order to avoid lengthy repetitions, this bipartite system has frequently been more simply expressed by the term *joint management.*

The choice of terms has sometimes been problematic, and this is no doubt reflected in the final text. The Introduction, Chapters 3 and 6, parts of the Conclusion, and to a lesser extent, parts of Chapters 2 and 4, were translated from the French. The rest was all written in English and with the exception of Chapter 1, by non-native speakers whose English was revised. While we have made every effort to harmonise the whole, we hope that the reader will bear with the inconsistencies that remain, and will have no difficulty in understanding the meaning.

CHAPTER 1

Rights over Resources

Mark HARVEY and Robert MAIER

Introduction

In the last two decades or more there have been major changes in the welfare regimes of Europe, affecting millions of people. Many differing interpretations have been offered (Esping-Andersen, 1990, 1996, 1999; Goodin *et al.* 1999; Crouch and Streek 1997; Hall and Soskice, 2001). Some have viewed the changes as a response to a generalised crisis of the "post-war settlement" of the welfare states that came to typify the different European polities and economies. Slower growth, increased global competition, demographic shifts, decline of manufacturing capacity, have all been invoked as either core components or exacerbating factors underlying this crisis. Others have seen change in terms of a re-alignment of the balance of forces within capitalism, seeing the rise of neo-liberal politics, personified by Reagan and Thatcher, as a recapturing of ground lost by the capitalist classes deemed necessary to recapture the dynamics of capitalism suffocated by the rigidities and protectionisms of welfare states. It is a reading of history in terms of trench warfare, territory being gained and lost in the unchanging battleground of class war.

There can be little doubt that something of major importance is happening in the nature of the diverse changes that are being experienced across Europe. In this book we offer a particular angle of vision on these processes of change in a comparative analysis of different European welfare regimes. No claims are being made to a comprehensive view or explanation. Rather, a partial but distinctive perspective is developed in order to provide a set of arguments supported by comparative empirical descriptions to counter the perceived excesses and weaknesses of other approaches.

The central focus of the book is on the construction and institution of "rights over resources". That is to say, we ask *how* resources distributed by welfare states are organised, *who* has rights over them, and *why* these rights over resources are different in different countries and have been changing over time. These rights are not understood as purely individual rights, but as entitlements which are held by individuals or instituted groups or all members of a national society. These rights normally have some legal basis, but with a great variety of legal forms, including general laws, agreements or contracts concluded by parties, such as unions, having a binding nature and many other forms. These rights over resources correspond to some extent to the category of "social rights" introduced by Marshall (1964), but have also some characteristics of his concept of "political rights", because they presuppose some political participation of workers, both in the political community and at the workplace. This category of rights has been defined by some authors, such as Held (Held and Thompson, 1990), as "political-economic rights" which guarantee in particular the right of organisation at the workplace.

Welfare regimes are vehicles which themselves institute equalities *and* inequalities, inclusions *and* exclusions (Esping-Andersen, 1990, 1993). We interpret this in terms of the who, how, and why of rights over resources. Changing regimes means changing the equalities and inequalities, inclusions and exclusions (or as we prefer, differential rights) – no regime, in the past or on current horizons, has effectively eliminated these polarities, and we will examine whether changes may mitigate or exacerbate them. From our comparative perspective, different countries' regimes institute these polarities differently by the way that rights over resources are constructed in various institutional forms. But we should also insist that we are not attempting *either* a general theory of rights, *or* a theory of the distribution of societal wealth, *or* a general theory of inclusion and exclusion. We confine ourselves to this narrower, but we hope robust, manner of analysing rights in terms of rights over resources, which in turn we restrict to those that flow through the wage, or, more broadly, payments in exchange for the use of labour.

For these reasons, this approach is quite different from the theory of Esping-Andersen. His work was based on a global typology of Welfare Regimes (1990) based on "ideal types". In the present approach the central focus is on a conceptual framework permitting a detailed analysis of the intricacies of the flows of resources. In particular, we do not adopt the main distinction of Esping-Andersen between commodification and de-commodification, or between market and state, which in our view does not help to elucidate the complex working of different welfare regimes, but rather hides important characteristics of different welfare regimes.

Our chosen point of entry for this analysis, then, is the complex institution of the wage. The wage is a pivotal institution[1] in economies and welfare states, a fulcrum or point of purchase, in the sense both of the locus of exchanges through which labour, goods or services are bought, and the locus of leverage where resources funding welfare regimes are obtained through taxation (direct and indirect) or insurance. It is a central channel through which resources flow.

However, in its very centrality as a channel of resources, the wage has inherently contradictory implications for welfare state regimes, in the sense that it embodies a number of persistent tensions that make these regimes a focus of continuous conflict, and hence change. In a "rights over resources" perspective there are three central tensions:

- The tension between private disposable income and goods and services secured through taxation and insurance.

- The tension between the wage as an instrument for purchasing labour services and as a channel for resources supporting time out-of-work (retirement, holidays, sickness, child support, etc.).

- The tension between the wage as a vehicle of inclusion and exclusion, where differential participation in employment leads to differential access to rights over the resources that flow through the wage.

Whilst the conceptual framework will be set out more fully below, these tensions are both analytically distinct, and, in our view, form the basis of continuing political conflict. So a central proposition of our analysis is that changing institutional forms of resource flows, new societal resources and new channels, are formative of the very social groups concerned in the development and exercise of rights over those resources. The nature of resource question is intimately linked to the nature of power question. So, in stressing the contradictory nature of the central vehicle for channelling resources and establishing rights over them, we hope to avoid any functionalist interpretation of the relation between welfare regimes and capitalism. In broad terms these tensions can be seen to be expressed in the ways that different European countries have markedly varying proportions of GDP available for personal/ private consumption; that there are continuing secular changes in working time and retirement age; and that *all* the welfare regimes under consideration are inherently gendered by virtue of structural differences in participation in employment (labour market access; duration of continuous employment; inequalities of opportunity) (Sainsbury, 1999).

---

[1] Note that we choose the term wage and describe it as an institution – albeit economic – rather than as a price in a market, as some economists might have it.

The male breadwinner model of employment, almost unquestioned at the time of the institution of many of the European welfare regimes, however modified since, still has a pervasive presence in many of the rights over resources flowing through the wage.

This approach to welfare states thus pays particular attention to economic flows through economic institutions, but links these to how rights to those resources are established. The different systems must be economically sustainable as part of a complex dynamic of capitalist economies. Flows of resources, however they may be differently organised, must be kept flowing for a welfare regime to endure – and the question then becomes one of whether the flows of resources expand, contract, or remain stable. This places conflicts over these resources, and shifting social rights over them, at the centre of the political economies of Europe. There has been a tendency of some analysis to underemphasize this dimension by regarding the distribution of resources under different welfare regimes as more or less exclusively political settlements, outcomes of social and political struggles over resources (Esping-Andersen, 1990; Korpi, 1989) or historical political institutions (Skocpol, 1995; Merrien, 1997). Our focus on the wage and resource flows recentres the analysis on an economic institution and the institutional forms organising the resource flows.

But, conversely, emphasis on the instituted, hence socially variable, nature of the wage contrasts strongly with narrowly economistic interpretations of the economy typical of the neo-classical tradition. If flows and transfers were nothing other than different ways of channelling money, and were therefore nothing other than money flows, institutional form would make no difference[2]. By contrast we ask whether it matters that employers or employees, or both pay social insurance; whether pensions are paid through taxation or insurance; or whether taxation is on income or expenditure. Likewise it can be asked whether it matters that health services are received in kind or paid for by compulsory medical insurance and privately provided; whether minimum incomes are secured by minimum wage statute or by fiscal redistribution; or whether pensions are received as a continuation of salary or as a defined benefit similarly related to final earnings from an occupational pension

---

[2] A clear enunciation of this principle is given by John Hills (2000: p. 11): "Any tax, whatever it is called and however it is collected, puts a 'wedge' between people's income and the (pre-tax) value of the goods and services they purchase". And it "does not really matter" whether people pay direct or indirect tax for these purposes.

fund[3]. It is through developing the arguments about why institutional form does matter, that we seek to demonstrate that different kinds of rights, of inclusion and exclusion, are centrally constituted by different institutional forms of resource flow. These different institutional forms can then be related to ways in which different national systems of social rights are constructed.

An instituted economic perspective on the wage also allows us to go beyond the sharp dichotomies often made between the *social* non-market and the "economic" market. We find that much of the debate about state and market, commodification and de-commodification is vitiated by a view which takes market processes as "purely economic" on the one hand, and all forms of resources channelled through taxation/compulsory insurance as non-market, hence non-economic and social, on the other. By viewing the wage as an institutional complex which "combines" different resource flows in different ways, we are in a position to argue that the wage is a societal vehicle for articulating different types of exchange, and that in the case of labour markets the wage is central to the organisation of the exchange process itself. So, if we take two examples from very different welfare systems, the French pension system entails compulsory social insurance, but the pensions themselves are means of purchasing commodities in product markets; in the UK national health system, many medical services are free at the point of delivery, but taxation is deployed in specific ways in a distinctively instituted pharmaceutical market with the state acting as central purchaser from private providers. In both cases, viewed from the perspective of resource flows, it is difficult to put either example in a clear analytical box denoted "market" or "non-market", "commodification" or "de-commodification".

---

[3]   Of course, there are useful comparisons to be made about absolute quantitative levels of expenditure on these different aspects of welfare expenditure, and valuable tools for modelling the distributive effects of different institutional resource flows (Piachaud and Sutherland, 2000). It is merely our contention that such quantitative flows must also be understood in terms of the institutional forms in which they occur.

I. Conceptual framework

In this section, the conceptual framework unifying the chapters which follow is outlined. The concept of "rights over resources"[4] is one of social rights, whether these apply to private individual property[5] or public goods, to take two extremes. Given our attempt to go beyond the dichotomy between market and non-market forms, a central aim of our analysis is to provide a more differentiated approach to the analysis of those resource flows that can be termed generically "compulsory monetary transfers". The reason for choosing this term is twofold. Firstly, it seeks to avoid assumptions derived from any one national system of taxation or social insurance. That is precisely what we need to problematise if we are to analyse differences between systems of taxation and insurance comparatively. Secondly, it seeks to avoid some general assumptions that place some expenditures in the sphere of "the market" whereas in many ways these expenditures have many of the characteristics of expenditures organised through taxation and social insurance. Private medical insurance may be compulsory in the requirement, but to varying degrees discretionary in the choice of financial instrument and provider – as is car insurance, for example.

On the basis of this concept of compulsory monetary transfer, we seek to explore in what ways the "social" character of rights over resources involved is constructed in different ways. As a shorthand, it could be argued that any rights over resources flowing through the wage that are more collective than individual property rights entail a form of "socialisation". But, because of the many possible (nationally varying) connotations and definitions of "socialisation" we need to be quite explicit and precise about the use of the term. It could mean nationalisation, the acquisition of private property by the state. But as has been pointed out, nationalisation can entail very little effective social control over resources, and national enterprises can be set distinctly commercial, even profit-making, objectives (Leys, 2002). Besides the nationalisations in France, Italy, and the UK are quite different in character and their character changed over time. In many usages, a socialised service simply means one delivered as a "public good". Thus in the case of the UK National Health Service the free provision of medical services at the point of delivery would be sufficient to qualify as "socialised" provision.

---

[4] We shall see that the concept of "rights over resources" incorporates both the access to, and the power to manage, resources.

[5] Private property rights are viewed as necessary underpinnings of market economies by quite sharply opposing theoretical positions, for example, Demsetz and Hirsch.

In other usages, "socialised" could mean effective collective control over resources by those who have rights over them. In this usage, the entitlement to pensions under a social insurance scheme is a socialisation of resources. This can be combined with an interpretation that these entitlements take place "at the expense of" private property. In this connotation, these rights are inherently anti-capitalist, hence "socialised" in a double sense. But clearly, to qualify for this second dimension of meaning, it has to be demonstrated that the rights are indeed "at the expense of" capital accumulation, diminishing rates of profit, and so on, and not just "to the benefit of" those who exercise the rights. Resources can be socialised without being socialist – or even on the way to becoming socialist as most opponents of social provision like to project any deviation from individualised property rights. By defining the "social" in rights over resources, we aim to demonstrate the development of different modes of societal, mutual, or collective ownership.

As a counterpart to this exercise in unpacking the different varieties of what might be meant by the term "socialisation", a similar exercise can be undertaken in relation to "private property rights". For our analysis in particular it is important to be able to qualify what is meant by private property or personal disposable income in relation to medical insurance and pensions. Many of the institutions that channel these resource flows of "private disposable income" have characteristics that distinguish them from the free individual right to exercise unrestricted choice over the disposal and use of assets. In parallel to the discussion of socialisation, at a first level there can be restrictions on what might be purchased by private disposable income (drugs, pornography, guns). Much so-called private medicine is funded on payments to private insurance, often both by employers and employees, to specified insurance schemes which are linked to specified private health provision, as a condition of an employment relation. Similar conditionalities attach to many pension schemes, with the important difference that the pension itself, as with "socialised" pensions, is generally in the form of personal disposable income. But that too can be subject to further conditionalities, such as the form of annuities, the payment of lump sums on retirement, all of which define and hence condition, private property rights. Many occupational funds have forms of mutuality built into their property rights, with shared rights pertaining to particular groups of individuals (Blackburn, 1999, 2002b). Technical questions distinguishing Defined Contribution from Defined Benefit pension schemes are concerned with who bears the risk in relation to what entitlements over property, pointing to how rights to private property are distributed, hence not absolute in relation to the private individual. The Enron crash has generated much discussion, and will generate much further litigation, as well as some legislation, over the property rights and issues of governance over company pension funds (Blackburn, 2002a). As a counterpart to the collective, mutual or societal ownership, we therefore aim to view different modes of individual property rights as equally socially instituted. Indeed, individualisation of rights over resources is as much a social process as societalisation, collectivisation or mutualisation.

To develop an analysis of social rights over resources flowing through the wage, therefore, and hence different forms of socialisation, we need to specify the dimensions involved in their construction. The three main dimensions that we are using in this analysis are:

- The nature of the social units exercising the rights in terms of levels of generality of collective rights (individuals; collectives of various extents – e.g. employees in a firm, in a sector, all workers; all citizens within a national territory, all Europeans, etc.).

- The nature of the power exercised by those units, in terms of exclusivity, modes of exercise of power through legal or political processes, levels of participation in resource management, etc.).

- The nature of the inclusivity/exclusivity of social units, and in particular the articulation between participation in employment and rights over resources. For example, women and migrant workers have been to some extent excluded in the past from benefits of specific welfare regimes, but these exclusions have been modified in most countries during recent years.

These dimensions of social rights are then used to interpret the differences in social rights over resources in different societal systems. We are seeking to demonstrate that the nature of these social rights varies with the types of resources, and the entitlements that are established to goods, services, or purchasing power derived from them. Essentially we are arguing that different units, powers, inclusivities/exclusivities, are established in and through these institutionalised constructions of rights over resources. The units/powers/inclusivities do not precede – analytically or historically – the constitution of the rights over resources. So for example, the institution of a category of workers with a minimum salary guaranteed by the state through fiscal support from general taxation – the current SMIC in France[6]– creates a new social category, with some,

---

[6] The SMIC started out life quite differently, as the SMIG, when the social unit was identified simply as those people having a minimum wage guaranteed by the state as the floor below which payment scales could not go.

but by no means all, the rights of the core salariat. The emergence of new social categories occurs through the emergence of a new differentiation of rights over resource flows that have also been changed.

We distinguish the following variables which permit to study the institutional forms of regimes of social rights over resources:

(A) the sources of the flows (deductions, contributions, payment instalments, etc.)

(B) the benefits or provisions

(C) the general characteristics of the linkages between sources and benefits

(D) the forms of power and types of exclusion.

A. *Resource flow sources*

The list below contains some of the main types of compulsory monetary transfer or deductions:

SOURCES

Tax on income

Tax on goods and services

Social insurance:

employee

employer

Compulsory

(pension) funds

Private/occupational

Pension funds

Compulsory

Medical insurance

DISCRETIONARY

INCOME

These items are just well-known exemplifications of some of the principal types; it is by no means an exhaustive list. Moreover, it should be clear that the last item, "discretionary income" is not defined as residual, because as we shall see, some forms of benefits, such as the complements or substitutes may form part of discretionary income.

It can be argued that different types of source are constitutive of different types of social units[7]. Five broad categories have been identified making up a range of possible compulsory monetary transfers. Each of them can be briefly considered in turn.

- Tax on income is a form of deduction which in some countries is universal to all income derived from employment and unearned income (rent, dividends, pensions, etc.). If at a standard rate, it can be seen to include and socially constitute a broad band of 'citizens' as taxpayers as all contributing on the same basis. Only those without income are excluded. That said, the core of income tax payers are employees, which makes the citizen-employee the central figure of this system. Where tax thresholds are part of the system of contributions, we would argue that those receiving income but below the threshold are included. Where there are differential levels of taxation for different levels of income, this form of deduction can be seen to do two things. First, it classifies and differentiates citizens – average, well-off, super-rich, etc. Second, it creates the basis for a system of redistribution of earned income (and only earned income) that embraces all citizens included within the deduction system *at the point of deduction.*

- Tax on goods and services, or indirect taxation, by contrast is a form of deduction on consumption, and although it encompasses almost all within society – including those without any sources of earned income – it appears to be less strongly constitutive of citizenship. Partly this is because most indirect tax systems do not have standard rates across all commodities and services, partly it is because important items of standard consumption shared by all are frequently excluded (food, education, housing), and partly because indirect tax remains a minor component of overall deductions in spite of a tendential rise in most European states. Unlike previous eras, prior to the dominance of waged income, indirect taxes (such as taxes on salt) are less likely to socially mobilise cohesion either in impact or in public reaction.

---

[7] We consider here primarily financial resources and their funding. It should also be recognised that just as there are benefits in kind, so also is there sourcing in kind, by voluntary or compulsory provision of services.

- Social insurance contributions based on income earned through waged employment differ "at source" in three significant ways from income tax. Firstly, and most obviously, they only fall on those engaged in the employment relation. Secondly, they normally fall on both sides of the employment relation, employers and employees, often according to "linked" (not the same) percentages, although ratios between employer and employee percentages may vary enormously. Thirdly, as a consequence, they are not deductions from "income" or "earnings", but are mandatory contributions constituting a part of the total cost of employment. These features of social insurance mean that employers and employees are mutually subject under the same system. As such, in different ways these systems are constitutive of employment relations, to varying extents, in a way that income tax is not.

- Compulsory savings in pension funds take various forms, all of which significantly differentiate these savings from discretionary rights over individual assets. In most contemporary societies which have this form of compulsory saving, there is a wide range of disparate forms of deduction. They can range from being compulsory alternatives to state pensions, where the state makes such payments compulsory, to being compulsory by virtue of employment within a given profession or occupation or by a given employer. If we take the latter case, as a system of deduction it creates a social identity of the company employee, as against the general form of social insurance, where social identity might be of a French employee. The effect of these forms of compulsory deductions is generally to constitute a multiplicity of heterogeneous groups under differing deduction regimes. The deductions are narrowly hypothecated, with deductions being linked strictly to the type of possible benefits at the point of deduction.

- Compulsory minimum medical insurance also may take a very wide range of forms, from state to company or individual based schemes. As with compulsory minimum savings for pensions, these systems can often be a compulsory alternative to state provision based on an alternative system of deductions. They also create a multiplicity of heterogeneous groups through narrowly hypothecated deductions related to differential expectations of possible benefits, at the point of deduction.

From this analysis of different forms of compulsory deduction/contribution, it can be seen that social identities are differently constructed even at the source of compulsory monetary transfer. But up to this point nothing has been said of possible linkages to possible benefits, and nothing has been said of how systems of sourcing might change or be combined with each other. The sourcing system is distinct, but only within an overall institutional framework that constitutes social rights to resources generated by deductions.

B. The benefits

We now turn to the benefits dimension of this institutional framework, where we have identified the following major types of benefit:

BENEFITS

Services in kind
(education, health, care of elderly and disabled,
childcare, law enforcement, etc.)

Wage equivalents (including earnings-related),
Complements,
Substitutes

Cost of living supplements (housing, children)

Services for hypothecated cash

- Services in kind cover an enormous range of social provision, for which no additional payments are made at the point of delivery. Although this is not here our primary concern, there can also be a wide range of possible institutions and organisations, public and private, involved in the provision of these services. Some services free at the point of delivery provide a general and standard provision to all recipients "in principle", although in practice establishment of norms and standards may be variable, according often to socio-economic characteristics of the recipient population. This type of provision, again in principle, treats all citizens as equal and assumes equal access, and so from the point of provision more or less creates a category of citizen. However, it needs to be recognised that, depending on economic development and growth, societal resources available for generalised provision are always limited, and equally, within the economic system at any given historical point in time, strategic decisions can be made about how much societal resources are made available. Free provision of "universal" education, accompanied by free provision of "selective" education is therefore an example of an historically moving "civic stratification". School leaving ages, the extension of universal education, and systems of selection for levels of higher education or different branches of education, divide citizens into those who have access to different levels of education. The creation of a stratified citizenry is nonetheless within a system of citizenship provision, but only if one accepts that opportunities for selection are equal for all citizens. These are therefore two examples of different rights over societal resources, one generalised the other stratified.

- Wage equivalents, substitutes and complements constitute a very broad category of benefits in cash. The strongest indication of equivalence to wages occurs when benefits are earnings-related. Describing them as equivalents, substitutes or complements also signifies that they constitute a transfer of cash for discretionary income of individuals to be used in generalised private consumption. Pensions are an example of this type of provision, where the transfer of cash does not in any way hypothecate the form of expenditure that recipients may choose to enjoy. Unlike free provision, this form of benefit can vary greatly, may be more or less redistributive, and can be the basis of creation of new categories of recipient of each form of cash benefit. Some forms of benefits can apply to all employees, whereas others may apply only to those of low income. When this type of construction of difference is made by the way benefits are defined, new social categories and inequalities may be created.

- Cost of living supplements are forms of benefit where the provision takes the form of cash payments for specific, and hypothecated, expenditure. In this case, the individual has not got discretion over the form of expenditure of the received cash benefit. Recipients and non-recipients are defined by different criteria, which form part of the process of institutionalising social categories at the point of provision.

- Provision of services under dedicated insurance schemes involves a level of mutualisation of risk between those that are included in those schemes. Medical insurance schemes are typical of these forms of provision, but they too can vary from being generalised state compulsory schemes, to employer-based compulsory schemes.

The way such schemes are constructed, in the US or France for example, demonstrate the variability of institutional possibilities from one that creates considerable inequalities in provision to one that ensures similar provision for a large proportion of the population. This variability therefore also demonstrates the role of the provisioning system in social categorisation and the creation of equalities and inequalities.

C. Linkages between deductions and benefits

Above, it has been shown how modes of sourcing and modes of provision constitute societal resources through the wage. Both at source and at the point of provision, there is a process of social categorisation, which will form part of the basis of our concept of regimes of rights over societal resources. But clearly, the third variable – linkages – is also central for the constitution of the overall regimes, insofar as the way modes of sourcing are linked to modes of provision in different societal arrangements reinforces or diminishes the social categorisation through the establishment of rights over resources. The nature of the linkages has been differentiated according to different types of conditionality of entitlement either qua deductee/contributor or qua recipient, or both. Here again, we exemplify these forms of linkage as the basis for the creation of rights over societal resources:

LINKAGES

Universal

Conditional upon resources
(means test)

Conditional upon attributes
(e.g. status, children, disablement)

Conditional upon qualificatory employment

Conditional upon contributory payments

Conditional upon expenditure

- Universal or unconditional rights obtain by virtue of living in the national territory, irrespective of being or not being a taxpayer or social insurance contributor, and no matter what social attributes the person might have. Put in this absolute way, these rights would make us citizens of the world, and clearly few such completely unconditional rights have been institutionalised. In terms of European welfare regimes, universality or unconditionality is generally *within* nationhood, buttressed by state-to-state agreements, notably also the creation of reciprocities at the European level. This form of universality or unconditionality is therefore an entitlement based on recognised nationality status of the person, a citizen-basis for a linkage between payers of some form of deduction and receipt of a range of benefits.

- Conditionality based on resources is a linkage established on the basis of the financial characteristics of the recipient, rather than characteristics of the contributor/deductee. This form of linkage sets different kinds of test on the assets or income of the recipient and thereby demarcates a social category of the "poor" and "deserving", "low income" or no-income. The specific measures used to define such linkages vary over time and between countries, and are thereby different social modes of categorising the entitlements. (It should be noted that we are only specifying the type of linkage here, not the type of benefit that might be received as a consequence, which also may vary).

- Conditionality based on status is again a linkage established on the basis of characteristics of the recipient, but in this case characteristics which are socially defined. Some of these can be seen as "derived" rights, if the status is defined in by a recipient's relation to a principal person's rights, and derived rights may or may not be diminished as a consequence of being derived. Marital status in relation to pensions of various kinds is an example, as are children's rights to benefits of various kinds. Primary rights for the disabled, as a socially defined condition, are an example of status-based conditionality. Primary rights to pensions are generally established by the institution of a legal age of retirement that accords a status to those above a certain age – a moveable definition, and one that may distinguish between men and women. Many of these status-based linkages, however, can be seen in terms of supplements or complements to rights based on an underlying model of income earned from employment.

- Conditionality based on qualificatory employment is a linkage related to characteristics of the deductee, and specifically to the length of time in employment, full-time or part-time. This form of conditionality particularly emphasises the model of the male bread-winner in full-time continuous employment over a working life as defined by the rules of linkage. But it is not a right established strictly according to a contributory principle, merely "time served". On this basis, the linkage may establish entitlements to income based on current income norms rather than contributions based on historic income norms. Again there are societally various institutional forms of such arrangements, which depend on varying deduction systems. Here the focus is on the nature of the linkage.

- Conditionality based on contributory payments is a linkage based strictly and proportionately to payments made by the recipient of benefits. It can be seen how this type of linkage might be inappropriate for medical insurance, where risks are unpredictable and frequently mutualised in various ways. Generally, this form of linkage relates more to insurance against discontinuities of employment, and especially discontinuation of employment in retirement. The contributions may be shared by employers and employees, and be voluntary, conditional to employment with a particular employer, or made compulsory by the state.

- Conditionality based on expenditure in personal consumption is perhaps the least well-defined right linking entitlements to benefits to payments of deductions through indirect taxation. Unlike linkages based on qualificatory employment or contributory payments, there is no established relation between the amounts consumers spend and the level of benefits to which they are entitled. This is the negative way of stating the positive proposition that a shift to indirect taxation as a means of generating societal resources leads to more diffuse rights over those resources. In many discussions of indirect taxation, the assumption is made that they are negatively redistributive, as the same or greater proportion of income is paid by those at lower levels of income. This assumption is valid on condition of there being no linkage establishing rules relating indirect tax paid to benefits received in cash or kind, which may negatively or positively redistributive. The establishment of conditionality to benefits based on resources of recipient is possibly the closest to establishing such a rule, but means testing more usually relates to low income level than to low spending power.

As before, it should be noted, that this list has no pretension to be exhaustive. All kinds of conditions can be defined, such as for example the condition of the number of years of residence within the nation-state[8].

As an analytical tool, these variables suggest that deductions, linkages and entitlements are first each considered separately, in their own terms, and without making prior assumptions that one type of deduction is necessarily tied to one type of entitlement through one type of linkage. There are no necessary, a priori, linkages between one type of compulsory monetary transfer and one type of enjoyment of a resource. How the resources are established, how the linkages are instituted, and the manner in which resources are received and enjoyed as benefits are all historically and societally variable.

Some ideal types of social rights

Having set out in particular the different types of resourcing, benefits, and linkages, it is possible in a preliminary way to construct some ideal type rights over resources involving a particular type of resource, a particular type of linkage, and a particular type of benefit. For example, nationality status may be the basis of a (national) universal right to a benefit received in kind (such as a medical service or education) funded by general taxation (direct and indirect). This might be termed a *citizen based right*. Or, social insurance paid for by the employee and employer through the wage may be linked conditionally on a continuity of employment over a qualifying period to the receipt of proportional wage equivalents, such as pensions. The benefits too are in the form of cash functioning as disposable income, analogous to earned income. This might be termed an *employment based right*. Private payment by an individual from personal disposable income for training in a skill might lead to a certificate from a private educational service, more or less widely recognised in specific labour markets. In this case, the right to skill formation is a private property right, and its subsequent use in exchange in labour markets can be seen as being turned to purely private advantage. Personal discretionary contributions to an individual annuity fund might result in deferred benefits, depending on the development of stock markets. These might be termed as being *private property based rights*.

---

8 In the Netherlands, the basic pension, which is independent of employment relations, is built up by living in the Netherlands between the age of 15 and 65, and for each year the resident builds up 2% of this basic pension. This condition can have quite dramatic consequences for migrant workers who came to the Netherlands say at age 35 or 40; they can loose up to 50% of the basic pension rights.

However, in talking about different types of rights, it should be emphasised that they refer to systematic and institutionalised linkages between a flow of resources and entitlements to benefits. As such, they do not describe different welfare systems as such. Nor, as yet, do they specify the different types of power or management upon which they may be based. Most national welfare systems contrast most strongly in the different ways these different rights may be combined, and their relative weighting. Moreover, any one individual within any societal resource regime is likely to be defined by multiple rights, combined in different ways and with different relative weighting. People are citizens *and* employees *and* individual property owners, but how these identities are combined and instituted vary considerable both within and between societies. Much of the book will consider different aspects of this variation.

1. Forms of power in establishing rights over resources

If one can broadly distinguish between citizenship-based rights, employment-based rights and private property based rights, they can be seen to relate to different forms of power. As each type of right is also a way of defining social categories, therefore, we suggest it is also a way of exercising different forms of power related to the different forms of rights. We would argue that there is a relationship between the relative importance of citizenship-based rights and employment-based rights and the dynamics and forms of parliamentary and industrial power. Again in very broad terms, it can be argued that if national budgets are primary instruments for establishing certain types of resource generation and rights over them, citizenship-based rights are most clearly affected, positively or negatively, by political parties elected to power in parliamentary elections. It can also be argued that private property rights are also enshrined and protected by legislation passed by political parties in power as governments. Indeed an argument could be made that there is a political zero-sum game between citizen-based rights and private property based rights, along the lines of a social democratic versus liberal welfare state regime. The higher the level of deductions of any kind, the higher the level of societal resources over which citizenship rights can be exercised. Conversely, the lower the level of deductions of any kind, the lower the level of societal resources, and the higher the level of available resources for private property rights based systems. In the political swings and roundabouts, a rise in liberal free market politics from the Reagan-Thatcher period marked a decline in social democracy. But, beyond and above the question of the levels of societal resources mobilised through forms of socialisation, there also remains a question of the effective powers citizens exercise over those resources through systems of parliamentary representation. Thus, we would argue that changes in social rights over resources – both citizen-based and private property based – cannot be fully characterised simply in terms of pro-market, anti-market, or erosion of one system of rights at the expense of the other.

If we turn to employment-based rights, the modalities of power are exercised much more centrally between organisations representative of employers and employees, however much these are given the sanction of state legislation. For this modality of power, relative strengths and mobilisation of the negotiating parties are central to the development of social rights over resources generated through social insurance deductions. From the standpoint of a citizenship-based system (such as the Scandinavian social-democratic one) employment-based rights regimes, by privileging the socialised wage as the principal societal resource over which employees and ex-employees may exercise rights, appear "corporatist" (Esping-Andersen, 1990, 1996; Goodin *et al.*, 1999) or "social capitalist" (Bussemaker and van Kersbergen, 1999). This is a portrayal based on an assumed dichotomy of state versus market, of commodification versus de-commodification. In these terms, anything less than universal citizenship rights over societal resources is deemed a restriction of rights in a zero-sum equation. We are arguing rather that there has been an evolving socialisation of employment-based rights over resources, in relation to which development of tax-based resources and rights over them may involve an erosion of employment-based rights without an equivalent gain in citizenship-based rights.

Through our focus on different modes of socialisation of resources that flow through the wage, however, we emphasise both the common centrality of the employment relation to both types of rights regime, and the differences in ways societal resources are generated and distributed. The contrast between the modalities of power of the two systems, however, is one where one form of rights is mobilised and exercised through parliamentary political systems, and the other through employee and employer organisations. There are always tensions between these two modalities of power, played out in different ways in different countries.

Moreover, it is important to consider how the general modalities of power are realised in institutional arrangements. These arrangements can take a multiplicity of forms, at one extreme as pure state institutions, with maybe some European-level aspects, or at the other extreme as institutions managed by representatives of employees and employers, but there is also the possibility to involve private enterprise, such as insurance companies or private training centres. For all these cases, there may be legal constructions (laws, directives, agreements between social partners having a binding status, etc.) which guarantee these institutional arrangements. Furthermore, it is necessary to study how the institutional arrangements will be managed in practice, with questions such as: how is the board chosen? Or is it elected? (by the state or by the organisations of employees and employers or both? by the members?); and: what kind of range of liberty does the board and the direction have in decisions concerning the attribution of benefits or in the choice of specific linkages between deductions and benefits. For example, in some countries, unemployment benefits can – to some extent – be used by the institution in charge for other purposes, such as subsidised work[9]. In short, these concrete exercises of power in the institutional arrangements can have far-reaching consequences for the regimes of welfare, because a general societal conception of a welfare regime can be transformed in practice into a regime with quite distinctive characteristics.

2. Access and exclusion from power: gender and ethnicity

The centrality of the wage as an institution around which social rights of resources are articulated has specific consequences for access to and exclusion from the power to exercise and develop rights. The two main structural exclusions from equal, full and continuous participation in the labour market – gender and ethnicity – thus have distinct implications for the modalities of power. Social movements and political organisations have emerged outside the main political frameworks of the salariat or parliamentary elections in many countries to address these issues. O'Connor has argued that a full range of social rights that afford economic independence without links to the labour market "is in general not realised in any welfare state" (O'Connor, 1999: p. 47; Sainsbury, 1999). Such a statement accords with an analysis that sees all societal resources generated from and passing through waged employment as essentially gendered. The key point relates to equal access to, and participation in labour markets, and so this analysis of the essentially gendered nature of welfare state arrangements, the gendered socialisation of resources in modes of deduction, linkage, and distribution, can be extended to all social groups where there are institutional and societal blocks to access and participation in labour markets. In particular, migrant workers have been in subtle ways partially excluded from various forms of benefits. Given our analysis of societal resources involved in skill formation, the same argument can also be extended to

---

[9] For example, the Netherlands.

44

differential access and participation in educational resources both in their own right, and as a basis for subsequent access and participation in labour markets. Although both gender and ethnicity are inadequately developed in our empirical work so far, they remain central to this type of analysis.

Concluding remarks

In this introduction some elements of a conceptual framework have been developed. These elements should be seen as useful starting points for an analysis of welfare regimes, but it should also be evident that these elements only offer partial and limited instruments of analysis.

Firstly, these instruments are above all useful for a quantitative and qualitative analysis of specific welfare provisions, such as one type of pensions. This first remark is intended to specify the possibilities and the limitations this approach. It should be evident that compulsory monetary transfers can be studied in a quantitative way, but also in a qualitative one, by analysing how new social groups are constituted by new modes of sourcing and type of benefits. By looking at changes in systems of compulsory monetary transfers over time, it is at least possible to get an idea of transformations of the quantitative and qualitative nature of welfare provisions, but also the changing social constituencies of welfare regimes. By making comparisons not only over time but also between different countries, we can take into account the inherent tensions arising from new social configurations – of a political, demographic and economic nature – which have been pointed out in the beginning of this section. Indeed, these tensions and conflicts exclude any stable arrangements, they point to an ongoing dynamic and process of transformation of welfare regimes.

The other elements of the conceptual framework, such as the linkages, the forms of power and the inclusions and exclusions are intended to develop the qualitative side of our analysis. We have emphasised the dual bases of power (parliamentary and industrial), and the tension between them, and have suggested that these take very different forms in our different countries, generating different types of conflict. The continuing and contrasting political battles over pensions in France and the United Kingdom are a case in point. But we have also suggested that the very way in which different institutional arrangements for the flows of resources occur, and changes in them, constitute new social categories of people that in turn form a potential social basis for new power conflicts over rights.

In short, in order to really analyse welfare regimes, a lot of other instruments will be needed, which permit to study the complex intricacies of any welfare regime combining a multiplicity of specific welfare provisions. There is a strong interdependency of the different institutional forms managing the various resource flows within a welfare regime, because of the interferences of the flows and because of the necessity to presuppose that these flows have to have a self-sustaining quality without any guarantee of a stable equilibrium. Therefore, although it is rather artificial to isolate one specific dimension of welfare provision for study, our approach has the advantage of focusing on the relation between resource flows and social change. Within these self-imposed limitations, it is hoped to combine quantitative and qualitative characteristics of elements of welfare systems, and also to study to some extent their inherently dynamic nature. However, we are also aware that a lot more has to be done. Conceptual instruments have to be developed in order to analyse (1) the interdependencies between the various welfare provisions and their institutionalisations, (2) the composition of the various welfare provisions into a system, and (3) the properties of a complex welfare regime, combining a great number of specific welfare provisions. It should be evident now that the properties of such a regime should be conceived as (a) being in partial conflict with each other, (b) dynamic, with variation in time and (c) as being of a mixed nature, with political, economic and social aspects. In short, the conceptual framework suggested here is a useful starting point for addressing these key issues.

We are not, in the grand manner, attempting to define or contrast a welfare regime such as France as an "employment-based rights" welfare regime to the United Kingdom as a "citizen-based rights" welfare regime, let alone establish these as types of welfare regime encompassing an institutional architecture of politics, economics and social policy. We are not attempting to develop a counter-typology to replace Esping-Andersen's Three Worlds (1990), for example, but are more interested in understanding the different dynamics of change. In focusing on the modes of resourcing, benefit distribution, and linkages between them, we are firstly rather aiming both to contrast different forms of "socialisation" of societal resources generated by deductions, and to see how these may change over time. Thus, the establishment of compulsory monetary transfers from one generation of employees to a generation of ex-employees may occur either through income tax systems or through employer/employee social insurance funds. Both forms of socialisation (as defined earlier) involve a transfer of purchasing power from the group defined by deductions to recipient social groups who then purchase commodities. This is not a picture of simple de-commodification, or socialisation taking resources outside the market economy altogether. They are rather societally instituted forms of resource flows, over which there are very different types of rights, and over which new types of conflict emerge between new social constituencies.

So, secondly, by looking at how systems of resourcing, benefits and linkages have developed and changed over time, we are attempting to analyse how social groups defined by these systems change along with changes in the nature of social rights over resources. We can take the emergence of groups not, or only partially, covered by the French social insurance system as an example of how new forms of exclusion are developed in relation to that system, as well as new forms of rights over social resources to which the excluded are entitled. Low-income employment subsidised from general taxation at the same time creates a social group whose rights over resources generated by the social insurance system are limited. Employees are divided in a way they were not before, and at the same time the nature of societal resources and rights over them are changed and recombined. How pensioners are formed socially and institutionally in different countries, with different relations to those currently in employment, and with societal, mutual, or individual property rights, conditions the way in which political battles over pension rights occur or not as the case may be. The way that resource flows are institutionalised is formative of the social groups that battle for rights over them, and the modalities of power they may exercise. Thus, by analysing systems of generating societal resources, modes of distribution of these resources, and linkages between them we can establish a conceptual framework for exploring changes in the nature of social rights and of the groups defined through the establishment and exercise of these rights.

References

Blackburn, R. (1999), "The New Collectivism. Pension Reform, Grey Capitalism and Complex Socialism", *New Left Review*, January-February 233.

Blackburn, R. (2002a), "The Enron debacle and the pension crisis", *New Left Review*, 14, March-April.

Blackburn, R. (2002b), *Banking on Death. The Uses and Misuses of Pensions Funds*, London, Verso.

Bussemaker, J. and van Kersbergen, K. (1999), "Contemporary social capitalist welfare states and gender inequality", in Sainsbury D. (ed.), *Gender and welfare state regimes*, Oxford, Oxford University Press.

Crouch, C. and Streeck, W. (1997), *Political Economy of Modern Capitalism. Mapping Convergence and Diversity*, London, Sage.

Esping-Andersen, G. (1990), *The Three Worlds of Welfare Capitalism*, Cambridge, Polity Press.

Esping-Andersen, G. (ed.) (1993), *Changing Classes: Stratification and Mobility in Postindustrial Societies*, London, Sage.

Esping-Andersen, G. (ed.) (1996), *Welfare States in Transition. National adaptations in Global Economies*, London, Sage.

Esping-Andersen, G. (1999), *Social Foundations of Postindustrial Economies*, Oxford, Oxford University Press.

Goodin, R.E., Headdey, B., Muffels, R. and Dirven, H-J. (1999), *The Real Worlds of Welfare Capitalism*, Cambridge, Cambridge University Press.

Hall, P.A., and Soskice, D. (2001), *Varieties of Capitalism. The institutional foundations of comparative advantage*, Oxford, Oxford University Press.

Held, D. and Thompson, J.B. (1990), *Social Theory of Modern Societies: Anthony Giddens and his Critics*, Cambridge, Cambridge University Press.

Hills, J. (2000), *Taxation for the Enabling State*, CASE Paper 41, Centre for Analysis of Social Exclusion, London School of Economics.

Korpi, W. (1989), "Power, politics and state autonomy in the development of citizenship: social rights during sickness in eighteen OECD countries since 1930", *American Sociological Review*, 54, 3, pp. 309-28.

Leys, C. (2002), *Market-Driven Politics*, London, Verso.

Marshall, T.H. (1964), *Class, Citizenship and Social Development*, New York, Doubleday & Company.

Merrien, F-X. (1997), *L'État-providence*, Paris, PUF.

O'Connor, J.S. (1999), "Employment equality strategies in Liberal Welfare States", in Sainsbury, D. (ed.), *Gender and welfare state regimes*, Oxford, Oxford University Press, pp. 47-75.

Piachaud, D. and Sutherland, H. (2000), "How effective is the British Government's attempt to reduce child poverty?", CASE Paper 38, Centre for Analysis of Social Exclusion, London School of Economics.

Sainsbury, D. (ed.) (1999), *Gender and welfare state regimes*, Oxford, Oxford University Press.

Skocpol, T. (1995), *Social Policy in the United States. Future possibilities in historical perspective*, Princeton, Princeton University Press.

CHAPTER 2

A Work-Welfare Nexus at the Heart of the Social Construction of Employment: New Perspectives on Labour Market Changes and Social Exclusion

Nathalie MONCEL, Margarida RUIVO
and Enrico FRAVEGA

Introduction

The present chapter will focus on employment and will seek to develop new categories for the analysis of labour market changes. We use the analytical framework developed in the previous chapter, and our discussion will be centred on the wage relation and its transformations, and in particular, on how this relation serves to define social units and forms of inclusion/exclusion. These two dimensions are at the core of an original approach that views employment as a social construction and takes as analytical entry point the linkages between employment and social protection.

Employment growth and social protection reforms are key items on the European employment and social agendas[1] and there is a burgeoning literature on these topics. However, the predominant trend is to treat these two spheres separately, and the relationship between them is rarely considered. Salais and Whiteside (1998: p. 151) have attributed this bias to the historical separation between social welfare and labour market regulation characteristic of Anglo-Saxon countries: "State welfare is perceived as a drag on economic performance [...] this juxtaposition of

---

[1] Notably in the framework established by the European social agenda, published by the European Commission in June 2000 and adopted by the European Council in Nice in December 2002, and in the European Employment Strategy initiated at the beginning of the 1990s (Summits of Essen in 1994 and Luxembourg in 1997). See Chapter 6 in this volume for more details.

the state and the market is the product of an Anglo-Saxon perspective which takes a restricted view of social and economic relations and the role of government in regulating them".

Similarly, in their analysis of the British system, Deakin and Wilkinson (1994: p. 143) note that "the relationship between social policy and the labour market has been comparatively neglected in studies of the welfare state. One reason for this is the institutional separation of social security from labour market regulation".

By contrast, our perspective stresses the centrality of the linkages between employment and social protection, and the four-step investigation developed in this chapter seeks to establish a basis for future research on these linkages. In the first section, we review current debates on labour market developments and social protection reforms. We highlight the predominant tendency to view these two spheres as distinct, although historically they have played a tightly interconnected role in the emergence of the employment status, especially through the institutionalisation of resources that flow through the wage and finance social rights.

We then focus on two specific issues in order to illustrate the strength of our analytical approach. Thus, in section II, we show how active labour market policies contribute to changing the nature of resource flows and how these changes are captured through current data on employment. In section III, we discuss the emergence of the notion of social exclusion and its relation to changes in employment and social protection.

In the final section, we develop the notion of a "work-welfare nexus" in an attempt to account for the two main features generated by the linkages between employment and welfare forms: societal diversity and social differentiation.

I. Analysing changing linkages between employment and social protection

The key developments in European labour markets have been widely documented over the last decades: the decline in the overall employment rate; persistent unemployment; shifts between sectors of activity from industry to services and in the structure of jobs from less skilled to more skilled; greater flexibility in working time arrangements and employment patterns; and growth of wage dispersion and the working poor. However, few of these studies see social protection as an integral part of the way labour use is organised or as an integrated factor of labour market functioning. Social policies are predominantly considered in an instrumental way: on the one hand, they are seen as possible responses to labour market transformations, especially the rise of unemployment or the renewal of the labour force; and on the other, they are turned into one of the causes of labour market dysfunction, because of assumptions of how they shape labour supply and demand.

Similarly, the major changes in welfare systems have been closely scrutinised since the 1970s, with the focus shifting from the issue of retrenchment to include more recent arguments for a trend to welfare state revival. These studies provide exhaustive descriptions of differences between countries as regards the development of welfare systems and their transformations over the last decades (Esping-Andersen, 1990, 1999; Pierson, 2001; Kuhnle, 2000). The majority focus on social protection and related social policies: labour market developments are apparently taken for granted and, to put it briefly, are seen as related predominantly to economic forces existing outside of the scope of politics.

Recently, however, two parallel trends of research dealing explicitly with the links between social protection and employment have emerged. The one analyses the extent to which welfare systems are "employment friendly" based on their impact on employment levels and economic growth (Atkinson, 1995; Scharpf, 2000); and the other focuses on how to reconcile work flexibility in the production sphere with adequate protection for workers in a context of increasing risks (Bosco and Hutsebaut, 1997; Esping-Andersen and Regini, 2000).

The first trend focuses on the level of resource flows linked to social protection funding and expenditure. The predominant economic approach here reflects the neo-classical account of labour market functioning, and analyses are based on the main assumption that wages are market prices resulting from an adjustment between labour demand and supply. Financing social protection through wage-based contributions is seen as creating a "wedge" between labour cost and labour productivity levels that disturbs the price mechanism. Thus social contributions are perceived as a burden on employment and an obstacle to job creation. This approach has contributed to the widespread acceptance of the definition of social contributions as "non-wage" costs, whereas they are clearly part of the total wage (comprising direct and indirect wages) paid to employees. At a macro level, it is argued that increased global competition and labour market efficiency in terms of job creation call for a reduction of these "non-wage" labour costs. However, there is no strong evidence to support the claim that there exists a direct causal relationship between employment levels and types of mechanisms for funding social protection. The correlation between labour cost levels and components is not clear, at least in the European Union countries. For instance, data for 2001 show that Denmark and Germany had similar hourly labour cost levels but very different labour cost structures (with social contributions representing less than 10% in the first case and more than 20% in the second). The same can be said when Italy and the UK are compared. Indeed, a low level of social contributions is usually compensated by a higher level of direct wages, which becomes necessary in order to finance social protection through income tax.

A similar criticism can be levelled at the analyses of the micro-level effects of social protection on labour market functioning, and more precisely the impact of social benefits on labour supply behaviour[2]. It is commonly held that a higher level of unemployment compensation leads to longer periods of unemployment[3]. This simplistic conception of job search motivation was criticised by Solow (1998) who stressed the importance of occupational status as a driving factor to get out of unemployment. Moreover, recent comparative research between European labour markets has highlighted the lack of clear-cut evidence of a lower commitment to work among the unemployed or of the disincentive effects of generous benefits (Gallie, 2000).

The second area of research deals with the consequences of flexibility on the labour market and develops a more micro-level point of view. Investigations focus on how social security systems cope with and should be adapted to the new developments in European labour markets. Three major normative proposals can be distinguished.

First, a transitional labour market approach is used to address the complexity of worker trajectories (Schmid, 2002). It is argued that current patterns of mobility in and out of the labour market contrast with the established model of lifelong stable and full-time employment and that "risky" labour market transitions require a redesign of unemployment insurance. The proposal is for a management of social risk sourced by a mix of tax-financing and personal savings. However, there is little evidence for a general destabilisation of employment status: permanent

---

[2] While the debates over this issue are intense, it should be noted that unemployment benefits account for only 7.5% of social expenditure (Eurostat, "Social Protection in Europe", Statistics in Focus, 2/2000) and are provided to roughly only one out of three unemployed people (Grimshaw and Rubery, 1997).

[3] This hypothesis is related to the job search model, according to which compensation acts as a disincentive to work because it increases the reservation wage (the minimum wage level for an individual to take a job), and delays acceptance of job offers. However this presupposes the existence of a uniform system of compensation covering all the unemployed with no limits on duration and regardless of their past and present labour market behaviour, which is a far cry from reality.

full-time employment remains the standard in most European labour markets, and unstable and risky trajectories concern specific segments of the labour force, predominantly women and young people (who are over-represented in precarious and part-time jobs). In promoting individual management of the resources sustaining time out of employment, this proposal advocates changes in the nature of employees' resources. But it overlooks the consequences of this in terms of changes in the status of employment, not least of which is the blurring boundary between waged employment and self-employment.

In the second, the theme of "flexicurity" is used to address such different issues as access to social protection for people in low-paid precarious jobs, the question of minimum benefits, the individualisation of benefits, and activation policies. While this approach includes the need for making labour market transitions more secure, it goes beyond the transitional labour market framework and develops a different perspective. The main issue here is how to extend the principles of regulation associated with the standard full time job (sufficient income and full access to social protection) to other forms of employment and adapt this regulation to the new needs engendered by discontinuous biographies (Klammer, 2000).

The third proposal, presented in a comprehensive study conducted by Alain Supiot for the European Commission, advocates a fairly similar position. The aim of the study was to examine perspectives for labour law reform, and to reconsider the employment status in view of changes in the realms of work, employment, and household structure. The "Supiot report" (Supiot, 1999) proposes replacing the employment contract by a *statut professionnel*[4] which would link social and economic rights to individual histories not only of waged employment but also of training, education and participation in socially useful non-waged work, thereby extending the linkages between work and welfare to non-employment activities. However, the report does not suggest how this should be financed, and this issue seems to be at the heart of current debates.

These approaches raise major questions. Does flexibilisation justify changing the whole social security system or would it only require integrating the new forms of employment into existing schemes? If so, why not channel the resource flows needed to finance new situations

---

[4]   The French expression *"statut professionnel"* could be translated literally by "occupational status" but it is more significantly expressed by "labour market status" according to Deakin (2002). In the English version of the Supiot Report it was translated as "membership of the labour force".

through the wage, as this path has already proven successful in the institutionalisation of the modern wage relation?

At the moment, it is apparent that social policy studies are dominated by the influence of economic determinism. The discourse on the disincentive effects of unemployment compensation has been given more weight than the issue of social protection for precarious workers. This is particularly visible in the emphasis placed on the activation of labour market policies and the tightening up of conditions of entitlement to unemployment benefits (Bosco and Chassard, 1999). These reforms play a crucial role in the reshaping of the linkages between employment and social protection and therefore in the definition of social rights, employment status and social divisions.

II. Labour market policies: impacts on resource flows and social categorisations

This section will examine recent transformations in the linkages between employment and social protection resulting from public labour-market policies implemented in the countries examined by our network. These policies have modified the nature of employees' resources, leading to new categorisations across the working population.

A. Subsidised jobs and subsidised workers

The European Employment Strategy has defined the objectives for public intervention in the labour market that are to be delivered through the National Action Plans for Employment. The latter adopt a broad definition of labour market policy that has increasingly come to encompass social policy and employment policy as well as structural reforms.

In the continental countries considered here, where social contributions are the traditional basis for financing social protection (France, Italy, Spain and, to a lesser extent, Portugal where a larger share of social protection is tax-financed), one of the major objectives is to tackle simultaneously the problems of insufficient employment growth and the "insider-outsider" structure of the labour markets. The line of approach adopted centres on the reduction of direct and indirect wages, either by general measures applied to the labour force as a whole, or by selective measures targeting what are termed "disadvantaged" groups with a view to improving their access to employment. In the UK, on the other hand, public intervention in the labour market tends to focus more on poverty, inactivity and unemployment traps than on job creation. Programmes aim to "make work pay", and focus on in-work benefits and welfare-to-work policies[5].

These measures all clearly modify the nature of resource flows linked to employment and social protection, either by financing a share of labour costs through public funds via policies geared to reducing these costs, or by financing an increasing share of the cost of the reproduction of labour through in-work benefits. In both cases, the mechanisms used reduce the role of the wage as a central vehicle for resource flows. However, a broad distinction can be made between subsidised employment in the first case and subsidised workers in the second, although these two categories clearly overlap (Moncel and Ruivo, 2002).

The category of subsidised employment concerns paid work activities for which the cost is partially or totally financed through taxation[6]. Subsidised jobs are defined as benefiting from the following measures:

- total or partial exemption from social contributions;
- monetary subsidies paid to the company to cover a part of the direct wage and/or social contributions, and often for the employment of targeted categories of workers;
- subsidies received by companies in exchange for expenditure on recruitment, employee training, job creation, start-up initiatives, etc.

These three types of measures constitute the preferred instruments for employment policies in the continental countries[7]. In Italy, Portugal and Spain, they are mostly targeted at specific populations such as young people and the unemployed, and at specific activities or regions. In France, on the other hand, their scope has been expanded to apply to low-paid workers, notably within the framework of agreements on the reduction of working time. Subsidised employment is less frequent in the UK, where labour market policies have always favoured supply-side schemes. Nonetheless, jobs paid below the "low earnings limit" have

---

[5] The notions "welfare to work" or "workfare" and "activation" are used to characterise the trend in social policies to increase the role of individual engagement in work-related activities. See Barbier (2001) for a discussion on the fuzziness of these expressions and the different meanings they are given depending on the societal context.

[6] Or by social contributions in the case of policies activating passive labour market expenditures.

[7] For an exhaustive description of labour market policy schemes, see the appendices to the final report by Clasquin and Friot (2001).

been exempted from social insurance contributions (National Insurance) since 1977: in 2000, two and a half million employees – and close to 20% of female employees – received a weekly wage below this limit (Equal Opportunities Commission, 1998). The more recent "New Deal" programmes introduced in 1997 provide subsidies for the employment of target categories of the labour force as well as for work experiences in a voluntary organisation or an environmental task force.

The category of subsidised worker is applied to two types of situations: workers whose wage is topped up by a tax-financed allowance conditional on their holding a job, and workers who draw a social benefit such as a minimum subsistence allowance concurrently with a low wage. These schemes are thus distinct from passive income support policies for the unemployed.

The second type of public intervention is the most recent, at least in the continental countries (minimum income benefit like the French RMI or an unemployment benefit drawn concurrently with earned income, notably in the case of part-time jobs), and has shown a marked increase thanks to the activation of employment policies and the introduction of "workfare" measures. In the UK, these have been more widely implemented via "in-work benefit" schemes such as the Working Family Tax Credit (WFTC).

The WFTC was introduced in October 1999 in order to reform the system of means-tested benefits for working families with dependent children that had been in place since 1971, first as Family Income Supplements until 1988, and then as Family Credit (Dilnot and McCrae, 2000). The salient characteristics of the new system are increased in-work benefits, called tax credits rather than social security benefits, which remain means-tested on family income, and channel extra money through the wage packet. In this sense, the benefits will effectively act as a wage subsidy and, as the UK National Employment Plan (2001) has noted, increase the risk that some employers will seek to take advantage of the scheme by lowering wages. The extension of this type of measure to low-paid workers in low-income households without children (Employment Tax Credit) is now under debate.

This form of income support for working people contributes to changing the nature of employees' resources by increasing the share of funding from the government budget. Moreover, the mechanism entails a two-fold shift in institutional forms: on the one hand, for redistributive purposes, tax-financed benefits tend to replace tax deductions and national insurance, and on the other, the scheme is implemented by the Inland Revenue services and not by the social protection administration.

In France, the new *prime pour l'emploi* is based on the same logic of topping up the low income of wage-earners' families via a tax credit paid by the income tax administration and thus bypassing the system of benefit provision financed by social contributions (see Chapter 3).

Between these categories of subsidised employment and subsidised workers, a number of hybrid situations exist, such as those covered by vocational training programmes and job-seeker allowances, or by employment schemes for the unemployed in the public sector. The latter, which are sometimes imposed by "workfare" policies and create a specific status that is not the employment norm in the public sector, are comparable to situations of subsidised employment, whereas the situations of job-seeking or training subsidised by public measures are closer to those of the "subsidised worker".

Subsidising employment and subsidising workers are also to be distinguished in terms of their effects: the first type of scheme tends to change employment rules whereas the second impacts on the structure of household income.

Subsidised employment programmes have entailed the multiplication of jobs that are constructed by specific rules for access to allowances provided on the basis of the characteristics of target populations or the particular objectives assigned to each policy measure. These rules, to differing degrees, provide dispensation from the norms governing the standard form of employment, and more generally, from the general rights linked to waged employment: we are referring in particular to the norms produced by collective agreements linking the wage to the qualification system; the minimum wage; termination of employment contract rules; and social protection.

The measures subsidising workers have no direct impact on the employment relation, the forms of wage determination, or contributions and entitlements to social benefits, since the schemes are applied to the individual's household income. However, they have an important impact on the functioning of the labour market: by topping up wages, they serve to sustain and organise the low-paid job segment.

Chapter 3 will provide a detailed analysis of how these differentiated forms of state intervention – subsidising workers or subsidising employment – are part of a trend to transform the nature of rights to national solidarity, to the detriment of rights based on labour law and citizenship rights, and to turn wage-earners and citizen-workers into benefit recipients.

The key question now is that of measuring the expansion of these programmes, and the problem is similar to that arising in the early 1980s with the growth of atypical forms of employment. We will thus turn to a close examination of comparative databases.

B. Contributions and limits of comparative data on labour market policies

A new Eurostat database was constructed[8] to serve as a source of information for monitoring the implementation of the European Employment Guidelines on labour market measures in the member states. The measures included in the scope of this Labour Market Policy (LMP) database were defined as follows:

> Public intervention in the labour market aimed at reaching its efficient functioning and to correct the disequilibria and which can be distinguished from other general employment policy measures in that they act selectively to favour particular groups in the labour market. Public interventions refer to measures taken by general government in this respect which involve expenditure, either in the form of actual disbursements or of forgone revenue (reduction in taxes, social contributions or other charges normally payable). General government should be understood as including central government, state/regional government, local government and the social security funds. The scope of the database is also limited to labour market measures which are explicitly targeted in some way at groups of people with difficulties in the labour market – referred to here as target groups. (Eurostat, 2002: p. 4)

These target groups concern the unemployed, employed at risk, inactive and registered job-seekers. Other more specific categories are sometimes also considered, such as youth, the disabled, or older workers. The database uses a narrow perspective on LMP which does not include general schemes or measures targeted at low-wage employees.

The data on LMP expenditures make a clear distinction between active and passive measures. The latter include out-of-work income maintenance and support (unemployment benefits, redundancy and bankruptcy compensation) and early retirement. Recent trends towards the activation of passive policies do not necessarily reflect a transfer of expenditures between these two categories, since the changes largely concern the conditions of access to certain measures. Active expenditures may increase if unemployment benefit recipients are under obligation to participate in training or counselling programmes[9].

---

[8] This database was constructed using the OECD Labour Market Programmes database.

[9] "In some cases participants [in active measures of direct job creation] may continue to receive an unemployment benefit instead of receiving a wage. In this case the

Table 1. Share of total expenditure by category, 2000
% total expenditure (categories 2-7)

	Spain	France	Italy	Portugal	UK	EU-15
2. Training (exc. Sub-category 2.4)	24.1	29.8	26.1	55.4	51.6	34.5
3. Job rotation and job sharing	0.7	–	0.3	0.1	–	0.8
4. Employment incentives	41.8	16.7	52.1	15.3	8.3	18.8
5. Integration of the disabled	10.2	9.5	0.8	4.5	25.9	15.6
6. Direct job creation	17.1	43.8	11.9	20.5	13.6	27.4
7. Start-up incentives	6.1	0.3	8.8	4.2	0.7	3.0
Total categories 2-7	100.0	100.0	100.0	100.0	100.0	100.0

Excludes sub-category 2.4. (Special support for apprenticeship). –: zero.
Source: Eurostat (2002a).

Active measures comprise a wide variety of schemes (Table 1): some provide counselling and training to improve the employability of the unemployed and other target groups (codes 1 and 2), while others seek to facilitate the integration of individuals into the labour market by subsidising employment (in the broad sense of the term) (codes 4 to 7). Subsidising employment consists of: i) providing support for recruitment and employment maintenance mostly in the private sector; ii) creating new jobs that are generally socially useful or of benefit to the community, where the bulk of the labour cost is usually covered by public finance; and iii) promoting entrepreneurship by providing start-up incentives, such as direct cash benefits, business advice and other indirect support.

From Table 1 it can be seen that the distribution of active expenditures by category is consistent with traditional views of LMP in the selected countries. The UK and Portugal place more emphasis on supply-side policies like vocational and educational training. Spain, France and Italy, on the other hand, tend to prioritise employment incentives or direct job creation, which are typically demand-side policies.

The analysis of the ways in which public funds are distributed to the direct recipients – individual beneficiaries, their employers, or the service providers supplying benefits in kind (Eurostat, 2002) – provides insight into the modalities used to formalise the policies in each country.

---

amounts received should be included in the measure reporting on the unemployment benefit" (Eurostat, 2002).

Table 2. Share of total expenditure by type, 2000
% total expenditure (categories 2-7)

	Spain	France	Italy	Portugal	UK	EU-15
Total	100.0	100.0	100.0	100.0	100.0	100.0
Transfers to individuals	**5.4**	**18.2**	**18.6**	**29.2**	**8.1**	**26.7**
Periodic cash payments	0.8	17.3	12.6	24.2	7.2	25.4
Lump-sum payments	4.3	0.8	6.0	5.0	0.9	1.2
Reimbursements	0.2	0.1	–	–	–	0.1
Reduced social contributions	–	–	–	–	–	0.1
Reduced taxes	–	–	–	–	–	–
Transfers to employers	**71.0**	**67.5**	**72.6**	**18.7**	**32.2**	**38.6**
Periodic cash payments	18.8	47.5	0.2	5.2	32.2	23.3
Lump-sum payments	3.5	1.8	4.7	13.1	–	1.2
Reimbursements	–	–	–	0.0	–	0.1
Reduced social contributions	47.6	17.8	67.8	0.4	–	13.6
Reduced taxes	1.1	0.3	–	–	–	0.4
Transfers to service providers	**23.6**	**14.2**	**8.8**	**2.6**	**11.3**	**27.0**
Not specified	–	–	–	**49.5**	**48.4**	**7.7**

Excludes sub-category 2.4. (Special support for apprenticeship). –: zero.
Source: Eurostat (2002a).

Table 2 shows that the organisation of transfers in the countries examined corresponds roughly to the overall logic reflected in Table 1. Transfers to employers represent about two-thirds of total active expenditure in Spain, France and Italy. This is associated with the predominance of employment incentives or direct job creation measures. (The quality of the data does not permit to draw conclusions concerning Portugal and the UK). The salient feature in Table 2 is the major role played by reduced social contributions in active expenditure, particularly in Spain and Italy. This clearly shows how resource flows that should be going from employers to the social security administrations are interrupted.

While the Eurostat data remain useful for the framework designed to coordinate employment policies, they present an important limitation. The resources allocated to policies directed at low-wage, low-income workers – a target group benefiting from state transfers – are not accounted for. Consequently, if the share of active LMP expenditure (categories 2-7) is measured in relation to GDP in 2000, the figures remain within proportions ranging from a minimum of 0.089% in the United Kingdom, to a maximum of 0.931% in France, with an average of 0.511% for the 15 EU member states (Eurostat, 2002a: p. 14). National figures have to be consulted in order to obtain the financial data corresponding to total expenditure on subsidised employment and workers[10]. It thus appears necessary to develop further indicators to assess the impact of public policies on resource flows. This also holds for the workers targeted by public policies whose resource flows are conditioned on their status in the labour market and their position in the wage or income hierarchy. While the Eurostat database does permit to measure the number of participants in LMP programmes, its scope needs to be broadened if it is to serve the purposes of our research objectives.

III. Reconsidering social exclusion and social integration through employment

Changes in labour market policies and welfare systems give rise to new forms of inclusion and exclusion and contribute to the processes of construction and deconstruction of new and old rights over resources[11].

The notion of "social exclusion" was developed in the mid 1960s to mid 1970s in response to the liberal view of *poverty* as an individual phenomenon. The aim was to stress the social nature of the "dropping out" processes observed among certain populations (such as drug addicts or people suffering from psychiatric conditions) and to reveal the existence of social groups without access to the economic and social benefits provided by welfare systems. Its widespread acceptance is due not only to its effectiveness in explaining social change, but also to the fact that public policies have set a priority on the "fight against social exclusion" both for state intervention and for research[12] (Bruto da Costa, 1998; Pererinha, 1996; Procacci, 1998).

---

[10] For example, in France, the DARES data on employment expenditure (DPE) cover a broader scope than that adopted by the OECD (and now Eurostat) for labour market policies (Roguet, 2001: p. 9).

[11] See Chapter 1 in this volume and Esping-Andersen, 1999.

[12] Research studies financed by the European Commission during the 1990s contributed substantially to disseminating the social exclusion concept in the European Research community. It should be noted that the Commission has recently changed its agenda – and its vocabulary – passing from *social exclusion* to *social inclusion*.

Social exclusion will be considered here from two points of view: A) as an outcome of changes in labour market inequalities and participation; and B) as a social status calling into question the inclusive power of employment.

A. Social exclusion as an outcome

The *social exclusion* concept was initially based on a binary logic (in/out); it was intended to replace the concept of *inequality* and to introduce a plurality of dimensions to which social exclusion/inclusion indicators should refer. The significance of this change is that it reflects a shift from a vision based on society "as a whole" – in which differences between diverse groups were related to one dimension only (generally income) – to a vision focused on the living conditions of the lower social strata (considered as a heterogeneous collection of "target groups").

Two types of research approach have contributed to the widespread diffusion of this concept. The first focuses on socio-economic aspects with an emphasis on three main ideas:

- the social nature of processes of impoverishment (Procacci, 1998; Saraceno in Negri, 1995);
- the precariousness of employment (Peña Casas and Pochet, 2001);
- the breakdown of the citizenship pact underpinning societal solidarity, and the effect of income polarisation in creating a "social divide" (Capucha, 1998; Procacci, 1998).

The second is related to studies on social cohesion showing:

- the breakdown of social ties, the incapacity to engage in active social life, the processes of exclusion from the social, economic, political and cultural systems of society; (Duffy, Walker A., Walker C. in Levitas, 1999);
- the relevance of spatial and urban dimensions (Procacci, 1998).

What is common to these studies is the view that *social* exclusion and *economic* exclusion represent two distinct but correlated dimensions. The literature relates *social exclusion* to: consumption levels; education and training; family structure; health; housing conditions; income levels; employment and labour conditions; life expectancy; ownership of goods; security; social networks and social ties (Peña-Casas and Pochet, 2001). From a socio-economic point of view, these dimensions are to be linked to the following factors: social and demographic trends (family structure); personal disposable income levels (for example, consumption levels, ownership of goods) and rights/access to social resources (for example, health, education and training, housing, security). It must be observed that negative access to social resources correlates with the largest number of indicators of social exclusion. While the question of poverty refers solely to economic resources, social exclusion and poverty are clearly interrelated: the ways in which goods and services are commodified or decommodified through the welfare system produce different effects on – and different boundaries between – these two dimensions.

Social integration therefore depends on *economic integration* – as the access to standard income/consumption levels – and on *social integration* – as the access to social rights/resources/protection. From this perspective, being socially excluded does not necessarily mean to be poor. And to be poor does not automatically mean to be socially excluded. We therefore consider these two dimensions as complementary. The following schema shows the variety of situations that can be produced by the combination of exclusion and inclusion factors:

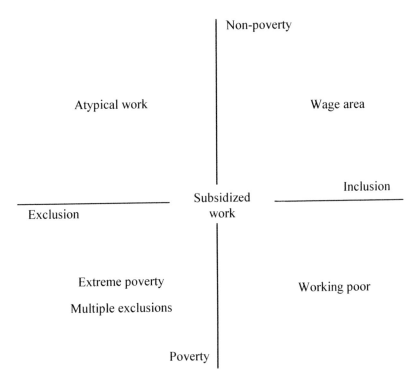

Four main zones are defined:

1. *Inclusion/non-poverty/wage area:* The wage relation ensures access to standard income/consumption levels (non-poverty) and the right to social resources;

2. *Inclusion/poverty/working poor:* This configuration demonstrates the possibility of being *included*, despite not being able to reach an ordinary standard of living. It shows the path to impoverishment via the precariousness of so called "bad jobs"

3. *Exclusion/poverty/extreme poverty and multiple exclusions*: This identifies the groups traditionally targeted by social assistance policies.

4. *Exclusion/non-poverty/atypical jobs:* This zone reveals the existence of non-poverty situations associated with weak entitlements to social resources.

In the central part of the schema, the presence of a wide galaxy of *subsidised jobs* can be observed. This category includes many different forms of subsidised employment that are not easily comparable and that link to all four parts of the schema. *Subsidised work*, therefore, beyond the changes it produces in the industrial relations system and in the construction of wages, work and unemployment, also challenges the idea of work as a *vehicle of inclusion.*

This typology is fairly close to Castel's analysis of the current situation[13], in which he distinguishes:

–   a zone of social integration characterised by stable, long-term employment and social protection; this zone is no longer as compact and homogeneous as before and no longer functions as an aggregation model for the whole society;

–   a zone of "social vulnerability" in which precarious jobs are the common situation and social protection coverage is highly variable;

–   a zone of extreme poverty/exclusion in which people suffer from the combined effects of unemployment, social isolation and low standards of living.

The zones of vulnerability illustrated by the schema clearly show that the growth of *atypical jobs* and the creation of new kinds of *subsidised jobs* are based on the same logic: the breakdown of the relationship between employment status and social protection. In the first case we

---

[13]   Castel in Fundacion Foessa (1994).

are dealing with a redistribution of social risks to individuals: atypical workers in precarious situations have limited or merely nominal rights and are relegated to the fringes of the welfare system. In fact, the spread of *atypical jobs* means a displacement of "non-wage costs", making this kind of contract attractive for employers and "reducing" remuneration to personal disposable income only. *Subsidised jobs*, on the other hand, tend to generate new forms of employment associated with specific forms of resources and social rights. Here, access to remuneration/social rights is not linked to a universal status, such as "worker" or "citizen", but to social stigma: the long term unemployed, single mothers, etc[14].

Despite the different psychological situations of *self-employment/atypical jobs* and of *subsidised jobs*, both situations provide limited access to social protection and contribute to the construction of weak socially inclusive identities. In conclusion, the emergence of the *working poor* can be considered as evidence of the recent failure of the wage to act as a vehicle of inclusion.

B. The question of social status

According to Paugam (1996), the existence – and persistence – of various forms of poverty (and social exclusion) is an outrage for the ideal of equality on which modern democracies are founded. The growth of a "risk culture" and the multiplication of new opportunities or intermediary spaces between work and unemployment that permit to experiment new ways of working have not diminished social inequalities and will lead to a fragmentation of the labour market and an increase in the disparities within and between the social classes.

The situation described in the schema above produces:

–   the emergence of a category of workers with limited access to social resources; according to Marshall, these would be workers without, or with lesser *industrial citizenship rights*[15];

---

[14]   This marks a return to the stigmatisation associated with the "Poor Laws" (Marshall, 1950).

[15]   From this perspective, comparing recent trends to Alfred Marshall's vision, we should observe a regression in the social rights development process. Thomas H. Marshall used the expression to designate rights that, during the 20th century, permitted to improve civil life, increase equality and reduce risk and uncertainty for the future. All this has profound repercussions on the representation and self-perception of the social and personal identity of *workers* and *citizens*.

- the reduction of the potential for social integration of work experiences; the existence of *working poor* in the world's richest societies, as Ehrenreich (2001) points out, attests to this.

In traditional societies, social status served as a bond to the social hierarchy while providing individuals with a specific "position" and a social identity. Therefore social status and its peculiar "immutability" functioned as a link to the symbolic identity and unity of the community. In contemporary states, an individual's position within society depends on his or her access to civil, political and social rights (Marshall, 1950)[16]. Civil and political rights, due to their earlier institution and entrenched universality, are now no longer considered as factors of social differentiation. Social rights concern the entitlement to that share of collective resources required to attain what is to be considered a minimum level relative to the average standard of living in a given society. In contemporary societies, *social status* is linked mainly to an individual's position in the productive and social protection systems (Schnapper, in Paugam, 1996). The fact that the question of *social exclusion* has been raised is in itself evidence that the principles of solidarity and inclusion are in crisis.

As we have seen, the social exclusion concept was developed thirty years ago in response to a morally unacceptable situation: the existence of groups without access to the fruits of economic progress or to the distribution of social benefits. How has the situation evolved since then?

A parallel can be drawn between the current transition from a Fordist to a post-Fordist society and the passage from traditional to industrial society. In both periods, the social question can be characterised by the following features: precariousness, dequalification, unemployment, uncertainty for the future and poor life conditions in terms of material deprivation, moral degradation and desocialisation. *Pauperism* was the concept created to express the social question during the entry into the *industrial society* while *social exclusion* defines the social question at the time of the emergence out of the industrial/Fordist paradigm. Social exclusion can therefore be considered the sign of a disaggregation produced by the social and economical order, the evidence of its fallibility (Donzelot, in Paugam, 1996)

With the progressive "escape" from the welfare system – through the creation of new forms of employment relations with limited access to social resources – it has become the individual's responsibility to deal

---

[16] Dupuy (1996) refers to: individual rights, chances/opportunity and access to social and economic resources.

with the risks society continues to produce. This is what Bauman (2000) has defined as *liquid modernity*. Social exclusion is therefore to be considered as a socially constructed process operating through the fragmentation of the labour market and the deconstruction of social protection, and implying the loss of *industrial citizenship rights*.

The consequences of combinations between situations of *inclusion/exclusion* and *poverty/non-poverty* reveal the limits of the inclusive power of work and forces welfare systems to face a new generation of social risks. The (re)definition of the linkages between work and the access to social resources is an urgent issue for research.

IV. Societal diversity and social differentiation of the work-welfare nexus

The two previous sections illustrate the relevance of an approach that takes into account the linkages between employment and social protection: these linkages are a blind spot in evaluations of labour market policies and appear to be central to the issue of social exclusion. We would like in this last section to elaborate on the notion of a "work-welfare nexus" in order to develop an approach that accounts for societal diversity and social differentiation as essential features of the relation between employment and social protection. The idea is to consider that this nexus constitutes the defining dimension of the employment status in comparison with other labour situations, self-employment, contracts of hire or for services[17]. As Deakin (2002) notes:

> The 'contractualisation' of the employment relationship was associated with the gradual spread of social legislation in the fields of workmen's compensation, social insurance and employment protection. The terms 'contract of employment' and 'employee' came into general use as a description of wage-dependent labour only as a result of this process. Contractualisation had two central aspects: the placing of limits on the employer's legal powers of command [...]; and the use of the employment relationship as a vehicle for channelling and redistributing social and economic risks, through the imposition on employers of obligations of revenue collection, and compensation for interruptions to earnings. (p. 3)

The close nexus between work and welfare is a central and distinctive dimension of the modern employment relation; it is supported by the wage as a central vehicle for the channelling of resource flows

---

[17] In some countries, compulsory contributions have been extended to the self-employed in order to maintain a certain level of security for these employment situations.

which constitute both employees' direct remuneration and social benefits. The instituted forms of the work-welfare nexus apply to the way in
which the wage relation has been constructed as the dominant social
category of the market form of work, and reflect societal diversity and
the variability of the wage relation within a given division of labour[18].

Thus the work-welfare nexus refers to the linkages between labour
markets and social protection systems at a macro-social level, and to the
social status related to employment at a micro-level. It is proposed as a
device to analyse the diversity, variability and evolution of the wage
relation in such a way as to account for the complex process of institutionalisation of these linkages. This process presents two important
features: it is a societal construction and it is interconnected with the
social division of labour.

The progressive extension of the wage relation and the institutionalisation of the work-welfare nexus were common developments in most
Western European societies during the post-World War II period. But
countries obviously developed specific patterns of this nexus that
stemmed from long-lasting institutional traditions, political and ideological positions and mobilisations "from below" around management,
work and welfare issues (Carpenter and Jefferys, 2000). The persistent
diversity of the work-welfare nexus is the argument against the existence of a universal type of relationship between labour market and
social protection system, such as is assumed in neo-classical accounts.
Moreover, although the construction of stable forms of social and
political regulation were the preconditions for the economic and technological developments that took place, this diversity reveals the relative
autonomy with regard to capitalist technological systems of the processes instituting societal configurations of the work-welfare nexus.
Using a comparative perspective, we argue that the work-welfare nexus
is part of the societal configuration of the *fait salarial* developed by the
societal effect approach, which stresses not only the social "embedded-
ness" of phenomena but also the social construction of actors and of the
space in which they act (Maurice, 1995). In terms of analytical perspectives, this means considering employment as an instituted economic
exchange; the focus of analysis turns to the processes and mechanisms
of institution of this exchange, their variation across countries and
dynamics over time.

---

[18] Given our focus on employment, we do not deal with the distinction between paid
and unpaid work, although this is crucial in the construction of the wage relationship
and welfare systems and their gendered patterns. For a comprehensive presentation of
this aspect, see Lewis (1992).

The second central feature of the work-welfare nexus is its heterogeneity: the social division of labour is reflected in a social division of welfare. Titmuss (1958) was the first to highlight this division of welfare, which he argued derives not from differences in intended function or aim but "from an organisational division of method, which, in the main, is related to the division of labour in complex, individuated societies" (p. 42). His study of the British welfare system showed how different systems operated in different social spheres to meet similar needs: he used the term "social" welfare to designate publicly provided funds and services (such as Social Security, local authority housing, the National Health Service, and personal social services); "fiscal" welfare to describe "allowances and reliefs from income tax"; and "occupational" welfare to cover a whole range of employer-provided benefits. Comparing public social expenditures to allowances and tax reliefs, Titmuss highlighted the importance of institutional forms of welfare provision:

> The first is a cash transaction; the second an accounting convenience. Despite this difference in administrative method, the tax saving that accrues to the individual is, in effect, a transfer payment. In their primary objectives and their effects on individual purchase power there are no differences in these two ways by which collective provision is made for dependencies. (pp. 44-45)

These different forms of welfare were prevalent for different social classes: public expenditures aimed more at sustaining working class incomes whereas tax allowances were targeted at middle-class groups and occupational welfare tended more to benefit upper professionals. Titmuss also observed that public debates tend to focus on "a stereotype of social welfare which represents only the more visible part of the real world of welfare" (p. 53) namely public expenditures commonly known as the "welfare state". Finally, he argued that while these three systems operated "as separate and distinctive attempts to counter and to compensate for the growth of dependency in modern society [...] they are simultaneously enlarging and consolidating the area of social inequality" (p. 55). Another analytical perspective of the work-welfare approach is therefore to understand the mechanisms and systems of distribution and redistribution that generate and maintain social, political and economic inequality (Sinfield, 1979).

Research on labour market segmentation has highlighted some of these mechanisms. Access to employment for young people and women and their position in the labour market are good examples of how the social division of welfare and the social division of labour both shape and generate social inequalities. Social benefits are indeed related to other forms of labour market segmentation (position in the productive system, wage determinants, mobility scales, employment contract and tenure, working time). So-called "atypical" forms of employment (temporary contracts, part-time work or self-employment) entail not only employment instability but also insecurity of income because they are coupled with restricted access to social benefits. In most of the European countries, precarious and part-time workers face reduced entitlement rights to income protection while unemployed and to pension income when retired (Grimshaw and Rubery, 1997).

Conclusion

We have sought here to show that the linkages between employment and social protection – or more to the point, the rights to social protection – are facing major challenges in contemporary societies. The search for flexibility via atypical forms of employment often entails reduced access to social protection, which in turn can create phenomena of segmentation, or even exclusion if unfavourable factors are accumulated. The linked transformations of the labour market and social protection systems raise the question of how to ensure social protection coverage for workers with complex trajectories in and out of the labour market and notably with long periods in training or long or frequent periods of unemployment, or for workers at the bottom of the ladder in terms of remuneration and conditions of work and employment. The financing of social rights thus becomes a crucial issue, and we have seen how public intervention in the labour market to subsidise employment or subsidise workers changes both the source and the direction of resource flows. The solutions adopted serve to destabilise the existing resource regimes.

Thus it can be asked whether the process instituting the wage relation is being reversed: are we witnessing an erosion of employment-related social rights? If so, are new social rights emerging, and what kind? These questions open up a new line of research around three connected issues. The first relates to the destabilisation of the linkages between the labour market and social protection systems resulting from changes in the division of labour. What are the new divisions of labour that entail new social divisions of welfare? And are these processes of social differentiation similar across countries? The second concerns the possible emergence of new social rights, for instance the right to life-long training promoted by the European agenda: how will these rights be deployed over the population and which political institutions will support, finance and assess their implementation? Finally, the third research topic deals with a broader issue at the core of the work-welfare nexus: if the role of the wage as a vehicle for channelling resources is reduced, what political choices in terms of distribution and redistribution would need to be made in order to ensure access to resources and social rights for social units having no direct relation to the productive sphere through waged employment?

References

Atkinson, A.B. (1995), *Incomes and the Welfare State*, Cambridge, Cambridge University Press.

Barbier, J.C. (2001), *Welfare to Work Policies in Europe – the Current Challenges of Activitation Policies*, Document de Travail du Centre d'Études de l'Emploi No.11, November.

Bauman, Z. (2000), *Liquid modernity*, Italian edition: Bari, Laterza.

Bosco, A. and Chassard, Y. (1999), "A Shift in the Paradigm: Surveying the European Union Discourse on Welfare and Work", in European Foundation for the Improvement of Living and Working Conditions, *Linking Welfare and Work*, Luxembourg, Office for Official Publications of the European Communities, pp. 43-58.

Bosco, A. and Hutsebaut, M. (eds) (1997), *Social Protection in Europe – Facing up to changes and challenges*, Brussels, European Trade Union Institute.

Bosco, N. (1998), La povertà economica in Italia. Dati, risultanze empiriche, tendenze, in *"Quaderni di Sociologia"*, Vol. XLII, n. 17.

Capucha, L. (1998), "Pobreza, Exclusão Social e Marginalidades" in J.M. Leite Viegas and A. Firmino da Costa (org.), *Portugal, que Modernidade?*, Oeiras, Celta Editora, pp. 209-242.

Carpenter, M. and Jefferys, S. (2000), *Management, Work and Welfare in Western Europe*, Cheltenham, Edward Elgar Publishing.

Castel, R. (1995), *Les Métamorphoses de la Question Sociale. Une Chronique du Salariat*, Paris, Fayard.

Clasquin, B. and Friot, B. (dir.) (2001), *La Construction Sociale de l'Emploi*, Final Report of the TSER Network, contract ERB SOE-CT-97-3041.

Bruto da Costa, A. (1998), *Exclusões Sociais*, Lisbon, Gradiva, Fundação Mário Soares, Cadernos Democráticos.

Deakin, S. (2002), "The Evolution of the Employment Relationship" paper presented at the Symposium on *The Future of Work, Employment and Social Protection*, Lyon, 17-18 January 2002.

Deakin, S. and Wilkinson, F. (1994), "Labour Market Regulation, Social Policy and European Integration", in J. Perris and R. Page (ed.), *Social Policy in Transition*, Aldershot, Avebury, pp. 143-164.

Dilnot, A. and McCrae, J. (2000), "The Family Credit System and the Working Families Tax Credit in the United Kingdom", *OECD Economic Studies* No.31, 2000/II, pp. 69-84.

Donzelot, J. (1996), "Les Transformations de l'Intervention Sociale face à l'Exclusion" in S. Paugam. *L'Exclusion, l'État des Savoirs*, Paris, Éditions La Découverte.

Dupuy, J-P. (1996), "La Philosophie Sociale et Politique Face à la Misère de l'Economie" in S. Paugam, *L'Exclusion, l'État des Savoirs*, Paris, Éditions La Découverte.

Ehrenreich, B. (2001), *Nickel and Dimed. On (Not) Getting By in America*, Italian edition: Milano, Feltrinelli.

Equal Opportunities Commission (1998), *Low Pay and National Insurance System: A Statistical Picture*, E.O.C. Research Findings.

Esping-Andersen, G. (1990), *The Three Worlds of Welfare Capitalism*, Cambridge, Polity Press.

Esping-Andersen, G. (1999), *Social Foundations of Post-industrial Economies*, Oxford, Oxford University Press.

Esping-Andersen, G. and Regini, M. (ed.) (2000), *Why Deregulate Labour Market?*, Oxford, Oxford University Press.

European Foundation for the Improvement of Living and Working Conditions (1999), *Linking Welfare and Work*, Luxembourg, Office for Official Publications of the European Communities.

Eurostat (2000), "Social Protection in Europe", *Statistics in Focus, Population and Social Conditions*, No.2/2000, Luxembourg, Office for the Official Publications on the European Communities.

Eurostat (2002), *Labour Market Policy. Database Methodology*, April 2000, Luxembourg, Office for the Official Publications on the European Communities, 2002.

Eurostat (2002a), *European Social Statistics, Labour Market Policy. Expenditures and Participants. Data 2000*, Luxembourg, Office for the Official Publications on the European Communities, 2002.

Fundacion Foessa (1994), *Informe sociologico sobre la situacion social en España*, Madrid.

Gallie, D. (dir) (2000), *Employment Precarity, Unemployment and Social Exclusion*, Final report of European Research Network EPURE, April 2000.

Grimshaw, D. and Rubery, J. (1997), "Workforce Heterogeneity and Unemployment Benefits: the Need for Policy Reassessment in the European Union", *Journal of European Social Policy*, Vol. 7, No.4, November 1997.

ISTAT (1999), Rapporto annuale, *La situazione del paese nel 1998*, Roma.

Klammer, U. (2000), "Working women in the Age of Flexibility – New diversities, new needs for social protection" in thematic Network "Working and

Mothering: Social practices and social policies", 4th report to the European Commission, Frankfurt, pp. 133-162.

Kuhnle, S. (ed.) (2000), *Survival of the European Welfare State*, London, Routledge/ECPR Studies in European Political Science.

Levitas, R. (1999), "Defining and measuring social exclusion: a critical overview of current proposals", *Radical Statistics*, No.71.

Lewis, J. (1992), "Gender and the Development of Welfare Regimes", *Journal of European Social Policy*, 2 (3), pp. 159-173.

Marshall, T. H. (1950), *Citizenship and social class*, Italian edition: Bari, Laterza.

Maurice, M. (1995), "Convergence and/or Societal Effect for the Europe of the Future?", in Cressey P. and Bryn J., *Work and Employment in Europe – A New Convergence?*, London, Routledge, pp. 28-40.

Mingione, E. (1999), *Le sfide dell'esclusione: metodi, luoghi, soggetti*, Bologna, il Mulino.

Moncel, N. and Ruivo, M. (2002), "L'impact des politiques d'emploi sur la socialisation des ressources des travailleurs dans cinq pays européens", *Sociologia del Lavoro* No.85, 2002, pp. 195-206.

Negri, N. (1995), "I concetti di povertà ed esclusione", in *Polis*, IX, n.1, April.

Paugam, S. (1996), *L'Exclusion, l'État des Savoirs*, Paris, Éditions La Découverte.

Peña-Casas, R. and Pochet, P. (2001), *Les indicateurs monétaires et non monétaires de pauvreté et d'exclusion sociale dans une perspective européenne*, Bruxelles, Observatoire Social Européen.

Pereirinha José, A. (1996), "Pobreza e Exclusão Social. Algumas Reflexões sobre Conceitos e Aspectos de Medição", in J.M. Carvalho Ferreira, *Entre Economia e Sociologia*, Oeiras, Celta Editora, pp. 208-232.

Pierson, P. (ed.) (2001), *The New Politics of the Welfare State*, Oxford, Oxford University Press.

Procacci, G. (1998), *Governare la povertà*, Bologna, Il Mulino.

Raveaud, G. (2000), "Dynamics of the welfare state regimes and employability", A study based on the National Action Plans for Employment, 1998-2000", Paper presented to the EISS Conference, Goteborg, September 7-9th, 2000.

Roguet, B. (2001), "La Dépense pour l'Emploi en 1998", *DARES, Premières Synthèses*, April 2001, No.15-1, p. 10.

Rossi, N. (a cura di) (1998), *Il lavoro e la solidarietà sociale: 1996-1997*, Bologna, Il Mulino.

Rossi, N. (1997), *Meno ai padri, più ai figli*, Bologna, Il Mulino.

Salais, R. and Whiteside, N. (eds) (1998), *Governance, Industry and Labour Market in Great-Britain and France*, London, Routledge.

Scharpf, F.W. (2000), "The Viability of Advanced Welfare States in the International Economy: Vulnerabilities and Options", *Journal of European Public Policy*, 7, 2 June 2000, pp. 190-228.

Schmid, G. (2002), "Employment insurance in critical transitions during the life-course", paper presented at the Symposium on *The Future of Work, Employment and Social Protection*, Lyon, 17-18 January 2002.

Schnapper, D. (1996), "Intégration et exclusion dans les sociétés modernes" in Paugam S. *L'exclusion, l'état des savoirs*, Paris, La Découverte.

Sinfield, A. (1979), "Analyses in the Social Division of Welfare", *Journal of Social Policy*, 7, 2, pp. 129-56.

Solow, R. M. (1998), *Work and Welfare*, Gutmann, A. (ed.), Princeton, Princeton University Press.

Supiot, A. (ed.) (1999), *Au-delà de l'emploi. Transformations du travail et devenir du droit du travail en Europe. Rapport pour la Commission Européenne*, Paris, Flammarion.

Titmuss, R. M. (1958), *Essays on "The Welfare State"*, London, Unwin University Books.

Torrens, F.J.A., *Reflexiones sobre pobreza y exclusión social en España. Nuevas formas y nuevas respuestas.*

Touraine, A. (1992), *Critique de la Modernité*, Italian edition: Milano, Il Saggiatore.

Touraine, A. (1997), *Pourrons-nous Vivre Ensemble? Égaux et différents*, Italian edition: Milano, Il Saggiatore.

United Kingdom Employment Action Plan 1999 and 2001.

United Kingdom Employment Action Plan 2001, http://europa.eu.int/comm/employment_social/news/2001/may/naps2001_en.html

CHAPTER 3

Resource Regime Reforms
and Worker Status

Bernard FRIOT

We consider that the predominant interpretations of social protection reforms are based on economistic postulates (management imperatives, the demographic crisis, competition from countries with low-paid labour, new information technologies, the shift from Fordist to property-based capitalism). By contrast, the research programme that we propose places the confrontation between capitalist accumulation and the assertion of workers' rights at the forefront.

It is our postulate that in the course of the 20th century, through both their union and their political struggles, the workers in the countries currently involved in the construction of the European Union obtained resource regimes which, at the beginning of the 1970s, constituted a potential basis for challenging financial accumulation, capitalism's dominant logic. And that, at the end of that decade, the European ruling classes seized the opportunity of the construction of a single market for capital and the providers of goods and services to launch a counter-revolution aimed at shifting these resource regimes in a direction favourable to financial accumulation.

It is these "resource regimes" that serve as analytical categories for the interpretation of the reforms discussed here. As explained in Chapter 1, resource regimes are defined by four variables: the mode of financing (sources) and the mode of distribution (benefits) characterise the types of resources; the other two variables are linked to the rights over these resources and distinguish between conditions of entitlement (or linkages between sources and benefits) and participation in the management of resources. Thus the issue of workers' rights linked to type of resource, while largely ignored elsewhere, is placed at the core of our work programme.

The present chapter analyses the shifts in these rights resulting from the reforms to the financing of employment and social protection introduced in France since the end of the 1980s, in a comparison with the Netherlands and Germany. It is based on a study conducted during the exploratory phase of our research programme[1].

The point of the comparison between these three high-wage-cost countries is to show that the different paths followed by the reforms all relate back to the same resource regime shifts. The resource regimes are designated here as: socialised wage, deferred wage, public insurance, tutelary allowance, pre-financed wage and employee savings regimes. The reforms are characterised as shifts

- from socialised wage to deferred wage (Part I)
- from socialised wage or from public insurance to tutelary allowance (Part II)
- from socialised wage or public insurance to pre-financed wage and employee savings (Part III).

The conclusion presents these shifts in resource regimes as an attempt to change workers' status, and therefore their rights.

I. From socialised wage to deferred wage

The *socialised wage* is the major resource regime in the continental countries of the EU. It encompasses not only the wage employers pay to their employees, but also the range of social benefits financed by the contributions they pay into the social security funds. The characteristics of the four variables defining this resource regime are as follows:

- Financing: For each job the employer makes two monthly payments – one to the employee (*direct wage*) and one to the social security fund in the form of social contributions proportional to the direct wage *(indirect wage)*; in France, for example, these *cotisations sociales*, which correspond to two-thirds of the direct wage and comprise an "employee" portion and an "employer" portion, represent 40% of the *total wage* (direct plus indirect wage).

---

[1] Christophe Nosbonne *et al.*, Enjeux des déplacements de l'articulation entre salaire, fiscalité et épargne dans les transformations de l'emploi, mise en perspective France/Europe du Nord, 2. Les transformations en cours dans le financement de l'emploi et des droits sociaux: comparaison France/Allemagne, Pays-Bas, by Bernard Friot (in collaboration with Gaël Coron), report submitted to the Direction Recherche, Ministère de la Recherche, Action concertée incitative Travail, Nancy, EPS-GREE-CNRS, July 2001, pp. 73-125. Readers are referred to this report for a fuller account of what is only briefly presented in this chapter.

- Benefits: The socialised wage covers all forms of benefits, whether wage replacement, services in kind (hospital care), reimbursement of expenditures (housing, ambulatory medical care), or flat-rate cash payments (family benefits).

- Conditions of access: The direct wage and replacement benefits proportional to this wage (unemployment, invalidity, sick leave, pension) are determined firstly on the basis of the qualification of the job or the person (in the case of state employees), since this qualification corresponds to a position in the job classification grid set by sectoral collective agreements. The amount and sometimes the duration of replacement benefits are also a function of the contributions record as well as of the recipient's age (unemployment), marital status (survivor's pension, pension enhancement per child raised) or severity of handicap (invalidity). Benefits complementing the direct wage are either tied to expenditure for health care and housing, or determined by a set of attributes for family benefits (number of children, level of income, marital status, kind of child-care service used).

- Management: Inasmuch as the socialised wage is financed by employers on the occasion of the employment of their workers, but covers populations and situations which go far beyond the sole employment relation, it is managed by both the social partners and the state, in a range of forms going from strict joint management by the social partners to a quasi-administrative arrangement.

The socialised wage, although not universal, can in no way be considered as a market price (even an "administered" one). Its socialisation is three-fold:

- Its financing and the conditions of access are not based on a market exchange, but are determined by collective bargaining. Far from there being an exchange of equivalents between productive input and resource, the qualification grid governing the distribution of the direct wage or its replacement, as well as the expenses and attributes linked to complementary benefits, are determined in a political process in which evaluation of the productive input is either indirect (qualification system) or non-existent (expenditure and attributes).

- A portion of the wage (40% in France) is mutualised by employers through their contributions to a common pool that finances non-work situations: childhood and youth, old age, sickness and unemployment. While this common pool is constituted by a number of distinct funds, mutualisation operates on a truly national, cross-sectoral level due to the field of application and financial solidarity of these funds. Added to this is the total absence of savings: the contributions are immediately spent on benefit provision, which rules out any individual accounting of input and outflow and clearly establishes the fact that jobholders are at all times producing the value that finances benefits for non-workers.

- The institutions of the socialised wage, which are private institutions arising out of the relationship between employer and employees, fulfil a public service function, and are jointly managed by their respective representatives and the state.

It will be seen that the reforms, which accelerated during the 1990s, have aimed at replacing the socialised wage by the deferred wage, tutelary allowance, pre-financed wage or employee savings, depending on the particular case. This section will examine the shift from socialised to deferred wage.

The *deferred wage* is a resource regime that is financed like the socialised wage but the benefits provided are limited to wage replacements. Wage complements in cash or in kind, such as family, housing or health benefits, which are considered to have no connection to the employment relation, are channelled through the tutelary allowance or employee savings, as will be seen later.

The conditions of entitlement remain centred on the qualification system, but their contributory nature is reinforced. The implication is that the benefit should correspond to the recipient's past contributions, as if it were a deferred use of the indirect part of the wage not consumed at the time of its creation. That is, as if each jobholder was financing his or her own benefits, rather than financing the benefits provided to others – the nonworkers – via his or her social contributions and thereby acquiring rights over the contributions of the future working population. In short, as if the intergenerational socialisation of the wage was being replaced by a mere intragenerational smoothing-out of income.

Clearly, if the perspective is one in which individuals recuperate their investment, and this within the only field considered to derive from the employment relation (wage replacement for retirement, unemployment, sick leave or disability), then management of the scheme would be incumbent upon the social partners, and them alone. With the shift from the socialised to the deferred wage, the distinction between "universal risks" and "employment-related risks" is accompanied by a distinction between the sphere of competence of the social partners (and collective negotiations) and that of the state (and the law).

The reforms introduced in the 1990s tending towards the deferment of a wage that had, until then, been socialised, fall into two broad categories. In one, "universal risks" are totally or partially withdrawn from the field of the wage, and are no longer financed by social contributions but through taxation. In the other, the wage-based financing of "employment-related risks" (unemployment and retirement) is maintained but its contributory nature reinforced.

In *France*, the most emblematic measure was the creation of the *contribution sociale généralisée* (CSG) in 1991. This tax subsequently proceeded to swallow up a growing proportion of the *cotisation sociale*, and the rationalisation for the replacement of a part of the socialised wage by an earmarked tax was always the same: first, it was not right for the wage to finance family benefits (the CSG percentage point created in 1991 was earmarked for family allowances); then, pension enhancement for child-rearing and the *minimum vieillesse* old-age entitlements (CSG raised in 1993 to finance the *Fonds de solidarité vieillesse*); and then health care (the CSG replaced over one-third of the *cotisation maladie* in 1998). The contention each time was that the wage must concern only the employment relation and that its socialisation to include the full range of life situations is unwarranted. This same line of argument was used to justify tax-financing the allowance for disabled adults (AAH) from 1983, and the single parent allowance (API) from 1999, both previously financed through the *cotisation sociale*, on the grounds that disablement and single parenthood should not be financed through the wage since there is no exchange in work provided.

In a similar vein, the requirement of a strictly individual exchange between contributions paid and unemployment benefits received (deferment of the wage) marked the series of reforms to the national, social partner managed unemployment fund (UNEDIC, *Union Nationale pour l'emploi dans l'industrie et le commerce*). The Beregovoy decrees of 1982 introduced a principle of proportionality between the duration of contributions and the duration of benefit provision; in 1984, the contributory benefit financed through the *cotisation sociale* was first separated from a non-contributory benefit for the unemployed who have exhausted their entitlements (financed through taxation), and then, in 1992, made regressive to speed up the return to employment. In 2000, the principle of an exchange of equivalents served, once again, to justify the introduction of an employment incentive (PARE): the rationale was that if the unemployed receive a wage in the form of the UNEDIC benefit, then they must provide work in exchange or be actively preparing to do so. Pension reforms reflect the same move to replace the socialised wage by a deferred wage: some have already been introduced (progressive shift from the 10 best to the 25 best paid years for the basic pension formula, starting in 1993); others are on the drawing board (*à la carte* retirement; civil service pensions based on average lifetime earnings and not final wage; replacement of years of pensionable service by a point system in the basic scheme).

In *Germany*, measures reducing the field of the wage and transforming the socialised wage into a deferred wage were introduced somewhat later. In the early 1990s, reunification brought a brief inverse trend, with a sharp increase in contribution rates to compensate for the drop in the share of public financing due to the monopolisation of budgetary resources for reconstruction. But this increase merely gave stronger impetus to the debate over *versicherungsfremden Leistungen* (non-insurance-related benefits), with employers and unions alike calling for fiscal funding of these "unjustified charges". As Klammer (1997) so rightly pointed out, this poses the major problem of where to draw the line between what is insurance-related and what is not. The salary, as the central object of the employment relation, could not be less "natural". How then can a "natural" criterion be used to determine which social needs should be covered through the wage and which through taxation?

This notwithstanding, the red-green government that came into power in 1998 introduced several measures to increase the share of tax-financing in the pension system in order to reduce contributions: VAT was raised by one percentage point; a green tax was introduced to bring the pension contribution down from 20.3% to 19.5% of the wage; the inclusion of three years of child-rearing per child in the pension formula was financed through the federal budget (rather than through the pension contribution); and the additional pension costs stemming from reunification were charged to the federal budget. With the result that everything in the mandatory old-age insurance benefit that is not considered to be covered by an exchange of equivalents between work and pension is fully or partially covered by taxation (Klammer, 2001)[2].

The deferred wage argument underwrites the pension reform of 1997 (with effect from 1/1/99). The wage replacement rate of the standard pension (based on a full working-life at average wage) is scheduled to drop from 70% to 64% by 2015 in order for the same total pension to take account of the increase in life expectancy. This means that it is as if

---

[2] However, in an inverse trend, the dependency insurance introduced in 1994 with effect as of 1/1/95, was financed by social contributions. It must be noted that this benefit was created in exchange for unpopular health insurance reductions as of 1/1/93.

the pension was financed by a stock of accumulated contributions to be transformed when the time comes into lower life-time annuities as the anticipated life expectancy increases. This is the opposite of the social-lised wage, which is always based on an intratemporal reasoning. The new SPD government then continued with this line of reform: a further reduction in old-age benefits concerning the survivor's pension, consi-dered to be non-contributory, was introduced in February 2001 with effect on 1/7/2001.

In the *Netherlands*, there has been a similar trend to withdraw what are considered to be non-employment-related risks from the sphere of the salary. In 1989, financing of the family allowance, which theoreti-cally remains within the insurance system, was switched from social contributions to taxation. Similarly, the 1998 disability benefit reform replaced the general disability insurance (AAW) with a scheme for the self-employed financed through their contributions (WAZ) and a scheme for disabled youth financed through taxation (WAJONG).

The transformation of the socialised wage into a deferred wage in the sphere of unemployment is particularly visible in the tightening up of the controls that show that the recipient of a wage-related benefit must remain within a logic of subordinated employment. Between 1990 and 1993, the number of sanctions imposed increased 2.3 times. In 1997, these penalties were reinforced: since then, unemployed workers who refuse to take up a "suitable" job offer run the risk of having their benefit provision suspended for a period corresponding to the duration of the proposed employment. The argument for an equitable balance between contributions and unemployment benefits was invoked for the 1995 reform, which tightened the link between contributions paid and compensation provided (although not nearly to the same extent as in France).

In a similar vein, the transformation of the pension into a deferred wage was on the agenda of the 1994 liberal-socialist government, who pushed for the pension formula to be based on average lifetime earnings rather than final earnings. This shift from the pension as a continuation of the wage to a pension as an exchange for a working record was reinforced by measures facilitating the transfer of rights from one scheme to another in the event of a change in employer; and by includ-ing periods of unemployment while terminating the exclusion of work under fixed-term contracts, thereby tightening up the relationship be-tween the working record and a defined-benefit pension.

Thus, in the 1990s, all three countries introduced reforms that were bent on tightening the individual link between wage and work provided. Situations defined as being "unrelated to employment" were switched to tax financing, while those social benefits that continued to be financed through the wage were tied to individual contributions records. These reforms countered the trend of the earlier decades in which labour law had tended to turn the socialised wage into an instrument for the immediate distribution to the whole population – whether working or non-working – of a growing share of the value added through collective work. This fundamental transformation of the wage (from "socialised" to "deferred") has changed the basis of workers' rights to resources. They no longer receive benefits on an intratemporal basis as members of a "collective worker" and according to the rules of labour law, but as owners of human capital that they valorise intertemporally on the labour market according to the rules of profit-making property rights.

II. From socialised wage or public insurance to the tutelary allowance

Public insurance, the other major resource regime alongside the socialised wage, is mostly present in the Anglo-Nordic countries of the EU. The four variables that define it can be characterised as follows:

- Financing: In its initial Beveridgean form public insurance was financed by a flat-rate or earnings-related tax on income, thus clearly establishing this resource regime as a right of the citizen-worker; subsequently, financing by progressive or indirect taxation components was sometimes added.

- Benefits: These consist both of free public services providing broad coverage of an overall need (health, child-rearing) and flat-rate wage replacement benefits (in the case of unemployment, sickness, disability or retirement); the level of these replacement benefits relative to the average wage depends on the accepted level of taxation.

- Conditions of entitlement: The initial contributory conditionality has given way to a universal scheme opening up basic public insurance to all residents; possible complementary benefits can be conditional on specific attributes (such as family configuration or disability)

- Management: As a public service, public insurance is managed by the public authorities, in particular by a social security administration.

It must be emphasised that public insurance, like the socialised wage, has a broad, generalist scope. From its inception, both the financing and the provision of benefits have concerned the whole population; overall health coverage has been provided; and although the flat-rate wage replacement income is low, it progressed in the decades subsequent to its creation.

Several of the reforms implemented since the 1980s have, by contrast, been marked by a "targeting" approach. They underwrite a shift in resource regime from public insurance and the socialised wage towards the *tutelary allowance*. What are the defining features of this currently expanding regime?

The mode of financing is not a decisive characteristic of this resource regime. It can be financed through taxation (and here direct, proportional taxation plays a lesser role than in public insurance financing): in this case "tutelary taxation" must be distinguished both from the "general taxation" of public insurance and the "tax-funded wage" of state employees. It can also be financed through the wage, either when social contributions finance targeted benefits, or when the direct wage is disconnected from the collective agreement wage for target populations.

Complementary benefits, whether in cash or kind, do not cover a whole need, but what is considered a basic "basket of goods and services" (such as for health care). Replacement benefits concern target populations. It must be emphasised that alongside the social benefits covering time out of work, the tutelary allowance also pays for work situations: as a flat-rate tutelary wage replacing the wage defined on the basis of the qualification system (minimum wage disconnected from the collective agreement wage); or as an allowance paid by the state to jobholders (allowances for the working poor) and their employers (in the form of exemptions from social contributions, which are replaced by a budgetary allocation to social security funds).

The conditions of access are fundamentally different from those governing the distribution of the socialised wage or public insurance. In the case of the socialised wage, the qualification grid is the decisive factor, and in the case of public insurance, it is citizenship (through payment of a proportional direct tax): qualification and citizenship are *positive* bases underwriting the right to resources. Here, on the contrary, a *negative* characterisation of the recipients serves to target them for entitlement to national solidarity, as "victims of globalisation", "poorly employable", "unskilled", "inexperienced", or "having insufficient income". Their entitlement is thus not to a solidarity between equals, whether as taxpayers or as employees pooling a portion of their wage – but to the solidarity of the rich towards the poor, singled out on the basis of their family status, age, or geographical or occupational sector. It should be noted that the negative definition of benefit recipients is what the reforms present as "positive discrimination": the positive nature of the measure is precisely based on its refusal to recognise the qualification or the active citizenship of the workers that are its "beneficiaries".

Management of this resource regime is also different: sectoral or cross-sectoral employee and employer organisations are replaced by company-level actors (in the case of exemptions from collective agreements) together with the state in its "tutelary" role responsible for vertical redistribution, with a strong presence of local authorities and local partners that are more management-oriented than political. The tutelary state is not the minimal state reduced to its essential functions, for its intervention on the market is considerable. Nor is it the charitable state: benefit-recipient employees are not limited to the working poor but form a growing part of the working population (about half of French employees, for example), and are affected less by a cut-back in their resources than by a change in the basis of these. Although the state intervenes massively in the financing and the definition of the resources of the lower paid half of the working population, it is not the state-as-employer (like other employers) mutualising the wages of its employees (that is, the state as guarantor of the socialised wage in the continental regimes), nor as the state expressing the public power of citizens, its defining trait in the Anglo-Nordic countries. It is as the tutelary state or *État providence** for workers whose identity as wage-earners and as citizens is negated. This *État providence* is new to Europe. Far from being in crisis, it is only now being constructed in order to take charge of categories of populations or basic needs falling within its tutelary function as guardian and protector.

For the three countries analysed here, it is in *France* that the construction of the tutelary state during the 1990s was the most marked (Palier and Coron, 2001). We have already seen how the CSG was extended throughout the decade to partially substitute for the *cotisation sociale* in the financing of family, old-age and health insurance benefits. It must be emphasised that the CSG thus serves to finance benefits that are increasingly means-tested (family allowance); non-contributory solidarity benefits (*Fonds de solidarité vieillesse*); and benefits provided by a basic health care scheme that only covers what is considered to be vital medical care.

The role played by the tutelary allowance in the remuneration of certain populations was, to a large extent, sparked off at the end of the 1970s with the invention of the category of "youth", through specific

---

* *Translator's note*: While this term is the commonly accepted translation for "welfare state", it has somewhat pejorative connotations, and the emphasis is more on the role of the state-as-provider than on the well-being of citizens.

measures "to promote the employment of young people". These "youth plans" served as a test for a range of subsidised employment situations that have subsequently become increasingly less targeted on age. Tutelary taxation, through subsidies paid either to the employer or the employee, substitutes – partially of course – for the wage (although sometimes at a high rate, with employers financing only 50% of the wage in the case of *emplois familiaux* (home service jobs) or even only 20% in the case of *emplois-jeunes*). Subsidised employment, such as the well-known *contrats-emploi-solidarité (CES)*, initially took the form of subsidies to the employer which were targeted on a particular sector, or type of employer (artisans hiring their first employee, for example), or type of employee (young people between 16 and 18 or the long-term unemployed). Since 1993, however, positive discrimination measures have given way to generalised measures granting regressive exemption from employer contributions: for wages below 1.33 times the *SMIC;* for part-time jobs; then on all wages for full-time jobs under 1.8 times the *SMIC* in companies that have switched to the 35-hour work week, which will ultimately concern 70% of private sector employees. To which must be added the tax bonus for all jobs concerned by this reduction in working time.

The logic here is thus no longer to provide hiring incentives (employment flow) targeting marginal populations that are the traditional clients of public assistance, but to provide fiscal support for the lowest wages, the employment stock. Furthermore, this support has taken a form that conflicts ever more sharply with the continental tradition of incompatibility between salary and social assistance. To begin with, the law to combat exclusion (1998-99) extended the possibilities for a worker paid a half-SMIC to concurrently draw the *revenu minimum d'insertion (RMI)* – a social assistance benefit created in 1989 for the unemployed who lost entitlement to UNEDIC benefits after the 1982 reform. This opened up a breach, albeit to a limited extent since concurrent drawing was only authorised for a relatively short period. Then, in 2001, the *prime pour l'emploi*, an employment incentive bonus in the form of a tax credit restricted to jobholders (earning between 0.3 and 1.4 times the SMIC) succeeded in turning the wage-based logic upside down: now people have to be earning a salary in order to receive social assistance!

The SMIC has become the central component of this arrangement and has effectively been transformed into a tutelary wage. The progressive broadening of the scope of discriminatory measures has made it possible to institute a benefit-recipient career that looks like the wage-earner career, but that excludes the population concerned from access to the latter. The fact that these two careers are identical in form is clearly crucial to the effectiveness of a discriminatory arrangement centred on what is called the "minimum wage" but that no longer presents the common characteristics of the wage. True, its mandatory indexation guarantees that its level remains attached to the collective agreement wage. But it constitutes a tutelary wage because it departs from the latter in two essential ways:

- An increasing share of its financing derives from tutelary taxation. The budgetary subsidies to social security funds to replace exempted employer contributions, the subsidising of the 35-hour work week, and the *prime pour l'emploi* tax credit all illustrate the extent to which the state contributes to the income of workers paid the SMIC whom it does not employ and whom their employers finance at very low levels.

- The link to the qualification system is ever more tenuous, and the SMIC functions increasingly as a flat-rate wage. This is particularly visible in the case of the *emplois-jeunes*, but is also true for the numerous precarious jobs systematically paid at SMIC level or a very low multiplier thereof. The SMIC impacts strongly on employment flow: many recruits enter at SMIC level, regardless of their qualifications. It also impacts on the employment stock, for the flattening of the wage hierarchy for the lower paid half of the salariat, due to collective agreements maintaining minimum pay levels below the SMIC, means that differences in the qualification grid have very little effect on the wage. Actual career development is far more compressed than the theoretical working career set in collective agreements.

It is of interest to note that in *Germany*, where the construction of benefit recipient workers is less developed, there is no national-level, multi-branch minimum wage (minima vary from sector to sector). But the debate has now precisely been opened over whether this would not be an appropriate way to create a visible reference wage for the "second labour market" that the *Bundnis für Arbeit* experts are pressing for.

In Germany, positive discrimination could not be constructed around youth as it was in France, at least in the industrial sectors. The German dual training system ensures an excellent liaison between the unions and young workers, and instils an early attachment to the principle of qualification, the core component of the socialised wage. Moreover, both the *Betriebsräte* and the sectoral union federations push for apprentices to be hired in order to avoid a floating workforce that would serve to depress wages and labour rights. It is women, whose labour force participation rate is relatively low (particularly when they are mothers) and workers in East Germany who have served as vectors for the construction of benefit-recipient workers.

After reunification the unions' immediate concern was to maintain uniform standards for wages, a major condition of the socialised wage. The battle to align East German wages with those in the Western Länder became a key theme in pay negotiations from 1991. In April 1993, the employers' refusal to implement the schedule for harmonising wages provoked IG Metall's first strike in East Germany: the two-week strike in the metalworking sector and three-week strike in the steel industry ended in a compromise to postpone harmonisation until 1996. Today, effective wage differences in the industrial sectors still reach 40%, despite a difference of only 8% between the pay levels set in collective agreements (Schäfer, 2000). East German workers are singled out for positive discrimination via "hardship clauses" that authorise plant-level agreements to save jobs in regions with high redundancy rates. Employers' associations, who complain that wages negotiated at branch level are too restrictive, have made a key issue of these "opening clauses", and are bent on obtaining exemptions at enterprise-level in order to negotiate lower pay rises in exchange for job security. The unions have put up a resistance, but the wage discrepancy between the Länder in the East and the West has created a vast space for workers who are denied access to the collective agreement wage on the grounds of their "disadvantages", and this is precisely the space of the tutelary wage.

Reunification thus played a decisive role in the construction of benefit recipient workers for whom the dominant mode of financing is the tutelary wage – through exemptions from the sectoral agreement wage – rather than tutelary taxation. True, subsidised employment also exists in Germany, and once again, largely in the Eastern Länder. The ABM scheme provides for public financing of jobs facing retrenchment to maintain pay levels at 100% of the wage when the employer is a city council or public service establishment, or at 75% in the private sector. At the beginning of 1997, the market subsidised by the Federal employment office concerned an estimated 1.3 million people (early retirement, training programmes, employment start-up contracts). But tutelary taxation plays a relatively secondary role for two reasons: 1) as we have seen, the substantial budgetary expenditures occasioned by reunification led to a drop in the public financing of social protection, and particularly in expenditure on employment incentives; and 2) more generally speaking, unions and employers alike are particularly wary of state intervention in wage issues, and perceive public financing of employment as a threat to *Tarifautonomie*. Consequently, both government and employers have preferred to focus their efforts on obtaining trade union consent to a policy of wage restraint, purportedly to defend employment and combat exclusion.

The Pact (*Bundnis für Arbeit*) has served as a useful instrument in this. True, Germany does not have a neo-corporatist tradition as in the Netherlands. But after the failure of the tripartite summit of 23 April 1996, and the SPD election victory of September 1998, Chancellor Schröder was quick to tout the Dutch Wassenaar Agreement (starting point in the early 1980s of the reforms leading to the "polder model") and to propose an ongoing tripartite co-operation.

For the first time, extensive measures were introduced that specifically targeted young people (but on a far lesser scale than in France, for although the plan was called "100,000 young people", only 40,000 would be concerned by these subsidised wage measures). The collectively agreed wage, when subject to social contributions, was to be subsidised at a rate of 100% for a newly created linked work and training placement (with 30-50% of time for training) or 60% for 12 months (and 40% for 24 months) in the other cases.

Geringfügige Beschäftingungen (GFB) or low-intensity jobs (less than 15 hours a week and 620 DM a month), which provided non-standard employment due to the initial absence of both social security contributions and entitlements, served as vehicles for the tutelary wage nation-wide. This type of job expanded substantially during the 1990s: it served as a substitute for full-time employment, essentially for married women and particularly in the commercial sector, and became just like any other job – but with reduced contributions and benefits (introduced after 1999). In order to avoid a threshold effect, some experts suggested the regressive subsidising of employee contributions for salaries between 630 and 1550 DM (for single people) and 3100 DM (for married people, with a modulation according to the number of children). Known as the "Mayence model", the plan presented by the Rhineland-Palatinate SPD at the end of 1998 included a further measure: family benefits for low-income employees were increased in order to align these with social assistance rates for child benefits and thus push recipients of the latter to take up employment (Klammer, 2000).

Finally, an intense debate arose over the need to create a second labour market by offering demand-side incentives in low-productivity service sectors. The new line of discourse of the *Bündnis für Arbeit* experts (Scharpf, 1999, see also Streeck and Heinze, 1999) focused on the need to construct a "low-wage sector". Its strength in the face of the unions lay in the fact that it carefully avoided challenging the industrial model as such. Rather, this model was declared unsuited to the service world: while the norm of high wages in the industrial sector was justified by high productivity, it was argued, general measures were needed to accompany the growth of job offers in the low-productivity tertiary sectors. Thus they proposed to fully exempt employer and employee social contributions on salaries up to 1500 DM, then regressively up to 2800 DM (thereby eliminating the specific character of low-intensity jobs).

In 2000, the Pact approved two regional experiments limited to the first 18 months of a new job. The one, in the Cologne and Brandenburg regions, was based on the "Mayence model"; the other was in Sarre and used contribution exemption modalities close to those recommended by Scharpf. It can be seen that while Germany has not as yet gone nearly as far as France, the conceptual framework for the tutelary allowance (through both the tutelary wage and tutelary taxation) is now in place.

In the *Netherlands*, the trend towards the construction of the benefit recipient worker is based on the same rationale that social protection must serve employment. Low-paid subsidised jobs have been created in the service sector, particularly in the labour-intensive social and health services. This notwithstanding, Dutch employment policy includes a relatively low share of what is commonly called "active" expenditure (31.5% in 1990, and 29% in 1996 compared to 42% in France). On the other hand, there is extensive recourse to financing the non-working time of the population of working age through sick leave and invalidity benefits in addition to unemployment. In 1984, benefits for illness (medical care and daily wage replacement compensation), unfitness for work and unemployment represented 18% of GDP compared to 12.2% in France and 13% in Germany. In 1993, for a population of less than 5 million employed workers (of whom only 3.5 million held full-time jobs), there were 392,000 unemployed receiving benefits; but also 338,000 years of daily sick pay benefits; 817,000 years of incapacity benefits; and 335,000 recipients of the basic social assistance benefit, which included large numbers of those not receiving the unemployment benefit because they had either exhausted their entitlements or had not yet been employed. And the unemployment benefit is high compared to other European countries: in 1996, the replacement rate was 46% of the last wage for a worker with a stable employment record compared to 38% in France.

What role does the minimum wage play in the construction of Dutch benefit-recipient workers? As in all countries with a Beveridgean tradition, that is, with both a universal public insurance system and occupational schemes based on the socialised wage, the minimum wage is classically disconnected from the sphere of the wage and connected to the sphere of public insurance. What distinguishes these two forms of insurance is that public insurance benefits are based on the minimum wage, whereas occupational benefits are earnings-related. The public pension, and public benefits for unemployment (or invalidity when these existed) correspond to 70% of the minimum wage, whereas occupational benefits for retirement, illness, invalidity or unemployment theoretically guarantee 70% of the recipient's last (or average) earnings. Moreover, collective agreements traditionally never set salaries at minimum wage level – effectively practised wages are at least 15% higher than the minimum wage. In other words, the minimum wage corresponds to what people are entitled to when they are not entitled to a collectively agreed wage.

For the hasty observer, the starting point here, then, is the intended point of arrival in a country with a continental wage tradition like France: the high visibility of the minimum wage as the reference income for benefit recipients. Except that these benefit recipients were, by definition, not employed, and that employees, for their part, benefited from generous time out-of-work pay through occupational schemes for sick leave, invalidity and unemployment that were only very slightly contributory. The reformers of the 1990s thus tackled the construction of benefit-recipient workers by focusing their efforts on pushing benefit recipients to work. They curbed their allowances and promoted jobs paid at a flat-rate minimum wage, which they effectively turned into a tutelary wage.

Thus, the average disability benefit (WAO) (socialised wage) dropped from 72% of average earnings in 1975 to 52% in 1998 (Wierink, 2002). Public insurance benefits linked to the minimum wage have, for their part, suffered considerably from the de-indexation of the minimum wage from real wage growth. At the beginning of the 1990s, it was decided that the minimum wage would only be indexed if the ratio of workers to non-workers remained below 0.86. As a result the minimum wage level dropped from 65% of the average wage in 1980 to 51% in 1996. Which means that workers paid minimum wage experienced a 20% drop in purchasing power (Valkenburg, 2000), and by the same token, so did public insurance benefit recipients.

The number of jobs paid at minimum wage level was expanded in two ways: through new job creation, and through the elimination of the discrepancy between minimum wage and the collective agreement wage.

At the beginning of the 1990s, half of "active" expenditures went to part-time community jobs managed by municipal authorities, paid at minimum wage level and financed by the state via a transfer of the social protection allowances which the new jobholders previously received. This was done through two schemes: *Banenpool* or "job pools" (1990) for the long-term unemployed (over three years), offering fixed-term contracts from which few manage to escape (80% of the beneficiaries remain in this type of employment); and the "youth employment guarantee" plan (JWG, 1992), 6-month contracts paid at minimum wage that young people who have been unemployed for six months and are receiving a minimum income benefit are under obligation to accept[3]. In 1997, the employees covered by these measures began to mobilise, particularly in the local government and hospital sectors where some 40,000 of these jobs were concentrated. In response to the strikes, the Union of Dutch Municipalities accepted to negotiate, and on 26 February 1998, signed an agreement to increase the wage to reach 120% of the minimum wage over ten years. Thus we see the construction, alongside the wage-earner career, of a flat benefit-recipient career (from 1 to 1.2) expressed as a percentage of the minimum wage. This benefit-recipient career is disconnected from the qualification grid that serves as reference in collective agreements.

These schemes, however, concern a relatively small number of employees (some tens of thousands), which is not the case for the general measure exempting employers from social contributions on wages under 1.15 times the minimum wage. During the 1990s, the successive ministers of social affairs pressured the unions and employers to align the lowest collective agreement wage with the minimum wage. In 1994 the new "purple coalition" minister threatened to refuse to extend those sectoral wage agreements that did not make provision for wages at minimum wage level. And in 1996, as part of the active employment policy – which had traditionally been concentrated on subsidised employment for target populations – a new measure was introduced: all wages below 115% of the minimum wage have been partially and definitively exempted from the employer social contribution. In 2000, this measure (WVA-SPAK) concerned 781,000 people (for a total of slightly over 6 million jobs).

In short, the populations serving as point of entry for the replacement of public insurance or the socialised wage by a tutelary allowance have varied from country to country: young people in France, women in Germany and, to a lesser extent, the Netherlands[4], or workers in East

---

[3] Subsidised employment in the Netherlands, as in France, has been marked by considerable institutional instability: Banenpool and JWG, together with the Regeling I/D are currently combined in the WIW scheme. For a complete overview, see Allaart *et al.*, 2002.

[4] Female participation in the Dutch workforce rose from 29% in 1971 to 60% in 1996, with a particularly high proportion in part-time employment (Hemerijk, 2000).

Germany. The paths followed have also been different. In Germany, reunification brought a clash between two worlds, which gave employers the opportunity to legitimate the tutelary wage via exemption from sectoral collective agreements. In the Netherlands and France this was achieved by shifting the nature of the minimum wage (and the nature of the shift has depended on whether the model was Beveridgean or continental). But, in each case, the aim has been to create a second-rate labour market via the tutelary allowance. Take the example of the French SMIC, which can arguably be said to no longer be the doorway to a collectively bargained wage: it has become a dividing line between benefit-recipient workers, for whom it is the reference wage, and other employees. It only plays this role effectively because it has all the legal trappings of a wage and concerns work situations that look like jobs. This is the crucial point: workers are paid in reference to the SMIC in general forms of employment ("particular forms" remain a small minority and are decreasing) without having access to the general form of the wage.

The focus of public debate on employment has thus made it possible for the ruling class to pull off a smooth counter-revolution by creating a tutelary wage alongside the collective agreement wage. And this has been accompanied by a major change in the basis of the rights to resources of the workers concerned: it is as if it were natural that they be paid not according to the qualification grid but in terms of their eligibility for national solidarity. The social violence that invalidates them by disqualifying them, in the strict (continental) sense of the term, is all the more effective in that it comes under cover of the fight for employment and succeeds in generating poverty without the traditional stigma.

III. From socialised wage and public insurance to pre- financed wage and employee savings

The development of the tutelary allowance, which concerns the lowest paid jobs, has been paralleled by the growth of two resource regimes based on financial accumulation (which is why they are dealt with together here): the pre-financed wage and, particularly among the highest paid workers, employee savings.

The *pre-financed wage*, unlike the tutelary allowance, resembles the socialised wage with regard to benefits and entitlement. The mode of financing, however, is different. The benefit (for instance the pension) is a function of the direct wage and provision thus depends on the conditions of attribution of this wage (the qualification system, in particular). However, the contribution paid into the social protection fund is accumulated rather than being immediately distributed, and the investment return serves to provide the benefit. Thus, investment income finances a benefit indexed on the wage (whence the term pre-financed wage). This impacts on the mode of management, for the finance industry enters the scene alongside the usual employee and employer bodies.

This advanced funding of the socialised wage, which is found for example in defined-benefit retirement schemes commonly referred to as pension funds, has its counterpart in funded public insurance schemes. In the latter, income from taxation is invested, and the return finances the public retirement or unemployment benefit.

Employee savings, on the other hand, differ radically from the wage, even though they also constitute an element of earned income, and are thus financed like the wage by employers. The benefits here supplement or replace the wage but have no relation to it. Entitlements are attached to the individual's presence in the firm, to the firm's financial results and to those of the financial market. Management of the funds is primarily in the hands of the finance industry, even when bipartite bodies or the unions play a role. The most common forms of employee savings are company-based medical schemes entrusted to private insurance firms, or company mutual funds which, when dedicated to pensions, are termed defined-contribution schemes.

In *France*, the recourse to financial accumulation is the least developed – although most controversial – aspect of the reforms to employment and social protection financing. Nonetheless, the freeze on, or scheduled cut-back of, wage mutualisation schemes reflects the plan to reduce the benefits financed by the wage in order to open up a space for benefits funded through financial accumulation. This was the goal pursued in the 1996 reforms of the AGIRC and ARRCO supplementary retirement schemes; in the current negotiations over the UNEDIC agreements; and in the extensions of the duration of contributions that are either already in effect (as of 1993 for entitlement to a full pension under age 65) or in the pipeline.

The pre-financed wage was introduced in 1998 with the creation of the basic pension scheme reserve fund which was designed to "fund pay-as-you-go" by accumulating a portion of the taxes earmarked for the basic pension: according to popular dogma, these investments will be used to top up the *cotisations sociales* when the demographic crisis hits.

Employee savings are financed through two schemes. On the one hand, there are tax incentives for property-based forms of remuneration that substitute for a raise in salary (various forms of profit-sharing including bonuses paid into a mutual fund with a possible company contribution, employee shareholding, stock-options). Until recently, these incentives had made little headway outside of a few very narrow segments of the salariat (apRoberts *et al.*, 2000). But they were given a boost in 2001 by the Fabius law aimed at small and medium-sized firms and encouraging long-term savings and inter-enterprise funds. Second, the introduction of a universal complementary medical insurance benefit (CMU) in 1999 was accompanied by mandatory enterprise-level negotiations over complementary medical schemes which thus became part of the pay packet. True, the CMU has been identified with free, means-tested complementary medical coverage, and as such, relates back to the construction of the tutelary state. But this is forgetting that its decisive effect has been to legitimate (by free affiliation for the "poor") the increasingly widespread existence of a second scheme alongside the basic medical scheme. While the basic scheme is financed through tutelary taxation and centred on a universal "basket of basic health services", the second scheme is occupational, provided by private insurance companies, mutual societies, or providential institutions managed by the social partners which – especially given the European directives on free competition in the single market – all operate on a logic of financial accumulation.

Germany has no supplementary retirement schemes equivalent to the French AGIRC or ARRCO. True, the social security contribution ceiling is much higher than in France, and this makes compulsory supplementary schemes unnecessary. But since contributions are not paid on wages above a ceiling (in contrast to France, where mandatory contributions for wages above the ceiling exist), optional occupational schemes have been created at enterprise level, and in most cases these are usually prefinanced on company accounts. As a result, employee savings currently represent about 20% of the pension system. Although this is extremely high compared to France where advanced-funding is still in embryonic form, a more measured interpretation of this figure is called for in terms of the viewpoint developed here: book reserves do not generate the same kind of financial accumulation as does the Anglo-Saxon form of prefinancing since they remain essentially a way for the enterprise to finance its assets, and these are not primarily financial.

Employee savings made a relatively late appearance in Germany. The Liberal Party together with a small number of employers had long called for tax incentives for funded pension plans (individual or company-based). And in the early 1990s, the Liberals advocated that the old-age dependency benefit be financed by tax-exempt insurance premiums; the Kohl government, however, remained true to the traditional wage-based logic and opted for financing through the social security contribution. But in February and May 2001, with the passing of two related

measures, one to reduce the basic state pension and the other to introduce funded private pension plans, the way was opened for earned
income to become the occasion for large-scale financial accumulation.
Between 2002 and 2008, the authorised rate for contributions to a
personal pension plan (not managed by the social partners) will rise
from 1% to 4% of the wage, and will benefit from a tax incentive up to a
limit of 2100 Euros annually.

The situation in the *Netherlands* is obviously very different. After the
UK, this is the EU country with the largest share of financial accumulation in employment remuneration. The Dutch pension system is based
on the three classical pillars of the Beveridge model: public insurance
(AOW), occupational pension plans (pre-financed wage) and individual
savings. The pre-financed wage in what are traditionally called pension
funds represents considerable financial clout, with a capitalisation equal
to 140% of the GDP. The total liabilities of the some 1000 jointly
managed sector-level or company-based occupational funds rank the
Netherlands fourth in the world, and given the small size of the population, the country ranks top for liabilities per capita. In 1996, pension
funds held assets of 604 million florins, compared to 293 million for
private insurance companies.

Nonetheless, advanced funding of the socialised wage and public insurance is subject to two contradictory trends. On the one hand, the pre-
financed wage has been promoted by two reforms. First, the public
pension system now contributes to financial accumulation. A few years
before the French decided to "fund pay-as-you-go", the first purple
coalition government introduced an old-age savings fund in order to
take advantage of high capital gains on the stock-market and avoid a
new contribution hike. Second, the introduction of an "own risks" policy
eliminated employers' mutualised financing of sick leave, and, to a
lesser extent, invalidity (which has erroneously been described as the
"privatisation" of these benefits): the stringent application of "the pollu-
ter pays" principle has caused employers to turn to private insurance
companies and, when they do, to the socialised wage being replaced by
a pre-financed wage.

On the other hand, defined-contribution pension schemes (employee
savings) have tended to replace defined-benefit schemes, leading to a
decline in the pre-financed wage. Occupational pension plans have
traditionally been "integrated schemes" paying the difference between
the guaranteed pension (70% of final earnings in defined-benefit
schemes, the vast majority) and the public pension. But more often than
not, pension benefits fall far short of this theoretical 70% (which is
based on a full working career in the same firm). In 1993, for example,

only one fourth of employees covered by this kind of occupational scheme (and not all are) had entitlement to the maximum replacement rate. Forecasts show that the current low figures are not set to improve much: only 31% of men and 24% of women born in 1970 will obtain a pension (public plus occupational) equivalent to 70% of their last wage (de Graaf and Maier, 2001). The low level of provision through the pre-financed wage is one of the sales arguments used by those seeking to promote employee savings. The rationale is that switching from defined-benefit to defined-contribution schemes means that stock market gains would be pocketed by employees regardless of the hazards of their working life. Theoretically, the employer can choose between a sector-level retirement fund, a company-based fund or a group insurance policy with a private insurance company. But in most sectors where pension funds exist, affiliation has been made mandatory by the extension of collective agreement arrangements, and joint management by the social partners has been set up. Employer and employee, nonetheless, retain the right to opt out (Lutjens, 1994). Competition between mandatory pension funds and private insurance companies is strong, given the enormous financial stakes, and their confrontation recently ended up in a case before the EU Court of Justice[5]. The insurance firms are trying to get a foot in on supplementary retirement plans, while the sectoral occupational funds are also keen to offer their members individual savings products. At the end of 1996, the law on "savings and retirement funds" allowed sectoral funds to enter the market for individual retire-ment products. At the same time, a unanimous agreement at the Labour Foundation opened the door for firms to opt out of the compulsory sectoral scheme if they could offer better protection or financial per-formance through their own scheme or by taking out a group contract with a private insurance company. This progressive confusion of the roles of jointly managed sectoral funds and private insurance companies essentially benefits the logics of financial accumulation, whether by bringing collective actors to accept insurance products as indispensable complements to occupational retirement schemes, or by introducing private actors into this field. It should be added that social security bodies and benefits have undergone such substantial reform that anxious individuals have been turning to private saving schemes (introduced in 1994) or to insurance products benefiting from strong fiscal incentives, especially when the combined amount provided by the first two pillars does not reach 70% of earnings. These developments are, obviously, not free of conflict, and not only between the sectoral bodies and the insur-

---

[5]   ECJ Albany International, 21 September 1999, C 219/97, Rec 1-6025.

ance companies. In March-April 1995, for instance, construction industry workers went out on their longest strike since World War II, in protest over the attempt by employers to finance early retirement through employee savings rather than through the mutualised wage.

In contrast to the tutelary allowance, the developments examined here primarily concern the highest paid employees. The reforms implemented in the 1990s vastly increased the proportion of investment yields, that is, profit-making property rights, in their income. This was done by the advanced-funding of benefits that have maintained their other wage-based characteristics (pre-financed wage); and by promoting employee savings schemes through strong fiscal incentives, thereby opening up the way for the pay packet to include property based income that is totally disconnected from the wage.

Conclusion: new statuses for workers?

In conclusion to this analysis of current shifts in resource regimes, this chapter will propose an interpretation of the transformations in workers' status that have been introduced by the reforms.

We have seen how the socialised wage and public insurance are being challenged today. Both these regimes show that large-scale, long-term commitments such as retirement pensions can be met by mutualising a portion of the value created during the year, either through the wage via social contributions, or through taxation earmarked for social security. There is no need for prior financial accumulation, since this only serves to accumulate future entitlements to be deducted from the value that will have to be created when the time comes for the pensions to be distributed. Thus, the socialised wage bases non-workers' entitlement to resources on labour law, just as public insurance bases this entitlement on citizenship rights. Financial accumulation bases the right to resources on traditional profit-making property rights, a key element in the capitalist logic since it is at the basis of the levy of rent or interest by the owners of finance capital. It is precisely this profit-making property right that was invalidated in the 20th century by the radical innovations concerning workers' resources, and that current pay reforms are attempting to re-establish.

The transformation of the socialised wage into a deferred wage asserts the wage as a price of labour power. Parallel to this, the property-owning worker, who is paid through the advanced funding of his or her earnings or through employee savings, becomes an auxiliary to financial accumulation, which he or she is induced to support. This has served not only to re-legitimate financial accumulation but to give it a considerable boost, for the pay packet has become essential to its constitution even though its token owners have no real rights over it.

The symmetrical counterpart of the property-owning worker is found in the benefit-recipient worker. Workers who have no access to a pre-financed wage, who are defined by what they "lack" and who have been disqualified as salaried workers or citizen-workers, are no longer the subjects of subversive labour rights or citizenship rights, but have become the object of national solidarity.

Workers' rights to resources have, until now, been based on the labour rights or citizenship rights won during the labour confrontations of the 20th century. Today, it would seem, these rights to resources are to be granted on the basis of national solidarity rights and profit-earning property rights. The European ruling classes are attempting to replace the anti-capitalist figures of the salaried worker and the citizen worker by those – fully coherent with capitalism – of the benefit-recipient worker and the property-owning worker.

The particular interest of the resource regimes defined here (social-ised wage, deferred wage, public insurance, tutelary allowance, pre-financed wage and employee savings) is that they permit a fine analysis of workers' resources. The traditional categories of "wage" and "social protection" used to analyse these resources present three major draw-backs: they are too broad; they introduce oppositions where these do not exist (between direct pay and redistribution) while masking those that do exist; and they are blind to the considerable transformations in workers' rights that financing reforms have introduced.

These resource regimes also permit a reading of European policy. The key cognitive tool for the legitimisation of current national reforms is the distinction the EU makes between two resource regime pillars: the first pillar basic schemes come under state tutelage, and the second pillar supplementary schemes are a matter for competition in the single market for capital, goods, services and labour. The first is the pillar of redistribution and the tutelary allowance. The second is the pillar of the pre-financed wage with its pension funds and of employee savings with their mutual funds.

This, of course, is the dream entertained by the European Union's ruling classes: the extreme political instability that the reforms are generating shows that there's many a slip twixt cup and lip.

References

Allaart, P., de Koning, J. and Theeuwes, J. (2002), *Gesubsidieerde arbeid in Nederland*, Den Haag, OSA.

apRoberts, L. *et al.* (2000), *Retraite et épargne salariale: les initiatives d'entreprise*, Rapport remis à la MiRe (Ministère de l'Emploi et de la Solidarité) et à la Caisse des dépôts et consignations (branche retraites), IRES-GREE, juillet.

de Graaf, W. and Maier, R. (2001) The Nederlands: a hybrid model for the regulation of the social salary, in *Salaires et protection sociale, qui paie ?*, sous la direction de B. Clasquin et F. Boughanémi, Luxembourg, Office des publications officielles de la Commission Européenne.

Hemerijck, A. (2000), Négocier les ajustements de la protection sociale aux Pays-Bas, in *La protection sociale en Europe: le temps des réformes*, sous la direction de Christine Daniel et Bruno Palier, Paris, Documentation française.

Klammer, U. (1997), Zur Umgestaltung der sozialen Sicherung und ihrer Finanzierung: Europäische Wege und ihre Relevanz für die deutsche Diskussion, *WSI-Diskussionspapier*, Hans-Böckler-Stiftung, Düsseldorf, Nr. 37, juni.

Klammer, U. (2000), Bas salaires: un défi pour l'État social, *La Revue de l'IRES*, No.33, pp. 97-124.

Klammer, U. (2001), Reforming Public Pensions: Equivalence versus Redistribution, in *Salaires et protection sociale, qui paie ?*, sous la direction de B. Clasquin et F. Boughanémi, Luxembourg, Office des publications officielles de la Commission Européenne.

Lutjens, E. (1994), Les régimes de retraite complémentaires aux Pays-Bas, *La Revue de l'IRES*, No.15, pp. 71-81.

Palier, B. and Coron, G. (2001), Les transformations du mode de financement des dépenses sociales en France depuis 1945, p. 37, ronéoté.

Schäfer, C. (2000), « Baisse des salaires: pour un monde meilleur ? », *La Revue de l'IRES*, No.33, pp. 57-97.

Scharpf, F.W. (1999), Gegen die Diskriminierung einfacher Arbeitsplätze, *Wirtschaftsdienst*, VIII, pp. 455-462.

Streeck, W. and Heinze, R. (1999), An Arbeit fehlt es nicht, *Der Spiegel*, 19, pp. 38-45.

Valkenburg, B. (2000), « Existe-t-il des salariés paupérisés aux Pays-Bas ? », *La Revue de l'IRES*, No.33, pp. 151-172.

Wierinck, M. (2002), Pays-Bas: la réforme du régime de l'inaptitude au travail (WAO), un chantier inachevé du second gouvernement Kok, *Chronique internationale de l'IRES*, No.76, mai, pp. 31-44.

CHAPTER 4

Skills and Credentials at the Core of the Relation between Resources and Employment

Joan Miquel VERD PERICAS and Coralie PEREZ

Introduction

This chapter examines the relations between training, skills, credentials and the wage in France, Spain and the United Kingdom. It focuses on recent changes in the different systems of vocational training and certification and their connections with the occupational classifications and remunerative systems of each country. From a perspective considering the total reproduction of labour, we concentrate on the articulation between the processes shaping the productive characteristics of labour and the processes resulting in the purchase of labour by companies.

Our particular focus means we have chosen to concentrate on a specific aspect of the training/employment relation. This relation has been approached elsewhere from multiple fields and points of view, one of the most recurrent being that of the role of training in labour market integration and career development[1]. The perspective adopted here contrasts with this and is based on a two-fold approach. We first examine the different institutional forms of skill production and certification and how they are related to and embedded in different societal logics; then we analyse the processes leading to the construction of occupational hierarchies and wage determination. These two aspects are finally

---

[1] The human-capital theory, despite its simplistic presuppositions, has been the most frequently used perspective. As Méhaut (1986) notes, research based on this perspective almost exclusively views training and education in terms of public economic policy and individual "investment".

examined together in order to better analyse the role played by skills and credentials as a link between employment and wage[2].

The chapter is organised into five main sections. The first section discusses the definition of occupational grids and the links between these and skills and credentials. The aim is to establish the terminology that will be used in the chapter as well as to introduce some of the elements that will be discussed in more detail in Section V. The following three sections present the systems of production of skills and credentials in France, Spain and the United Kingdom respectively, showing the connections between these systems and the occupational hierarchies and associated levels of pay (i.e. the direct and indirect resources received by workers at a particular occupational level). We are not concerned here with wage levels (in a macro perspective) or with skilling and deskilling processes, but with the institutional forms underlying the process of wage determination. Finally, Section V presents a comparative synthesis in which we attempt to identify the main trends of change with an emphasis on the principal actors and logics involved.

The analysis will focus on three of the five countries originally examined in a preliminary study conducted by the "Social construction of employment" research network[3]. These three countries show sufficient differences with regard to collective bargaining practices, the determination of occupational hierarchies and the production of skills and credentials to provide an appropriate basis for an international comparison – although the range of configurations covered is clearly not exhaustive.

In France and Spain, wage definition is generally based on occupational grids established through collective bargaining between workers and employers at a centralised level. However, the grids applied in each country differ with regard to their collective points of reference and their implementation at company level. The close relationship between credentials and position in the occupational hierarchy observed in many sectors in France produces a very different situation from that found in Spain. At the same time, the extremely high incidence of fixed-term contracts, the small size of many companies, and the multiple levels of bargaining that are characteristic of Spain result in a level of coverage by collective agreements that is qualitatively and quantitatively lower than that found in France.

---

[2] Our necessarily brief descriptions of the different systems of vocational education and training in each country do not do justice to the important role these play in the production of skills and credentials. For a fuller account, see Aventur and Möbus (2000), Otero (2001) and Twining (1999).

[3] The other countries were Italy and Portugal.

In Great Britain the role of collective bargaining is less visible, partly due to the voluntarist tradition of industrial relations, the less formal connections between training, recruitment and pay, and the different institutional levels for the setting of wage scales. Nevertheless, in the traditional British model, collective bargaining allows for the negotiation of a wage that provides some form of recognition of the productive knowledge collectively shared by groups of workers.

Despite these differences, certain transformations affecting the processes of wage formation are common to all the European countries. The most important of these is perhaps the trend towards the individualisation of the wage relation, a process attested to by the centrality of the discourse on competencies. It implies a progressive disconnection of pay determination from a collective point of reference, thus jeopardising the political character of the wage. The three countries analysed here each present specific configurations of this trend, and we will show how these are embedded in the particular systems of wage definition and related to the differences we have highlighted here.

I. Training, occupational hierarchies and pay: a complex relation

A. *Occupational classifications and wage scales*

The perspective we adopt considers the wage – that is, the total remuneration in cash or kind received by workers for providing the use of their labour – to be the result of political bargaining between workers and employers. The wage is thus taken to be a tariff, rather than a price (subject to the laws of supply and demand) for a measurable and exact quantity of work. Our particular interest here is in the processes leading to the placement of a worker at a particular wage level.

Traditionally, customary rules and practice played an important role in the determination of the "adequate" remuneration for a particular kind of work or post (Marsden, 1994). Today, however, wages in most countries are determined on the basis of occupational hierarchies: each occupational level has an associated level of pay. It is important to note that these hierarchies and the criteria on which they are constructed vary within and between countries, and it would be an extreme oversimplification to assume that they are established by similar processes or produce similar effects. In addition, labour market and employment policies contribute to diversifying the processes of wage determination and to rendering them more opaque; the traditional association of an employment with a particular wage level is being eroded (see Chapters 2 and 6).

Occupational and wage hierarchies are not simply the consequence of a particular division and organisation of labour, nor do they represent an irrefutable ranking of skills and qualifications. They are the result of political negotiations between workers and employers and reflect the balance of power between the two. They are also shaped by the role played by the state in these negotiations, and reflect the level of state intervention in the regulation of economic and social life. As Rozenblatt (2000: p. 141) points out, they are "rooted in the particular system of industrial relations developed within each national configuration". Occupational classifications, moreover, extend beyond the wage relation into many other domains of society. They serve to create social identities and meanings as well as to determine the position of individuals within the social structure – in short, they are one of the factors defining social hierarchies within a society.

Rozenblatt (2000)[4] has developed a typology of "systems of work valorisation" which serves to illustrate the different systems and logics underpinning the construction of occupational hierarchies. While the original typology presents three different systems, the discussion here will be limited to two of these: we will not consider the system under-writing the Japanese model where distinctions are based solely on the level of the workers' initial qualifications and the position reached in the life cycle. Although this model can also be found in large corporations world-wide, our focus on societal logics within the EU makes it less pertinent to the present analysis. On the basis of this typology, thus, two main systems, can be said to characterise the dominant frameworks structuring the hierarchies found in EU countries:

a) A system of valorisation connected to the organisation of work. It takes two forms: The *job evaluation system*, in which "the classification norm [...] seeks to specify the occupational attrib-utes of a job held by an employee through the use of job evalua-

---

4   An earlier version of this typology was published by Eyraud and Rozenblatt (1994). Marsden (1999) proposes an alternative approach showing how a company organises the totality of work that needs to be done into different jobs and categories. The dif-ferences between these typologies stem from the authors' different objectives: Mars-den analyses systems of construction of occupational categories mainly from the point of view of the organisation of work, the division of labour inside a company and job contents, whereas Eyraud and Rozenblatt are more interested in the implica-tions that the different occupational categories have in relation to the valorisation of work and the wages received by the workers.

tion techniques". And the system based on *category nomenclatures*, where "classifications are legitimated by an external stamp of recognition conferred directly or indirectly by the state, which acts as guarantor of a codified division of social occupations".

b) A system of valorisation centred on professionality. This model also takes two forms. In the *trade-based system*, "the figure of the skilled tradesperson, via the trade unions and their control over apprenticeship, shapes the organisation of labour and segments the classification applied to the various types of workers". In the *professional system*, "the skilled worker who has served an apprenticeship is at the centre of the hierarchical order and unskilled workers as well as manual workers attaining posts of responsibility are positioned in relation to this central figure".

These two main systems can be identified with particular countries. On the one hand, the *job evaluation system* is characteristic of Sweden, and *category nomenclatures* are used in countries such as France, Italy, Portugal and Spain. On the other hand, the *trade-based system* is the dominant model in the United Kingdom, whereas the *professional system* is characteristic of Germany.

As noted by Rozenblatt, these models – which are described in their pure forms – continue to evolve. Indeed, the changes occurring in industrial relations and employment throughout Europe have, in certain cases, produced rapid transformations that some authors have qualified as a structural change (e.g. Eyraud, 1998, for the British case). These changes and their implications for workers' resources will be examined in detail for each of the countries considered here.

B. Skills, credentials and workers' resources

In order to understand the implications and consequences of the different ways in which occupational and wage hierarchies are constructed, we need to consider the role they play in the socialisation of resources, on one hand, and their relationship to skills and credentials, and thus to institutional systems of vocational training and certification, on the other.

Wage grids are one of the factors contributing to a particular societal configuration of workers' resources, and are thus an element entering into the construction of resource regimes. A distinction has been made in Chapter 3 between the resource regime based on the socialised wage and that based on public insurance. In the former, employers pay not only the direct salary but also social security contributions, and consequently both kinds of resources can be seen as a product of wage conflict. Therefore not only do the wage grids that define the direct salary have a politically negotiated character, but so do the rules for entitlement to social protection benefits and for the calculation of pensions.

In the resource regime based on public insurance there is a clear distinction between the wage and the fiscal deductions financing cash benefits and services in kind. In this case taxation is an important vehicle for the socialisation of resources, and a significant share of resources is thus not determined by political bargaining between workers and employers. Here, wage conflict is concentrated on the definition of occupational hierarchies and their associated levels of pay.

Although the resource regime based on the socialised wage may seem more likely to be associated with a system in which occupational hierarchies are defined at a centralised level and guaranteed by the state (*category nomenclatures*) this is not always the case. The logics of the division of labour and occupational ranking are not always the same within this model, as has been clearly shown in comparisons between France and Germany (Maurice, Sellier and Silvestre, 1987; Maruani and Reynaud, 1991). As stated earlier, occupational and wage hierarchies and the way they are defined are ultimately shaped by the system of industrial relations and the historical development of workers' rights and state regulations in each country.

Wage and occupational hierarchies can also be considered as a means of social and economic recognition of skills and credentials and can be related to the institutional modes of production and certification of skills and knowledge – and hence to the organisation of and policies on this field developed in each country. The final reference in occupational grids – whether their underlying logic is centred on *professionality* or on *work organisation* – is usually the workers' skill level and/or credentials. These are the attributes that legitimate workers being placed at a particular level in the pay hierarchy, and thus the wage they will receive. However it should not be forgotten that access to training, skills and credentials is the result of institutional and social configurations that are mediated by social and economic inequalities and conflict.

As Recio (1997) has pointed out, workers acquire their skills through two major processes: formal vocational training on the one hand, and training on the job – which is difficult to disassociate from experience – on the other. We will focus on the first of these in an attempt to identify the links between training, credentials and occupational classifications, although we will also examine some of the procedures designed to certify and validate non-formal training or experience. We will thus distinguish between *formal training* and *non-formal training*. In the former we include the elements acquired in an institutionalised manner, and apply the usual administrative distinctions between *initial vocational training*, *continuing vocational training* and *training for the unemployed*. *Non-formal training* is used to cover the knowledge, capabilities and social skills that are acquired in a non-institutionalised way on the job, through the use of and adaptation to technology, through consultation of colleagues, or simply through the continuous performance of specific tasks over time. Nevertheless, not all skills are "trainable": the general socialisation process, mass media influences, and differentiated socialisation processes based on gender, social class or ethnic origin have a significant impact on the skills an individual may possess[5].

Another point should be made here: skills and credentials are not, as sometimes stated, two sides of the same coin. They are not uniformly appreciated at company level: companies may take account of credentials only, or skills only, or both (giving different weight to each) depending on the job to be filled (Martín Artiles, 1999)[6]. Moreover, not all credentials stem from vocational education or training, nor are they the sole outcome of these processes.

Finally it bears repeating that beyond the general trends observed in all the European countries, the relations between the organising principles underpinning occupational hierarchies and the institutional forms of vocational education and training take many forms. Countries such as Spain and France, that share a *category nomenclatures* system, show marked differences not only with respect to the role played by credentials in determining a worker's position in the hierarchy, but also regarding the kind of training situations that are considered suitable for recognition by a credential (Cachón and Lefresne, 1999; Verd, Gérardin and Barbera, 1999).

II. The case of France

A. Production of skills and credentials

In France, the systems for the production of skills provide initial vocational training, principally for full time students, and continuing vocational training for workers and the unemployed. In addition, a

---

[5] The concept of *tacit knowledge or skills* (Wood, 1987) corresponds fairly well to this idea of "non-trainable" skills.

[6] For a discussion on the analytical distinction between the skills and credentials required for *access* to a job and those required *on* the job see García Espejo (1998); QUIT (2000).

system called *formation en alternance* (work-based training) combines classroom instruction and on-the-job training under specific labour contracts – mainly *contrats d'apprentissage* (apprenticeship contracts) and *contrats de qualification* (training contracts). Initial vocational training constitutes a parallel itinerary to the general/academic route and is regarded as less prestigious. Moreover, there is unequal access to continuing training: higher level employees are largely favoured, as are workers in the larger companies which offer training to a broader range of employees compared to the smaller firms (Gahéry, 1998).

The national education system (*Éducation nationale*) offers three levels of vocational training credentials: at the first level, the *Certificat d'Aptitude Professionnelle* (CAP, Vocational Aptitude Certificate) and the *Brevet d'Études Professionnelles* (BEP, Vocational Studies Certificate); then the *Baccalauréat Professionnel* (Vocational Baccalaureate) and the *Baccalauréat Technologique* (Technological Baccalaureate); and finally, at the higher education level, the *Diplôme Universitaire de Technologie* (DUT, Polytechnic Diploma) and the *Brevet de Technicien Supérieur* (BTS, Higher Technician Certificate). It is noteworthy that the creation of the *Baccaulauréat Professionnel* in 1985 implied the formal recognition of the knowledge that – it is assumed – can only be acquired in a situation of real work (in the company)[7]. This reflects the trend towards a broader recognition of knowledge by the national education system.

The creation of the *certificats de qualification professionnelle* (CQP, vocational qualification certificates) in 1987, which introduced sector-specific skill certification, opened a breach in the monopoly held by the national education system. The idea was to diversify the paths for acquiring credentials, particularly for young people entering the labour force through the linked work and training *alternance* system. The CQP*s* were initially introduced in the metalworking industry, but are now recognised in the classification grids in close to forty sectors. They effectively reflect the companies' push to define a post in terms of capabilities and competencies: although they are in competition with the

---

[7] With this diploma, the national education system introduced a new conception of vocational training credentials, which included two major innovative elements: The first, *contrôle en cours de formation*, or continuous assessment throughout the training process, replaced examinations by *situations d'évaluation* and implied changing the way of assessing the knowledge acquired. The second, *délivrance des diplômes par unités*, made it possible to obtain a credential for a single unit, with each unit being assessed separately (Bouyx, 1998).

national education credentials, they are essentially dependent on company-defined needs and this raises the problem of their transferability.

It is also possible to obtain a credential from a training institution outside the national education system: the credential can, furthermore, be officially approved (homologated) by the *Commission Nationale des Certifications Professionnelles* (National Commission for Occupational Certification) which implies recognition at national level. Any private or public training provider can apply to the Commission for homologation of their credentials – on the basis of a number of criteria, but essentially that the training provided corresponds to labour market demands.

With regard to non-formal training, the system for the *Validation des Acquis de l'Expérience*, which validates the experience gained in a job or in voluntary work (with a minimum requirement of three years' experience), allows candidates to obtain the credits needed for a vocational credential[8]. This system is the outcome of recent thinking on the connections between training, certification and career, and the idea that training is first and foremost valorised in the firm: "From this point of view, negotiations on the accreditation of skills gained through experience (*les acquis*) is part of the same logic as that underwriting the development of 'management based on competencies'" (Merle and Lichtenberger, 2001: pp. 184-185). Candidates are now able to obtain a full credential (from the national education system or an approved training provider), or sectoral certification (such as the CQP) through this process.

Finally, the *Bilan de compétences* (Assessment of competencies) offers a form of recognition of skills and knowledge that have not been acquired through formal training. It is a formalised procedure assessing personal and professional skills by various methods such as interviews and tests. A *dossier* or "portfolio" is established, which is not a credential but is designed for the holders' personal use and can only be shown to third parties with their approval (Bjornavold, 1998). The procedure is available to private and public sector employees as well as to the unemployed, but the number of workers using it remains limited.

---

[8]   This system was adopted in January 2002 as part of the *Loi de modernisation sociale*. It was preceded by two lesser known arrangements: the *validation des acquis professionnels (VAP)*, adopted in 1985, gave employees and the unemployed who did not hold the required entry qualifications access to higher education on the basis of their work experience. In 1992, the VAP was extended to permitt candidates to submit a portfolio describing their work experience in order to obtain credits towards a degree without taking the examinations (Céreq, 2002).

B. Occupational hierarchies and the role of credentials and skills

In France there are three main types of classification grids: *Grilles Parodi-Croizat*, *Grilles à critères classants*, and *Grilles Mixtes.* All three grids can be classified as *category nomenclatures* systems although there are important differences between them.

The key characteristics of the *Parodi* grids are the hierarchical structuring of occupational classifications within different industrial branches (*filières*) and the emphasis on work experience as the main criterion for promotion. This system corresponds to a Taylorist-Fordist model of work organisation. The needs of each job are defined in terms of work station, job content and tasks, independently of the person performing it.

The *Grilles à critères classants* define each occupation in terms of the knowledge (*savoir*), technical skills (*savoir-faire*) and social skills (*savoir-être*) required, and thus go far beyond classifications based on the worker's technical knowledge. Classification is based on a scale of points – from 140 to 395 – attributed according to four main factors: a) knowledge, b) autonomy, c) responsibility, and d) kind of job or function.

Finally, the *Grilles Mixtes* combine elements from each of the above models. The structure of the grids is based on *filières* (industrial branches) like the *Grilles Parodi*, but the definition of occupations is more flexible, as in the *Grilles à critères classants*.

These three systems do not represent rigid models, as each company or sector has its own specific adaptation, which is set by collective bargaining. Collective agreement coverage is very high in France[9] and therefore most of the workers are included in one of the three main classification systems.

Credentials play a central role in the definition of the level at which the worker will be placed and constitute a point of reference for all the actors involved in collective bargaining. Nevertheless, the Parodi grids do not make systematic reference to credentials: when these are specified, they are considered as a personal attribute of the jobholder. In the "*critères classants*" grids, "the credential is not attached to the person

---

[9]   In 1997, 96.7% of workers employed by companies with 10 or more employees and 83.9% of those in companies with fewer than 10 employees were covered either by a sectoral or company-level collective agreement or by the status of a state-owned company (EDF-GDF, SNCF) (Combault, 1999). But this generalisation of coverage must be qualified by the large number of collective agreements and the diversity of their contents (Jobert, 2000).

but contributes to identifying the work post" (Jobert, 2000: pp. 114-115)[10]. It should be added that the traditional distinction between initial and continuous vocational training is coming under challenge due to developments such as the *validation des acquis*, the greater role played by the social partners in the production of credentials (joint consultative commissions), and the introduction of sector-specific certification (CQP).

It is important to note that the Parodi classifications are progressively being replaced by the *Grilles à critères classants* and *Grilles Mixtes*[11]. Indeed, the very principle underlying the appearance of the *critères classants* model foreshadows the end of the Parodi system and the wage order linked to it. The *Grilles à critères classants* base their legitimacy on a "technical operation" rather than on collective bargaining, which partially deprives the unions of their legitimacy and capacity for action. In addition, the "objective" criteria defining the work post are implicitly linked to workers' "individual" attributes, thus preparing the way for the discourse on competencies.

The shift from the Parodi to the classifying criteria grids also indicates a change in the *level* of bargaining, since consideration of individual attributes, as well as wage management, take place at company rather than at sectoral level. As a result, there is a shift in the focus of sectoral bargaining, which tends to centre more on the definition of procedures (for the construction of the classification of posts) than on the actual definition of posts and their hierarchy (Reynaud, 1988). This prefigures the trend towards the individualisation of skill recognition, as observed in the shift from qualifications to competencies: the link between credential and post is becoming looser, with the credential becoming a condition of access to an itinerary rather than to a position in the classification grid.

III. The case of Spain

A. *Production of skills and credentials*

The current Spanish system of initial vocational training was established in 1990; its implementation has been progressive, with completion scheduled for 2002/2003. Courses are organised in modules or

---

[10] These grids include entry thresholds which guarantee a minimum hiring coefficient for holders of a credential specified in the grid.

[11] The *grilles à critères classants* now represent just under one third of the grids in use in France (Jobert, 2000).

short-term training units, with a high degree of practical training and a significant portion of the instruction (around 25%) in conditions of real work. This has implied a move away from a more academically oriented system towards the acquisition of knowledge and technical and social skills geared to meeting the needs of companies (Otero, 2001: pp. 52-53).

Continuing vocational training and training for the unemployed constitute a sub-system called *formación no reglada* or "non-regular" training. One of the objectives of the second National Vocational Training Programme (1998-2002) was to establish a common system of accreditation for initial vocational training, continuing vocational training and training for the unemployed that would also recognise work experience. This same system would then provide credentials to students on completion of their initial vocational education, to workers who have had their professional skills validated, and to the unemployed for the training they have received. The aim of these policies on certification transparency and the validation of skills acquired on the job is to facilitate the process of entry or re-entry into the labour market (Planas, 1998). In 1999, the National Institute of Qualifications was created to further these objectives, but to date, the list of vocational credentials that are to form the axis of the national qualifications system has not yet been approved.

However, the general guidelines establishing the *certificados de profesionalidad* (certificates of occupational aptitude) were drawn up in 1995. These certificates, which are not equivalent to the initial vocational training diplomas, were designed to give formal recognition to the "non-regular" training system, and training centres have been awarding them since 1998, although only for *formación ocupacional* programmes (the main programmes for the unemployed). To date, the only form of recognition available to those engaged in continuing vocational training is an attendance certificate. In theory, the *certificados de profesionalidad* offer the possibility of obtaining a credential for knowledge acquired in a non-formal way by validating on-the-job experience. Nevertheless, the main difficulties seem to be the recognition of very diverse skills by the same credential and the disparity in equivalence criteria (Casal, Colomer and Comas, 1998; De la Torre, 2000: pp. 270-278).

B. Occupational hierarchies and the role of credentials and skills

Until 1980, when the law on Workers' Statute (*Estatuto de los Trabajadores*) was passed, everything relative to occupational classifications was specified in the *Ordenanzas Laborales* (labour regulations that had been in force since the 1950s). These regulations established detailed descriptions of posts and tasks and attempted to address issues such as knowledge and experience, seniority and hierarchical position for each individual working in a company. This extensive specification of details could produce 20 to 30 different occupational categories in a single company (Miguélez, 1993).

Since 1980 and particularly since the abrogation of the *Ordenanzas Laborales* in 1994, the specific occupational structure applied in a company has been set by collective bargaining. However, as negotiations are traditionally conducted at different levels (company, sectoral or cross-sectoral, sometimes also combined with national or regional levels) with no co-ordination between them, it became extremely difficult to identify the locus of wage determination. In addition, many companies continued to use the old hierarchical structures defined in the *Ordenanzas Laborales*.

In 1997, trade unions and employers signed the *Acuerdo sobre Cobertura de Vacíos* (Agreement on Gap Filling) in order to cover sectors where occupational grids were not regulated by collective agreements. The objective was to replace the occupational classifications based on the *Ordenanzas Laborales* and to "modernise" the grids. However, the model proposed in the Agreement largely reflects the proposals from employers to reduce the number of occupational categories and to extend workers' polyvalence and functional mobility.

This model, which also serves as a guideline for sectoral and company-level collective agreements, establishes a structure based on eight different occupational levels. Each level is defined by a set of "framework factors" (*factores de encuadramiento*): a) knowledge/experience, b) initiative, c) autonomy, d) responsibility, e) leadership and, f) complexity. Some of these "framework factors" reflect the trend towards a model of labour force management based on competencies and therefore organised in a more individualised manner.

The Agreement comprises an important innovation in that it allows for the occupational classification system to be completed by dividing each level into different functional areas. The classification implies far more than a simple enumeration of posts as it focuses on their contents. In addition, it recognises knowledge and skills that have been acquired both formally (vocational education or training credential) and non-formally (through experience or other non-certified practices).

The importance given to workers' credentials and the links established between these and occupational level is another notable innovation[12]. This represents a significant change in a country where workers traditionally acquired their skills within the company. Basic skills were acquired by performing tasks and consulting senior colleagues, or through in-house vocational training in the large companies. The posts requiring middle-level technical knowledge were covered by workers who had received on-the-job training and progressed up the company step by step promotion ladders (Köhler and Woodard, 1997: p. 69).

The Agreement on Gap Filling will expire at the end of 2002. In the cases where gaps in the definition of post and wage hierarchies remain[13] the Agreement provides for an extension of the existing collective agreements to the sectors without coverage (CES, 2001). This means – if things develop as agreed – that in the near future most of the companies will have wage grids in which the old occupational categories will have been replaced by the occupational levels proposed in the Agreement guidelines.

IV. The case of Great Britain

A. Production of skills and credentials

The reforms of the British system of vocational education and training introduced in the mid-1980s set up two major initial vocational training itineraries for 16- to 18-year-olds, offering the possibility of either continuing in full-time education at a college or of entering a government-supported training scheme. The focus of the reforms has been market-based training, which means that "private training is achieved by employers and employees making choices within a training market" (Tatch, Pratten and Ryan, 1998: p. 88).

---

[12] However, while a minimum credential requirement is ascribed to each level, this does not mean that the holder of the credential will automatically be placed at the corresponding hierarchical level. With the spectacular increase in the educational levels of the Spanish population in the 1980s, companies were unable to absorb the large numbers of well-educated youth entering the labour market: many were forced to take up posts below their level of credentials.

[13] The percentage of workers covered by collective agreements is disputed as the official figures do not exclude employees covered by more than one agreement. The most recent calculations suggest a range between 83% (CES, 2001: p. 359) and 85-90% (Fina, González and Pérez, 2001: pp. 40-42). The proportion of workers covered by collective agreements setting wage scales was 65.1% in 2000 (CES, 2001: p. 389) – but this figure has not been corrected for workers covered by more than one agreement.

These initial vocational training routes lead to two distinct types of credentials, which were created in 1986 with the aim of unifying the various existing vocational credentials. The main full-time courses lead to General National Vocational Qualifications (GNVQs) in England, Wales and Northern Ireland, or to the Scottish equivalent (GSVQs). To obtain this credential, students need not only to assimilate the knowledge included in units linked to specific occupational fields, but also to acquire certain basic communication and technical skills.

In the second route, government-supported training schemes such as Modern Apprenticeships, National Traineeships and Youth Training programmes lead to National Vocational Qualifications (NVQs). The NVQ system is defined by the government as the main vocational training itinerary for those who have left the full-time educational system. It is structured in units linked to a particular aspect of an occupational field. The evaluation process usually involves an assessment of the student's ability to perform specific tasks, called "the performance evidence". It can also include an informal questionnaire or written test for "the supplementary evidence". The NVQs focus on practical rather than analytical skills, which means that they recognise the ability to perform tasks but not necessarily to have a deeper understanding of these.

NVQ credentials are also used to certify continuing vocational training and training for the unemployed. Continuing vocational training up to technician or similar levels is organised in modularised courses, which makes it easy to apply the NVQ evaluation criteria. The programmes for the unemployed – which should, in theory, focus on training – often concentrate on motivation and guidance or simply provide poor quality training. The Training for Work programme (which was redesigned in April 1998 as Work Based Training for Adults) offers assistance in finding a job or on-the-job training. This service is combined with compulsory remotivation programmes and the development of a "personal responsibility" approach job creation (Jones, 1999: p. 146). The New Deal programme allows unemployed people to choose between subsidised employment, work for a charity, work for the government on environmental issues, or full-time education. In practice, it represents a way of introducing low-paid jobs into the market, as the option of full-time education is only open to people with very low level credentials.

The Training and Enterprise Councils (TECs) played a particularly important role in these government supported training schemes. The Councils were created in the early 1980s with the main objective of implementing a governmental educational policy that was essentially geared to the needs of local markets. They served as intermediary agencies between the primary funding bodies (government or enterprises) and the training providers (Atkinson, 1999). However, they came under heavy criticism, compelling the Labour government to launch a review process. This process – which was conducted by the National Skills Task Force composed of employers, special interest groups, voluntary organisations and trade unions – led to the TECs being replaced by Learning Skills Councils in 2001.

B. *Occupational hierarchies and the role of credentials and skills*

In the United Kingdom, occupational hierarchies were traditionally linked to the apprenticeship system. The figure of the skilled tradesperson was pivotal in the occupational classifications and their associated wage levels. Trade union influence on pay determination was substantial, both through wage bargaining at a multi-employer (trade) level and also through their control over apprenticeship.

The progressive dismantling of the traditional apprenticeship system and Conservative governments' attacks on trade unions from the end of the 1970s have produced a situation in which occupational categories and their contents are determined in a completely decentralised way or even unilaterally by employers at company level. The percentage of workplaces in which collective bargaining is the dominant mode of pay determination dropped from 60 per cent in 1984 to 29 per cent in 1998 (Millward *et al.*, 2000: pp. 186-187)[14]. Where pay bargaining exists in the private sector, it is conducted at employer or plant/establishment level and, in general, negotiations beyond the company level are extremely rare (Millward *et al.*, 2000: pp. 187-193; Crouch, 1992: pp. 402-417).

Single-employer bargaining has resulted in an organisation of the work process that can present substantial differences within the same trade or industry: occupational classifications and pay scales can consequently vary from company to company. Moreover, the only possible national common point of reference regarding skills and credentials – the NVQ classification – is not perceived as providing a basis for a shared classification system.

---

[14] The same authors calculated overall collective bargaining coverage (including workplaces where it was not the dominant mode of pay determination) to be 40% of workers in 1998 (Millward *et al.*, 2000: p. 197).

It is disputed whether these developments mean that workers' skills have ceased to be a basis for the wage levels paid by companies. The linking of pay to individual performance appears to be more frequent in workplaces without recognised trade unions (Millward *et al.*, 2000: p. 213). It also seems that large companies are making increasing use of schemes linking pay to appraisals of individual merit or performance. As noted by Edwards *et al.*, "jobs have come to be defined in terms of the internal requirements of companies, and pay systems have been oriented towards rewarding individual and collective contribution to company performance" (1998: p. 18). Schemes linking pay to performance are "particularly common for managerial or white-collar staff, though they also extend to manual workers" (Edwards *et al.*, 1998: p. 22). Different dynamics can be observed in small companies, but these have not had a significant influence on pay determination trends. Moreover, employers' associations have called for the almost complete individualisation of industrial relations, meaning "individual pay contracts and merit pay in place of national agreements and collective bargaining" (Howell, 1999: p. 39).

The limited recognition of workers' skill levels in pay determination – in favour of performance and other more informal features such as social skills, personality or motivation – has been attributed to the British voluntarist and market-based approach to training. Some authors stress the danger of Britain becoming locked in a low-wage, low-skills equilibrium:

> The failure of reward systems to link skill adequately with pay, the lack of ILMs [internal labour markets] and job structures that offer opportunity for advancement, the insecurity of employment in many sectors, the weak connection between qualifications and recruitment, the difficulties posed by the role of skills as positional goods and the threat effect of a more meritocratic approach to hiring and promotion, the uncertainty of the payoff from training *vis-à-vis* other forms of investment, the volatility of the UK economy and the product market strategies being pursued by firms in many sectors, all pose questions for the viability of a system geared solely to responding to market forces. (Keep and Mayhew, 1996: p. 320)

V. The role of skills and credentials in pay determination. Does the wage still have a political nature?

A. *Occupational classifications and the individualisation of the wage relation*

As we have seen in the preceding sections, the dominant organising principles underlying the construction of occupational classifications vary from country to country. The most obvious differences appear to stem from the particular work systems that set the framework for the definition of occupational hierarchies. As shown in Section I, the *trade-based system* characterising the British case and the *category nomenclatures system* that is characteristic of France and Spain have sharply contrasting logics. We will provide a general overview here of the role that credentials and skills play in these systems today.

In the United Kingdom the most frequent situation is that of companies defining occupational categories and the associated levels of skill in terms of their own needs, either unilaterally, or in collective negotiations. This situation is the result of the progressive weakening of trade unions in a context where bargaining was traditionally conducted at industry level without legislative backing, and where skills were acquired within the company without the endorsement of a homogeneous national system of credentials. Nowadays the existence of a collective point of reference common to different companies depends on the strength of the trade unions at industry level, as the relatively new NVQ system has received little recognition from companies and is not used as a basis for positioning a worker within the occupational hierarchy. These circumstances have led to an increasing individualisation of the wage relation. Companies have much more freedom to set pay based on individual performance, and career advancement (and thus pay) is frequently determined by attitude, personality, motivation and other more informal features rather than by skill levels (Keep and Mayhew, 1996).

In Spain and France the trend towards the individualisation of the wage relation is far less marked. The existence of a system of work valorisation with the external guarantee of the state has curbed this process. Wages are mostly the result of a collectively agreed occupational hierarchy, although the traditional role of credentials differs in these two countries. In France there is a dual point of reference: the knowledge and skills required for a particular post are socially recognised by a credential, and these credentials are taken into account in the classification grids. In Spain, credentials have traditionally played a far less important role, and have only recently come to be considered as a criterion for the placement of a worker in an occupational grid. However the introduction of the *grilles à critères classants* in France and the use of the Agreement on Gap Filling as a basis for collective agreements in Spain have entailed a progressive transformation of the role of collective bargaining in the wage relation. These "modern" classification systems primarily set the criteria and procedures for determining the pay received by a worker but do not establish guaranteed links between task, post and wage; credentials have become more of a condition of access to employment than the basis for a position in a hierarchical grid. These classification models clearly introduce a "logic of competencies" into the wage relation, although these "competencies" are yet to be clearly defined[15].

But the logic of competencies is not specific to labour force management in France or Spain, since it is just as evident among British employers. Nor is it simply a pervasive principle affecting the impact of occupational classifications on the definition of pay, as it is profoundly modifying the systems of the production and certification of skills. What are the principles underlying this logic and what are the issues at stake?

B. *From skills to competencies*

The discourse on competencies could be seen merely as a way of giving respectability to what has been known as "individualised management of the labour force". As Dubar (1996: p. 189) points out:

> The notion of competence serves [...] to indicate the highly personalised nature of criteria for recognition that permit to reward individuals on the basis of the intensity of their personal commitment and of their 'cognitive' capacity to understand, anticipate and solve problems related to their function, which are also the problems of their company.

The use of this logic in the wage relation has important consequences for the whole system of production and certification of skills as well as for the social order linked to occupational and wage hierarchies[16]. As Jobert (2000: pp. 90-94) has indicated:

---

[15] While we have mentioned schemes relating pay to individual merit or performance in the British case only, this trend, which is closely linked to the individualisation of the wage relation, is also evident – although apparently less frequent – in Spain (CES, 2001: p. 390) and France (Goetschy, 1998: p. 383).

[16] But classification grids are not only being weakened as a result of the introduction of the competence approach: the role of the occupational sector as a space of social regulation is being challenged (declining union influence, development of cross-sectoral skills, etc.) and manual-worker categories are losing ground to intermediate

The social exchange dimension is absent in the competence approach [...] and there remains an implacable opposition between classification and competence: the one is based on stable properties subjected to collective debate and negotiations providing legal guarantees for the employee; the other is based on unstable properties assessed by the company and requiring individual commitment.

In the competence model, remuneration is based on an appreciation of an individual's performance within a work collectivity. In other words, competencies are evaluated individually but in context. Evaluation is thus conducted on a one-to-one basis between employer and employee, without the possibility of a critical view from the outside on what is going on inside the company. Moreover, competencies always have to be proved. Contrary to the context in which credentials constitute a stable basis for determining wages, "management based on competencies" always implies the possibility of modifying the wage. The wage relation becomes uncertain and ultimately, the definition of the wage depends on the power relations existing within the company and the ability of the unions to present a united opposition to the employer's attempts to individualise pay.

In the logic of competencies, and from the employers' point of view, workers holding the same credential will not necessarily have the same "individual competencies" and will therefore not be ensured the same wage. The wage is no longer a tariff but a price paid for the worker's individual contribution to the company. The process for setting the salary that the worker will receive is seen as merely a technical and "objective" decision, and the wage relation loses its political character. The corollary to this is increased inequalities between workers:

> The legal figure of the worker that had been modelled by labour law has thus progressively given way to a Janus-faced figure: one face is that of the professional whose individual identity finds expression through work, and the other that of the isolated or insecure employee, whose work is once again being treated as a commodity. (Supiot quoted in Lichtenberger, 1999: p. 104)

This trend towards the individualisation and depoliticisation of the wage is restrained by the presence of trade unions and the limitations imposed by collective agreements, although the balance of power between the traditional actors is being tipped in favour of the employers.

---

and upper-level categories, which are most affected by policies aimed at individualising the wage and careers, and where collective rules have less sway.

C. Credentials and vocational training systems and the competence logic

The managerial use of the concept of competencies has also been introduced into vocational education and training programmes, affecting their contents and how they are taught and evaluated (Ropé and Tanguy, 2000). This can first be seen in the trend observed in all three countries examined here towards the extension of their certification systems to include any kind of "competencies": the rationale being that any kind of knowledge, capability or skills that can be used by companies should be recognised by a credential. Furthermore, vocational training courses are being partly developed at the workplace in order to adapt their contents to company demands; this is consistent with the systems validating prior experience or knowledge in which learning on the job is perceived as equivalent to formal learning in vocational training courses.

Beyond these general observations, the particular systems of vocational training and certification in each country must be taken into consideration. It can be argued, as Lefresne suggests, that there is a correlation (both negative and positive) between the legitimacy of the system and the emergence of the debate on competencies. More precisely:

> [When] the system of professionalisation is regulated jointly by the social actors and draws on strongly established professional identities [...] the debate on competencies has no real autonomy and the issues raised exist only in relation to the system of qualification that is endowed with a strong legitimacy (stable norms associated with a high level of recognition) and a certain flexibility (through collective bargaining) [...]. If the system of professionalisation and certification is still poorly structured, the debate on competencies remains a secondary one, the central question being that of the production of collective points of reference. (Lefresne, 2001: p. 7)

Thus, in the UK, "competencies" could be seen as constituting a possible model of correspondence between vocational training, credentials and pay in a system that is still in search of its collective points of reference. The British unions, more attached to a trade logic and the time spent in apprenticeship, did not mobilise around the issue of a homogeneous system relating skills, vocational training and credentials. The NVQs have introduced a system of credentials that is partially independent of the training institutions and companies, but which retains the traditional job/craft distinction. "A system implemented without the participation of the trade unions raises no real issues in terms of classification criteria since there is no collective agreement" (Lefresne, 2001: p. 13)[17].

In Spain, where the system of vocational training and certification is still poorly structured, the debate on competencies appears to be largely secondary. The major issue, in a context where a large part of the population holds no recognised vocational credentials, appears to be the construction of a more transparent and structured system of accreditation for initial vocational training, continuing vocational training and training for the unemployed.

The French debate thus appears to be specific, since the competence logic is now challenging a collective reference system based on the occupational sector as the key defining space. Management based on competencies echoes the debates over the respective roles of the company and the sector, the validation of experience (*acquis de l'expérience*) (which also concerns the unemployed), and the national *répertoire des certifications* (list of credentials) – that is, a heterogeneous mix of norms, actors and issues.

Conclusion

Three aspects have been emphasised throughout this chapter, and particularly in the last section: the transformation of the processes of wage determination, and the resultant individualisation of the wage relation; the emergence of political and economic inequalities between workers arising from this process; and the significant role of the state in the construction of vocational training and certification systems reflecting the logic of individualisation.

These changes have produced a significant shift in the role of skills and credentials as a link between employment and the wage (direct or indirect) paid by employers. Indeed, the "bargaining value" of workers' credentials and skills is being replaced by the rationale that each worker's salary should be the result of his or her individual abilities and performance. This serves to blur the political character of the wage and to minimise the collective rights (and struggles) of workers.

There are, however, some further issues related to the production of skills and credentials and the articulation of these with pay that we would like to mention here, although they have partly been raised elsewhere in the book (Chapters 1, 2 and 3).

---

[17] Lefresne emphasises that the good press received by the British system in Europe is paradoxical considering how little it is used by firms in the UK.

One of these issues is the importance given to training in employment policies at both national and European (EU) levels. This is due to European rhetoric attributing unemployment to inappropriate or inadequate training. This rhetoric is being increasingly intermingled with the discourse on competencies, a concept that tends to be dished up in every shape and form for employees and the unemployed alike. Underlying this is the idea that it is the responsibility of individuals to be employable or for their training to be adapted to the labour market. However, the debates on "employability" frequently ignore the unequal access to initial or continuing vocational training.

Another issue is the question of transferability. New systems of vocational training and certification have emerged that seek to provide a more "comprehensive" system of credentials geared to companies' demands, as well as to enhancing labour market "transparency" and worker mobility with a view to sustaining employment. The question arises here of the "quality" of the credentials that are granted. A vocational training system that offers credentials with lower social esteem to those who are excluded from the labour market or faced with job insecurity does little to remedy their situation.

These questions can be approached from the perspective of the construction of rights over resources. This framework places the conflicts and inequalities of access to training and employment within an analysis of the processes and institutions governing the distribution of resources. This will be the object of future research by our network.

References

Atkinson, D. (1999), *The Financing of Vocational Education in the U.K.*, Thessaloniki, European Centre for the Development of Vocational Training.

Aventur, F. and Möbus, M. (2000), "Formation Professionnelle Initiale et Continue en Europe: Synthèse Comparative" in Conseil d'Analyse Économique: *Formation tout au Long de la Vie*, Paris, La documentation Française.

Bjornavold, J. (1997), "La Evaluación del Aprendizaje no Formal: Calidad y Limitaciones de las Metodologías", *Formación profesional*, Revista europea, 12: pp. 58-75.

Bouyx, B. (1998), "L'Enseignement technologique et professionnel", *Cahiers français*, 285: pp. 37-42.

Casal, J., Colomer, F. and Comas, M.. (1998), *La Interrelación entre los Tres Subsistemas de Formación Profesional en España*, Bellaterra, GRET, Universidad Autónoma de Barcelona.

Cachón, L. and Lefresne, F. (1999), "Estrategia de los Actores, Lógicas y Políticas de Empleo Juvenil en Europa", in Lorenzo Cachón (ed.), *Juventudes, Mercados de Trabajo y Políticas de Empleo*, Valencia, 7 i mig.

Céreq (2002), "La Validation des acquis professionnels. Bilan des pratiques actuelles, enjeux pour les dispositifs futurs", *Céreq Bref*, 185, avril.

CES (Consejo Económico y Social) (2001), *Economía, Trabajo y Sociedad*, Memoria 2000, Madrid, CES.

Combault, P. (1999), "La Couverture Conventionnelle à la fin 1997", *Premières informations*, Dares, 29 (2).

Crouch, C. (1992), "Reino Unido: El Rechazo del Compromiso", in Guido Baglioni and Colin Crouch (comp.) (1990), *Las Relaciones Laborales en Europa. El Desafío de la Flexibilidad*, Madrid, Ministerio de Trabajo y Seguridad Social.

Dubar, C. (1996), "La Sociologie du Travail Face à la Qualification et à la Compétence", *Sociologie du travail*, 38 (2): pp. 179-193.

Edwards, P., Hall, M., Hyman, R., Marginson, P., Sisson, K., Waddington, J. and Winchester, D. (1998), "Great Britain: From Partial Collectivism to Neo-liberalism to Where?", in Ferner A. and Hyman R. (eds), *Changing Industrial Relations in Europe*, Oxford, Blackwell.

Eyraud, F. (1998), "La Négociation des Mobilités, Comparaison Internationale", in Bernard Gazier, David Marsden and Jean-Jacques Silvestre (eds), *Repenser l'Économie du Travail. De l'Effet d'Entreprise à l'Effet Sociétal*, Toulouse, Octarès.

Eyraud, F. and Rozenblatt, P. (1994), *Les Formes Hiérarchiques. Travail et Salaires dans Neuf Pays*, Paris, Minuit.

Fina, L., González, F. and Pérez, J. I. (2001), *Negociación Colectiva y Salarios en España*, Madrid, CES.

Gahéry, R. (1998), "La Formation Continue", *Cahiers français*, 285: pp. 108-112.

García Espejo, M. I. (1998), *Recursos Formativos e Inserción Laboral de Jóvenes*, Madrid, CIS-Siglo XXI.

Goetschy, J. (1998), "France: The Limits of Reform", in Anthony Ferner and Richard Hyman (eds), *Changing Industrial Relations in Europe*, Oxford, Blackwell.

Howell, C. (1999), "Unforgiven: British Trade Unionism in Crisis", in Andrew Martin and George Ross (coord.), *The Brave New World of European Labour. European Trade Unions at the Millennium*, New York, Berghahn Books.

Jobert, A. (2000), *Les Espaces de la Négociation Collective, Branches et Territoires*, Toulouse, Octarès.

Jones, M. (1999), *New Institutional Spaces. TECs and the Remaking of Economic Governance*, London, Regional Policy and Development Series.

Keep, E. and Mayhew, K. (1996), "Evaluating the Assumptions that Underlie Training Policy", in Alison L. Booth and Dennis J. Snower (eds), *Acquiring Skills. Market Failures, Their Symptoms and Policy Responses*, Cambridge, Cambridge University Press.

Khöler, C. and Woodard, J. (1997) "Systems of Work and Socio-Economic Structures: A Comparison of Germany, Spain, France and Japan", *European Journal of Industrial Relations*, 3 (1): pp. 59-82.

Lefresne, F. (2001), "Compétences et Enjeux Sociaux dans les Pays Européens", *Formation Emploi*, 74: pp. 5-20.

Lichtenberger, Y. (1999), "Compétence, Organisation du Travail et Confrontation Sociale", *Formation Emploi*, 67: pp. 93-106.

Marsden, D. (1994), *Mercados de Trabajo. Límites Sociales de las Nuevas Teorías*, Madrid, Ministerio de Trabajo y Seguridad Social.

Marsden, D. (1999), *A Theory of Employment Systems: Micro-foundations of Societal Diversity*, Oxford, Oxford University Press.

Martín Artiles, A. (1999) "Organización del Trabajo y Nuevas Formas de Gestión Laboral", in Faustino Miguélez and Carlos Prieto (dir.), *Las Relaciones de Empleo en España*, Madrid, Siglo XXI.

Maruani, M. and Reynaud, E. (comp.) (1991), *Debates sobre el Empleo. Francia y Alemania*, Madrid, Ministerio de Trabajo y Seguridad Social.

Maurice, M., Sellier, F. and Silvestre, J.-J. (1987), *Política de Educación y Organización Industrial en Francia y en Alemania. Aproximación a un Análisis Societal*, Madrid, Ministerio de Trabajo y Seguridad Social.

Méhaut, P. (1986), "La théorie du capital humain", in Lucie Tanguy (dir.), *L'introuvable relation formation/emploi*, Paris, La documentation française.

Merle, V. and Lichtenberger, Y. (2001), "Formation et Éducation tout au Long de la Vie 1971-2001: Deux Réformes, un Même Défi", *Formation Emploi*, 76: pp. 169-189.

Miguélez, F. (1993), "Clasificación, Movilidad y Relaciones Laborales", *Revista de economía y sociología del trabajo*, 21/22: pp. 8-18.

Millward, N., Bryson, A. and Forth, J. (2000), *All Change at Work? British Employment Relations 1980-1998, as Portrayed by the Workplace Industrial Relations Survey Series*, London, Routledge.

Otero, C. (2001), *El Sistema de Formación Profesional en España*, Thessaloniki, European Centre for the Development of Vocational Training.

Planas, J. (1998), *Formación Continua, Reconocimiento de las Competencias y Sistemas de Formación Profesional*, Bellaterra, GRET, Universidad Autónoma de Barcelona.

QUIT (Grup d'Estudis Sociològics sobre la Vida Quotidiana i el Treball) (2000), *Sirve la Formación para el Empleo?*, Madrid, CES.

Recio, A. (1997), *Trabajo, Personas, Mercados, Manual de Economía Laboral*, Barcelona/Madrid, Icaria/FUHEM.

Reynaud, J. D. (1988), "Les classifications: Quelques Réflexions", *Travail et Emploi*, 38: pp. 13-16.

Ropé, F. and Tanguy, L. (2000), "Le Modèle des Compétences: Système Éducatif et Entreprise", *L'année sociologique*, 50 (2): pp. 493-520.

Rozenblatt, P. (2000), "Occupational and Wage Hierarchies: an Historic Turning Point", in Linda Clarke, Peter de Gijsel and Jörn Janssen (ed.), *The Dynamics of Wage Relations in the New Europe*, Dordrecht, Kluwer.

de la Torre, I. (2000), "La Dimensión Social del Capital Humano. Formación Ocupacional y Formación continua", *Papeles de Economía Española*, 86: pp. 266-279.

Twining, J. (1999), *Vocational Education and Training in the United Kingdom*, Thessaloniki, European Centre for the Development of Vocational Training.

Tatch, J., Pratten, C. and Ryan, P. (1998), "Employment Structures and Labour Market Aspects Related to VET", in CEDEFOP, *Vocational education and training – the European research field*, Thessaloniki, European Centre for the Development of Vocational Training.

Verd, J.M.. Gérardin, F. and Barbera, F. (1999), *Formación y Cualificación: Elementos para la Construcción de una Tipología Societal*, Report presented at Porto for the thematic network "La construction sociale de l'emploi" (ERB SOE 2 CT 97 3041), April 1999.

Wood, S. (1987) "The Deskilling Debate. New Technology and Work Organization", *Acta Sociologica*, 30 (1): pp. 3-24.

CHAPTER 5

Unions and the Wage-Welfare Nexus

Roland ATZMÜLLER, Bernadette CLASQUIN
and Luca QUEIROLO PALMAS

In this chapter we will discuss some elements of the "forms of power in establishing and exercising rights over resources" (see Chapter 1). As the complex institution of the wage relation is our chosen point of entry for the analysis of social rights over resources, we will focus on the conflictual character of this relation and the actors involved in its institutionalisation. In particular we will examine the role of unions in regimes of resources and social rights, that is, their relation to and position in (nationally different) welfare systems. Though the role of the unions in the creation and sustaining of European welfare systems seems to be taken for granted, there is little literature on this topic. Industrial relations and welfare appear to be different research disciplines. However, from a rights over resources perspective, the power relations around welfare and collective bargaining appear fundamentally connected. Recent developments in the "crises of the welfare state" show that the question of social rights over resources does not simply concern technical matters such as finance, spending levels, or recipient groups, but is a deeply political problem. Thus, the role of social actors such as unions in the welfare systems has to be discussed.

This chapter will argue that the unions have different powers to influence the construction of social rights depending on the institutional configurations governing the resources flowing through the wage. Thus the different levels of collective bargaining, and participation in the management of social security funds or in the management of pension funds, define differentiated spheres of action that are to be related to historically constructed societal characteristics. The nature, scope and transformation of the powers exercised by the unions are to be taken into account as factors contributing to the shaping of resource regimes.

In the first part we will focus on general dynamics and review some of the research literature dealing with the role of unions in the welfare system. We will examine recent trends in industrial relations in Europe towards wage moderation, the re-emergence of coordination (such as in the form of social pacts), the development of so-called coordinated decentralisation and supply-side oriented collective bargaining focussing on employment levels rather than wages. We will end this part with a discussion of the impact of EMU on collective bargaining.

In the second part case studies on France, Italy and the United Kingdom will be presented and the issues we have raised here will be discussed from rather different points of entry, depending on the specific situation in each country. The French case study highlights current shifts in the balance of power between government, employers and unions within the framework of recent resource regime changes reducing the scope of the *cotisation sociale*. The Italian case study examines the emergence of a new resource regime and its difficult consolidation in a political cycle that restrains the role of social pacts and reduces the involvement of unions in the joint administration of welfare. The case study on the UK discusses the break up of the link between industrial relations, employment and the social security system through a fundamental reconfiguration of the regime implemented under the hegemony of neo-liberalism.

I. The unions' role in resource regimes: general dynamics and recent trends

As highlighted in Chapters 1 and 3, the configuration of resources that are exchanged through the wage implies a number of contradictions. Exchange processes that are channelled through wages are articulated with other social spheres, responsibilities (unpaid work in the household) or needs (time out of employment) and the conditions available to fulfil them. The debate thus necessarily enters the territory of political power relations, conflicts and the mediation and representation of different interests (Friot, 1999: p. 99). To emphasise the "instituted, hence socially variable" nature of the wage requires looking at those actors and institutions whose practices fundamentally shape and influence the contradictions of the wage relation and institutionalise particular *resource regimes* that reach well beyond the narrow confines of the workplace level.

A. The role of the unions in welfare state debates

Given the "ostensibly clear link" (Crouch, 1999) between welfare studies and industrial relations, discussion of the role of unions within welfare systems strangely lacks systematic and comprehensive treatment. Yet this could help shed light on the historical dynamics and trajectories of both areas. Ebbinghaus (2001: p. 6), when analysing the ambiguous role of social partnership relations in Europe, observes that welfare states "have also been realised through self-administration of publicly mandated social insurance, collectively negotiated private welfare funds or union-run employment schemes." However, Colin Crouch is right to call the link between these areas of social research "fugitive" as most analyses generally do not go any further. The question of how the social character of the origin of resources – considered as falling within the realm of industrial relations – is linked to the rights over them that are contained in welfare systems, is usually neglected.

Welfare studies frequently focus on institutional structures, the outcomes of social policies, and the populations concerned. Though they often criticise a simple focus on expenditure levels and certainly analyse qualitative aspects of transfers, they seem to regard the resources available for social policy as "neutral", or at best, debate these resources in terms of the problem of taxation levels and redistribution. The conflictual character of the resources contained in the exchange processes that run through the wage becomes separated from analyses of welfare policies. On the other hand, industrial relations studies usually focus on the role of unions in conflicts over employment relations, the representation of the interests of their members and – most crucially – the determination of wage levels through collective bargaining. But the role of unions within welfare systems is at best treated as one among many other fields. The current crises of industrial relations and welfare systems in Europe show that this separation is not just a question of scientific relevance:

> Given a widespread belief that welfare states, and especially their social insurance components, must be reformed, union participation in the reform process has become fundamental in all systems where unions and employer organisations have a formal role [...]. Unless governments are willing to risk the conflict that would ensue from expelling unions from social insurance management, they have to win union agreement jointly to make the reforms. (Crouch, 1999: p. 439)

Though we cannot claim to offer a satisfying and systematic account on this perspective, it is assumed here that the link between welfare systems and industrial relations is not arbitrary, as if the role of the unions in the flow of resources and the rights related to them would just be a question of management structures or the pressure a certain interest group can exert on the political system. Rather the unions (as well as other actors) fundamentally shape the character of these resources and vice versa[1].

B. Trends in industrial relations from a "rights over resources" perspective

Industrial relations in Europe have undergone a number of severe changes that have clearly affected the role and power of unions. Recently emerging regulatory devices, in particular different forms of "pacts" between employers, employees and the state at different societal levels (sometimes called "soft" forms of regulation), and the European macroeconomic framework have increasingly replaced traditional wage negotiation policies. These changes put severe constraints on pay bargaining at all levels and also affected the role of the unions in social policy making. According to Schulten, in the post-1945 "Fordist" phase wage developments and policies were linked to productivity gains – albeit differently from country to country. This guaranteed a certain participation of workers in economic development and removed wages (partially at least) from market competition. However, a fundamental U-turn has taken place, "which can be described as a transition from a productivity-oriented wage policy to a competition-oriented wage policy" (Schulten, 2001: p. 9).

Thus, competitiveness has become a legitimate benchmark in the negotiating process. Unions are forced to internalise the macroeconomic concerns of the current orthodoxy preoccupied with inflation rates (Léonard, 2001). In a context of slack labour markets, such policies create a strong incentive for unions to participate in new forms of co-ordination and corporatist forms of negotiations to compensate for their loss of power (Traxler, 2000a: p. 411). This is often described as the emergence of a competitive corporatism that has come to replace the social corporatism prevailing in the 1960s and 1970s.

On the whole, the social corporatism [...] was based on a 'political exchange' in which unions abandoned a 're-distributive' expansive wage pol-

---

[1]   The national unemployment schemes in Scandinavia (with the exception of Norway) and Belgium, which are run by the unions, provide good illustration of this (Crouch, 1999; Ebbinghaus and Visser, 1998; Ebbinghaus, 2002). Ebbinghaus and Visser claim that this institutional factor is one of the most important variables explaining the development of union membership in these countries. Union membership in the Scandinavian countries reaches 80% or more, and it continued to grow during the 1990s (Waddington and Hoffmann, 2001). In the light of our approach it would be interesting to ask whether and how union control of unemployment insurance schemes influences benefit levels, access, coverage and other issues.

icy [...] in favour of a productivity-oriented wage policy [...] for which they were compensated by tax benefits, the extension of the welfare state or an expansion of social rights to participation and codetermination. By contrast, the wage policy in the competitive corporatism [...] is fully committed to enhancing national competitiveness." (Schulten, 2001: p. 18)

In the following sections we will discuss three related trends in industrial relations in Europe: wage moderation, the emergence of social pacts, and the development of a coordinated decentralisation of collective bargaining. We then examine the impact of European Monetary Union.

1. Wage moderation

In the context of our problematic one of the most crucial factors shaping the role of unions in the wage-welfare nexus can be located in a shift in the hegemonic power relations between employers and employees, which comes to the fore in the predominant, neo-liberal conception of labour costs (see Chapter 2). A labour-cost understanding of the different components of the wage distinguishes direct pay for time worked and not worked (paid leave etc.), bonuses, payments in cash and in kind, costs of vocational training, social security contributions, costs of welfare services, and taxes. In our perspective different elements of the wage are seen as institutionalisations of the conflicts about "rights over resources". The neo-liberal understanding constructs them as cost factors which are said to be detrimental to competitiveness, economic growth and employment level/volume.

However, wage moderation is a central feature of recent trends in industrial relations. The pressure on unions all over Europe to support the profitability of companies and the whole economy by accepting moderate wage agreements to improve employment opportunities has considerably increased. Mermet (2001: p. 34) notes that, "[...] in the early eighties and nineties, real wages did not keep pace with productivity gains, thus causing a gap and delay in compensation for productivity. After the mid-eighties, wage increases did keep pace with productivity gains, but without reducing the gap opened up in the early eighties."

The following table (Pochet and Fajertag, 2000) clearly reveals the effect of wage moderation.

Table: The wage as a proportion of GDP

	1980	1980-1990	1990	1990-1998	1998	1980-1998
Austria	72.9	-4.1	68.8	-4.7	64.1	-8.8
Belgium	77.8	-8.3	69.5	0.1	69.6	-8.2
France	76.4	-8.0	68.4	-1.6	66.8	-9.6
Germany	74.5	-6.8	67.7	-2.7	65.0	-9.5
Italy	72.6	-0.4	72.2	-5.4	66.8	-5.8
The Netherlands	74.1	-9.3	64.8	-0.4	64.4	-9.7
Portugal	76.2	-6.9	69.8	1.0	70.8	-6.7
Spain	78.5	-7.9	70.6	-3.7	66.9	-11.6
United-Kingdom	72.2	0.7	72.9	-1.8	71.1	-1.1
European Union	76.0	-5.1	70.9	-2.7	68.2	-7.8
United States	70.5	-1.5	69.0	-0.2	68.8	-1.7

Source: Fajertag/Pochet, 2000: p. 24.

The data show a remarkable decrease of the wage as a proportion of GDP between 1980 and 1998 of up to 10%. The most notable exceptions are the UK and the US, where the reduction was less than 2%. However, it should be mentioned that these countries showed a steep increase in the wage spread – and hence in inequality – which served to sustain a highly segmented labour market and an increasingly polarised welfare system (Schulten, 2001; Glennerster and Hills, 1998, for the UK). Italy and Portugal also showed a somewhat lower decrease of the wage share compared to the EU average. Furthermore, these developments did not happen at the same time. Whereas most of the countries experiencing a marked decline of the wage share did so in the 1980s, in Italy the reduction occurred in the 1990s and was the highest in this decade. Austria showed a rather even decline over the period examined, which nevertheless meant one of the most pronounced reductions of the wage share in the 1990s. Germany and Spain also experienced a strong continuing decline in the 1990s.

To understand recent trends in industrial relations concerning wages it is also necessary to focus on so-called *non-wage labour costs* or the *tax burden on labour* which have entered centre stage in policy debates in most European countries and at Community level (Hassel and Ebbinghaus, 2000). In some debates about the employment record of continental Europe, high non-wage labour costs, as embodied in mandatory social insurance contributions and direct taxes on income paid by employers and employees, are depicted as a "continental dilemma"

(Scharpf, 1998). In this view, continental European economies have to increase their contributions to finance rising social costs, partly for passive labour market policies (unemployment and early retirement benefits), thereby driving even more workers out of their jobs, which in turn demands higher contributions. Therefore wage restraint alone cannot guarantee lower labour costs, if non wage labour costs continue to rise (Hassel and Ebbinghaus, 2000: p. 71)[2].

2. Coordination instead of conflicts? Social Pacts and (co-ordinated) decentralisation

Two recent industrial relations trends in Europe underlie the attack on wage levels. On the one hand, there is a re-emergence of "national corporatism" as a number of social pacts have been concluded in the wake of the implementation of EMU (Fajertag and Pochet, 2000; Kauppinen, 1998). On the other hand, collective bargaining is undergoing a continuing process of (so-called co-ordinated or organised) decentralisation (Waddington and Hoffmann, 2001; Traxler, 2000a+b).

According to Pochet and Fajertag (2000) social pacts aim at managing a combination of different features such as: reduction of labour costs; restructuring of welfare and extension of flexible working conditions; re-commodification of labour and support for a growing number of low-paid workers; convergence with the Maastricht criteria by cutting back welfare provisions; and preservation of social peace in the implementation of reforms. In this form of "soft" neo-liberalism the strategies of labour parties and unions are brought into line with mainstream discourses. Hence social pacts do not simply replicate the neo-liberal strategies prevalent in the Anglo-Saxon world. The differences appear in the role that the "social partners" – in particular the unions – acquire in the reform process and also in the concern regarding the social inclusion of groups with low income and skills[3].

Another central feature of industrial relations under the "post-Fordist" compromise is described as "co-ordinated" decentralisation towards lower levels of the economy (in particular the company level).

---

[2] According to Esping-Andersen, who has partly accepted this hypothesis, in Scandinavia the problem of low productivity/low income jobs is at least partly solved through public sector employment and training policies, which are far more developed in these countries compared to continental Europe where principles of subsidiarity often prevail (Esping-Andersen, 1992).

[3] It should be clear however that this marks a fundamental shift in the understanding of social policy. The goal to maintain and improve living standards is replaced by that of preventing poverty.

Nevertheless, this development is connected to the competitiveness orientation of macro-economic and employment-related policies, as has been clearly revealed by recent studies on pacts on employment and competitiveness (Sisson and Artiles, 2000; Freyssinet and Seifert, 2001). These pacts reduce the importance of more substantial or qualitative aspects of employment (such as pay, conditions). Agreements seek rather to increase or preserve employment levels, while strengthening competitiveness at the same time (Institut des Sciences du Travail, 2000: p. 52). However, bargaining on the topics of employment and competitiveness very rarely leads to increases in employment levels, not to speak of wage levels (Zagelmeyer, 2000). Rather employers offer to refrain from mass redundancies and to rely on different measures of voluntary redundancies (such as early retirement).

3. Industrial relations and European integration

The tight framework of the stability-oriented monetary and fiscal policy of EMU and the ECB (Kasten and Soskice, 1999) appears to be one of the deeper reasons underlying the trends outlined here. Member states can no longer resort to devaluation to alleviate an external economic shock and inflation cannot be used to reduce public deficits, which are limited to 3%, as price stability has become the prime target. Hence, wages, the labour market (employment levels) or social security are the main avenues for adjustment to an adverse economic shock (Kauppinen, 1998). This serves as a device to discipline workers to refrain from so-called excessive wage demands and stick to "responsible" forms of collective bargaining.

This macro-economic framework pushed unions to accept and implement welfare reforms, inflation control, reduction of labour costs and cuts in public expenditures. EMU and the Stability Pact (finalised in 1997 in Amsterdam) therefore altered the informal agreement on devaluation replacing it with internal depreciations. In the absence of an encompassing European-level regulation of wages, working time, labour rights and fiscal systems, the goal of this framework is to make national labour markets compete with each other. "With labour mobility as well as fiscal federalism so limited, the burden of adjustment is concentrated almost entirely on labour costs, including the social wage" (Martin, 1999: p. 7). Hence, it can be argued that this framework institutionalised the shift in the balance of power between unions and employers at the European level, revealing its political rather than technical or neutral fundaments.

II. France, Italy and the UK: societal differences

In each of the EU countries, the recent changes that have taken place are marked by the historical relations between employers, unions and the state. We have chosen below to examine three reform processes that involve the unions to differing degrees and that highlight current forms of wage conflict concerning wages and social protection. While national differences cannot be reduced to ideal-types, the three countries examined here serve to illustrate situations in which the processes used, although totally dissimilar, resulted in an erosion of rights.

A. *France: union divisions facilitate the development of the tutelary state*

There has never been mass unionism in France, even if the main decline occurred between 1977 and 1987 when membership rates dropped from 25% to 10% of the workforce (Labbé, 1998). Viewed from abroad, French unions appear particularly weak and divided. Yet they have demonstrated their weight several times over the last two decades, notably with regard to government attempts at pension reforms. Their power is an outcome of a historical construction and is deeply embedded in the French societal configuration: they acquired legitimacy to act as employees' representatives (well beyond their actual membership) not only at company and sectoral levels, but also at the cross-sectoral national level, and to act on the resource flows channelled through the wage. However, it is our contention that with the growth of the share of tax-financing in social protection at the expense of the *cotisation sociale*, the balance of power is changing and the union's scope for action is being reduced.

The institutionalisation of the complex power relations between state, employers and unions in the course of the 20th century permitted the construction of a resource regime based on employment rights. The state played an important role in this process, notably by entrenching the role of unions and employer organisations in negotiations over wage determination (Jefferys and Contrepois, 2000; Barrat, Yacubovich and Maurice, 2002) as well as in the management of social protection. However, it was also through these instituted channels that European objectives of wage moderation and the reduction of the "social burden" on wages could be achieved. Beyond the question of monetary stability, this particular configuration of institutions and power is probably one of the reasons why there was no need for a social pact to meet the Maastricht criteria.

This section will first briefly describe some aspects of the modalities of power exercised in the field of the wage and social protection. Then the reduction of working time (1996-2000) and the transformation of unemployment insurance (1999-2000) will be taken as examples of the role played by French unions in resource regime changes.

1. Employment-linked rights: recent dynamics in power relations

An examination of the evolution of the wage relation in France from World War II up to the early 1980s reveals a two-fold, and somewhat asymmetrical, role of the state. On the one hand, government intervention served to guarantee general employment rules: by acting on the minimum wage (through indexation and an annual nudge) and setting rules for collective negotiations (such as compulsory annual wage bargaining), the state provided a legal basis for sectoral collective bargaining. This in turn impacted on wage hierarchies. On the other hand, the state played a relatively limited role during this period in the wage-based social protection system (financed through the *cotisation sociale*, and centred on pay-as-you-go wage replacement): employers and unions were (and remain) the primary actors in the decision making processes concerning contributions, distribution of benefits and entitlement rules.

This seemingly contradictory role must be taken into account when analysing the significance of processes instituting the wage-welfare nexus. While wage conflict has been ensured a strong legitimacy through the participation of unions and employers in the management of the social protection system, the role of the state, which has maintained an attentive eye on the level of contributions, must not be forgotten. Moreover, differences have emerged between the unions over time with regard to wage bargaining and the joint management of social security: the latter has always been criticised by the CGT, the largest union in terms of membership, as having favoured employers. The other major unions – the CFDT, CGT-FO, CFTC and CGC have generally been more ready to seek a compromise[4].

---

[4]   The CGT (*Confédération Générale du Travail* – General Workers' Union), has traditionally been close to the Communist Party. The CFDT (*Confédération Française Démocratique du Travail* – National Democratic Workers' Union), is a reformist union close to the Socialist Party and favours co-operation. The CGT-FO (more commonly known simply as *Force Ouvrière* – Workers' Power), of anti-communist tradition, has a large constituency in the public sector. The CFTC (*Confédération Française des Travailleurs Chrétiens* – National Christian Workers' Union), campaigns for social integration. The CGC (*Confédération Générale des Cadres* – National Manager's Union) has defended the interests of managerial staff since their

Studies on collective bargaining and the social protection system – the two are generally treated separately – have highlighted a number of changes that have taken place in these fields since the 1980s.

Since the Auroux laws (1982), the relationship between the different levels of collective bargaining – cross-sectoral, sectoral and firm – have changed: firm level agreements have grown significantly in volume (Jobert, 2000) whereas, due to declining membership, unions have become more powerful at the sectoral than at the workplace level. Subsequent measures permitting to apply dispensatory agreements put the *ordre public social*[5] in jeopardy. New rules of representation were also introduced favouring the most representative unions at workplace level while at the same time permitting mandated non-unionised workers to negotiate at the small firm level. Bargaining topics changed as employment became a key issue for negotiations: in a context of huge membership losses and declining industrial action, unions gained increased responsibilities through their participation in decisions concerning the economic future of the firm; some saw this as an opportunity to enter into a partnership process with employers and the state, who are both keen to develop social dialogue[6].

The attempts to reform social protection in the 1990s (such as pensions) show how difficult it is for the government to exercise its power in this field. Nevertheless, several measures were introduced, and although the system remains essentially based on *cotisations sociales*, the share of tax-financed benefits grew significantly. This has resulted in a dual system: on the one hand, benefits financed by *cotisations sociales* are provided to workers on the basis of their employment status; on the other hand, tax-based social protection finances a growing part of the population whose participation in the labour force has become "precarious" or "atypical". Moreover, the complexity of the resource flows and the technocratic mode of management of the social protection system make for a lack of transparency: the decision-making processes, regardless of whether resources are financed through taxes or social contribu-

---

incorporation into the general salariat. For more information on French Unionism, see Jefferys (2003).

5   The "social public order" instituted a hierarchy between the different bargaining levels, with an obligation for a company level agreement to be more favourable to employees than those negotiated at a higher level.

6   On this notion developed to foster "social partnership" to achieve "consensus", as opposed to power relations between contradictory interests to achieve a compromise, see Chapter 6 in this volume.

tions, increasingly by-pass political deliberations and thus restrict the role of the unions (Volovitch, 2001).

Two further points concerning the current situation should be noted. First, the public sector, which still represents almost one fourth of employment in France, has always been strongly unionised, and remains an important arena for social conflicts over work issues. Privatisation and externalisation of public service employment has nonetheless tended to reduce the sphere of influence of both the state and the unions. Second, the 1990s saw the emergence of new social movements: some were organised on an occupational basis (the nurses' "*coordination*"), some formed new unions (*Groupe des dix*, UNSA[7]), and yet others represented previously unorganised groups (such as the unemployed). They have challenged the traditional unions' form of organisation, their action and representativity; the demonstrations they have organised (such as that of the unemployed in 1995) have sometimes compelled the dominant unions, as well as political parties, to take position on the issues raised. Major conflicts over reforms (unemployment benefits, pensions) have given rise to a strong mobilisation of the working population, and this has also led to changes at the political level. In France, pressure from the street influenced the political debates of the 1990s – and this remains true today.

Despite the European integration process, the influence of national actors over wage-welfare issues remains powerful. The instituted decision-making processes have created a specific space for changing alliances and coalitions between them. The two rounds of negotiations discussed below serve to illustrate the interweaving of power between government, employers and unions that shapes the current political debate over resources.

2. Wage moderation and active employment policy: the reduction of working time

One of the most important issues facing the unions in the 1990s was the obligation to negotiate on the reduction of working time. The negotiations on the 35-hour week were faced with three contradictory objectives linked to the dominant interests of the actors concerned: reduction of working time, organisation of working time and employment[8]. And as

---

[7] National Union of Independent Unions.

[8] In this case, the law on the 35-hour week preceded negotiations. Bargaining over working time, according to Bloch-London and Boisard (1999), followed three stages during the second half of the 20th century: first, unions sought to obtain a reduction in working time while maintaining pay levels; then, at the beginning of the 1980s, em-

a result, wage bargaining became dependent on these three terms of exchange.

Employment growth was the government's main objective, although the difficulty in measuring the effects of working-time reductions on job creation was well known. Furthermore, with a view to bolstering the effectiveness of its policy, the government introduced a 5-year degressive reduction of employers' social contributions partially targeted at young people, the disabled and the long-term unemployed. The reduction in working time in the French case can thus be seen as an activation policy. Further government objectives were to boost collective bargaining at sectoral and firm levels, and finally, to comply with the 1993 European directive on working time (Bohm, 1999). The legal framework for the reduction in working time was debated in the French Parliament[9], and collective agreements had to be approved by the Ministry of Labour prior to their implementation.

The laws on the reduction of working time and the obligation to negotiate led to a renewal of collective bargaining at sectoral level and a strong development of firm level bargaining; the unions nonetheless saw a decrease in the role of shop stewards in favour of mandated workers, especially in small firms. The laws also impacted on direct wages: most of the agreements included a wage freeze of one to four years coinciding with the implementation of the euro. Furthermore, the state stepped in to finance part of the employers' social contributions for target populations (as it had done for part-time employment since 1992) – thus encouraging the development of low-paid jobs for low-skill workers (Concialdi and Ponthieux, 1999, Chapters 2 and 3 in this volume). The government addressed this problem by partly exempting wages up to 1.8 times the minimum wage from social contributions. The reduction of working time thus also meant a reduction of labour costs for employers. But at the same time, a growing share of the social security funds jointly managed by unions and employers had to be tax-financed – which left the worker as taxpayer footing the bill (Radé, 2003).

---

ployers sought to adapt the organisation of working time to company constraints. Finally, in the 1990s, the state imposed employment as a topic of collective bargaining, with a view to promoting work sharing; it should be added that the beginning of the decade saw a growth in part-time work, largely due to the exemption of employers' social contributions (Audric and Forgeot, 1999).

[9]   Three laws were passed (1996, 1998, 1999) to reduce standard working time to 35 hours a week, two of which were passed under the Socialist government. The annual mode of calculation had been introduced by a separate law in 1995.

This example highlights the emergence of contradictory trends: the government restructured the framework for collective bargaining, creating spaces for new power relations based on alliances at sectoral and firm levels; but the scope of collective bargaining was reduced as the focus shifted to activating employment policy and wage moderation. The shift in the financing of resources from the *cotisation sociale* to taxation increased state power, but changed its role from that of arbitrator and guarantor of the generality of employment rules to that of provider of funds to support the reduction in working time. It should be noted, however, that in 2001, two years after the bulk of working time negotiations had been completed, wages returned to the fore as the primary topic of collective bargaining.

3. Joint administration: the unemployment insurance agreement of 2000[10]

The French unemployment fund, the *Union Nationale pour l'Emploi dans l'Industrie et le Commerce* (UNEDIC), is a jointly managed institution operating on the basis of an agreement negotiated between the unions and employers' organisations[11] that has to be approved by the government[12] to acquire force of law. The scope of the negotiations includes the setting of contribution rates, levels and duration of benefits and their entitlement rules[13]. The results of each negotiation process will obviously depend on the balance of power existing between the protagonists and between them and the current government. On 31 December 1999, the three-year agreement on unemployment insurance ended and a new one had to be negotiated.

At about the same time, the main employers' organisation came up with a new strategy[14]. Advocating the application of cost-benefit risk

---

[10] This section draws on the interesting historical work of J.-P. Higelé (2002).

[11] Who have equal representation on the board (*paritarisme*).

[12] After consultation of the Conseil Supérieur de l'Emploi formed by state representatives and the unions.

[13] The unemployed draw their benefits from the ASSEDICs (*Associations pour l'Emploi dans l'Industrie et le Commerce*).

[14] The National Federation of French Employers (CNPF) changed its name to the *Mouvement des Entreprises de France* (MEDEF), and led by its vice-president – president of the French Federation of Insurance Companies – proposed an initiative called "the social re-foundation" plan. Advocating a disengagement of the state, it called for social dialogue geared to creating a new "social constitution" within an "autonomous social sphere". Although employers had long been opposed to the cross-sectoral level of collective bargaining as this was seen to entail too strong a generality of rules, the MEDEF revised this position with the opportunity offered by

management to the social protection system in general, and to unemployment insurance in particular, it called for reforms in that direction: unemployment was accepted as a risk that had to be covered, but expenses were to be tightly controlled, strong incentives for job seeking provided – and the unemployed were perceived as being responsible for their situation.

A climate of tension thus prevailed over the negotiations. Three employers' organisations and five unions were gathered around the table; although the unemployed had their own associations, they were represented by the CGT, the only union to have a special section for them. The unions were divided: three signed the final agreement, but the other two refused.

Two preliminary agreements were rejected by the government. After the employers' representatives and the unions who had signed threatened to withdraw from UNEDIC, the Prime Minister intervened in person, and a third and final agreement was signed in October 2000. The government, in fact, had been in agreement with most of the provisions of the initial text, and particularly those concerning the development of targeted activation policies linking the receipt of benefits to an obligation to be actively seeking a job. But it objected that the planned reduction in employers' contributions would jeopardise the short-term financial equilibrium of the fund. Furthermore, it held that the agreement should not serve to create inequalities between the unemployed receiving UNEDIC benefits and those receiving a flat-rate tax-financed social assistance benefit. In the final agreement, the reduction of employers' contributions was delayed, with the stipulation that the resultant surplus budget be used to finance the unemployed who had exhausted their entitlements. The government also insisted on retaining state power to penalise the unemployed who did not comply with procedures, and on the state employment agency maintaining control over the job seeker. Finally, noting that acceptance of a new job initially had little to do with the unemployed person's skill level, the government reintroduced a reference to skill level in the final text, although in somewhat vague terms.

As a result of this agreement, the relationship between the job-seeker and the state employment agency has been strongly individualised, linking benefit entitlement to a "back to work" plan (PARE). In using the UNEDIC fund to partially finance the unemployed who no longer

---

the state to reduce employers' social contributions; for that purpose, national-level cross-sectoral bargaining was welcome. The aim was to combat the architecture of the 35-hours law which favoured negotiations at the sectoral level

have rights to benefits, the government introduced a mix between wage-based and taxed-based resources. Furthermore, the compromise between employers, the government and the signatory unions was reached by marginalising two major unions.

The two examples discussed here show that the state played a crucial role in introducing taxation into workers' resources. It promoted employment as the most important outcome for negotiations, acting as a tutelary state. The nature of the joint management structure, combined with the weakness of the unions, appears to facilitate an alliance against the more representative unions. Hence, in restricting the scope of the wage and fostering social dialogue, the tutelary state seeks consensus more than compromise, a trend that can also be observed in Italy, as will be seen below.

B. Italy: social pacts and the emergence of new resource regimes

During the 1990s, a succession of "social pacts" between employers, unions and the state permitted the implementation of income policies that produced a shift in the traditional resource regime based on the socialised wage and employment rights. In this process, unions gained a central place in the political system, albeit only through sustaining government policy on the gradual retrenchment of social protection. Some of the major trends marking this decade were: control of inflation, reduction of real wages, growth of the working poor[15] and persistent unemployment. The redistribution of income and wealth was accompanied by a clear reduction in industrial and wage disputes and a decrease in union membership (which dropped to about 36% of active wage earners).

A key feature of the decade was the growth of a culture and practice of *concertazione*. This was deemed crucial to meet the Maastricht convergence criteria and to cope with the political crisis that had destroyed the party system ruling Italy since 1945. The implementation of

---

[15] Between 1989 and 1998 real net monthly wages (without tax and social contributions) decreased by 8.7% (Banca d'Italia, Report of the Governor, 2000: p. 127). In that decade, wages did not compensate for inflation and did not recuperate productivity gains. The wage share of the GDP decreased. The number of low-paid workers (earning less than 2/3 of the average wage) grew significantly: in 1989, the working poor accounted for 8.3% of wage earners; in 1998 they represented 18.3% of the workforce (Banca d'Italia, 2000: p. 127). These rates were higher for part-time workers: non-standard work often induces new forms of poverty. There was also a 50% increase in low income families in the 1990s (Banca d'Italia, 2000: p. 69).

reforms was based on social pacts, and four key pacts served to effectively change the regulatory system after 1993:

- The first pact abolished the indexation of salaries to inflation: a category of *programmed inflation* (based on annual government forecasts) was introduced to set the upper limit to wage growth. Thanks to *concertazione* between the government and the social partners, the bargaining system became highly centralised and linked to governmental macroeconomic targets, while wage bargaining at enterprise level remained optional and limited to large companies with strong union representation. As a result, real wages have diminished constantly since 1993, while company profits have risen. Moreover, the unions failed to defend their goal to extend company-level bargaining and promote the unionisation of the small-sized companies characterising the productive structure of Italy.

- The second pact transformed the pension system. The public pension scheme was restructured and the remunerative system (the pension as a continuation of the wage) was changed to a contributory system (benefits based on total contributions paid) for all new entrants to the labour market[16]. Employee savings, private pension plans and occupational pension funds were introduced, with fiscal support from the state. Joint management of the occupational funds was instituted, as well as an advisory board including union and employers' representatives for the basic scheme. The pension reforms implemented under the centre-left *Ulivo* government thus provided an institutional framework ensuring unions a central role in the management of these compulsory transfers.

- The third pact transformed the labour market, fostering flexible work through massive fiscal support (to finance reductions in social contributions).

- Finally, the social partners, led by the government, agreed to shift the sourcing of some benefits from social contributions to tax-based funding (health care, maternity, family benefits). The idea was to cut total labour "costs", perceived as an obstacle to economic

---

[16] The new public scheme will cover roughly 50%-60% of final salary (compared to 80%-90%), thus pushing people to pay for private or occupational pension plans. To obtain the same pension as before, workers will pay higher contributions in a new institutional mode that channels money through the stock market and involves different actors (banks, insurance companies, unions and employers) and different responsibilities with regard to risk-sharing. Mostly high-paid employees, with standard jobs, will have access to complementary pensions, while low-paid employees, with flexible jobs, will be supported by tax-based provisions.

growth and competitiveness; social contributions were reduced from 44.5% of overall labour cost in 1990 to 37.2% in 2000 (Banca d'Italia, 2000: p. 127). The *Ulivo* government also increased the number of means-tested benefits.

Through these pacts, the unions confirmed and extended their institutional role in the emerging resource regimes. They became crucial actors in the reform process, whether this concerned social protection, industrial relations, labour markets, or monetary and fiscal policies. Trying to by-pass the unions proved fatal to the short-lived Berlusconi government, which collapsed in 1994 after its attempt to reform the pension system without *concertazione*.

In short, during the decade of the *Ulivo* government, the unions obtained new rights with respect to the management of some resource flows, training, flexibility, equal opportunity, and working time – but they lost control over the development of real wages. They were able to defend the socialised wage for the core salariat, but accepted new resource regimes for all new entrants to the labour market. They negotiated a reduction in social contributions as well as fiscal support for companies hiring particular categories of workers (the unemployed, women, young people).

The reforms introduced through the social pacts can be seen as producing a clear shift in resource regime: from socialised wage to deferred wage, pre-financed wage and tutelary allowance (see Chapter 3). The shifts concerned different categories of workers: the socialised wage remains predominant for the core salariat, the pre-financed wage is dedicated to high-wage workers and is under the control of the social partners, the tutelary allowance is gradually becoming the predominant regime for poor workers and the "unemployable", and the deferred wage is the new standard for all new workers. This means that each resource regime introduces a combination of different sources of financing, linkages and benefits for different categories of workers.

The strategy of *concertazione* – a closely intertwined mix of government policy, collective bargaining and tripartite coordination – was used to implement the new resource regimes. It enabled the government to adhere to the Maastricht criteria and to retrench the social protection system. The unions' influence on compulsory transfer flows (discussion of reform measures, social pact on financing social protection, role in the management of certain benefits such as occupational pensions, public pensions, or training) was nonetheless strictly dependent on the political situation, and therefore on the existence of a centre-left government. The unions adopted a dual strategy: on the one hand, they opted for support of the so-called general interest (complying with the

European agenda, control of inflation, budgetary recovery) at the expense of a short-term defence of wages. On the other hand, they managed to preserve the rights of workers in stable employment and pensioners in exchange for a casualisation of the employment situation for young workers and all new entrants to the labour market. By the end of the decade, they had become important political actors with a strong consultative role, reorienting and moderating welfare retrenchment. However, it must be emphasised that the social dialogue process took place strictly within the framework of the government's reform agenda, and that the unions had no power to challenge that agenda as such.

But this kind of social pact is closely dependent on the political context, and its instability is evident. As two moderate commentators on union questions argue:

> It is really not clear what the benefit is from the unions' point of view; of course they have gained political recognition, which offers the government some degree of social consensus in a period of economic austerity and gives the unions political honour in a period of uncertainty and weak representativity. But these are benefits for the unions and not directly for the workforce as under the corporatist model. (Accornero and Carrieri, 1997: p. 323)

The end of concertazione: extending and transforming the new resource regimes

One of the most important effects of the reforms implemented through the social pacts was probably the construction of shared beliefs and a climate of trust between the social actors. The model of *concertazione* contributed to establishing a cognitive framework based on the conviction that respecting the deadline for meeting the European criteria was crucial to *saving the nation*. Cognitive frameworks, to be effective, clearly require some form of institutionalisation: this was achieved through numerous forums, bipartite and tripartite committees, and such like, which served to spread the common language and grammar of *concertazione*. The hegemony of a *narrative* lies in its capacity to make other possible lines of action appear unnatural and inconceivable. From this perspective, *the logic of meaning* is first and foremost *a logic of power*. *Concertazione* serves as a powerful mechanism for the depoliticisation of political issues: the decision derived from a common definition of a situation is perceived as *the only thing to do*. And in the case of Italy, entry into the EMU can indeed be described as a symbolic narrative of an external constraint (Radaelli, 2000). For the unions, the result was the loss of an independent point of view and of the capacity to produce an innovative agenda not derived from technical necessity, in other terms the loss of the capacity to produce a different definition and representation of the situation, and to define new perspectives from which other policy guidelines could derive. These were probably the most detrimental effects of *concertazione* and social pacts.

Despite their declining representativity (due to the growth of atypical work, among other factors), unions gained political recognition through the social pacts and a form of incorporation into the political system. But the search for political recognition also created a dependency on political actors and the political cycle. This became particularly apparent during the pre-electoral period at the end of the 1990s. The completion of the process of entry into EMU together with the possibility of an electoral victory of the right-wing coalition destabilised the model of *concertazione*. The last pact signed during the D'Alema government, which sought to institutionalise the practice, was never implemented. The process underway towards a merger between the three main trade union organisations broke down. Debates arose within the left-wing CGIL[17] over future relations between the social actors and the need for another kind of action; other unions shifted to the right in anticipation of a change in government and in order to secure political recognition after the elections; new autonomous unions organised effective strikes in the public administrations, schools, transport, communications, and built up organisational power in other sectors. Widespread public discussion arose over the results of income policies for labour, symbolising the collapse of a shared worldview between the social partners and government. Furthermore, the employers' association withdrew from *concertazione*, and called upon the future government to implement a more stringent retrenchment of social protection.

The strategic remit of the new right-wing government can be characterised by the following features:

- Casualisation of work; generalisation of part-time and temporary work without negotiations with unions; introduction of jobs on call; fostering of competition between regions in terms of wages and employment rights; reform of the legislation on unfair dismissal; progressive shift from collective bargaining to individualised bargaining; privatisation of public employment services; undermining of collective bargaining and employment rights in companies leaving the informal economy, presented as a means to combat informal employment; fiscal support for employers for certain types of contracts and reduced social contributions;

---

[17] *Confederazione Generale Italiana del Lavoro* – Italian General Workers' Union.

- Introduction of a new system of taxation with a regressive profile and only two levels: 23% up to 100.000 €, 33% for all other taxpayers; abolition of inheritance tax; cuts in state transfers to regions and towns, thereby destabilising local benefit provision. The new tax system will clearly create a crisis in the financing of public expenditures that, in turn, will legitimise a further retrenchment of welfare provision;

- Reduction of social contributions for public pensions (by 4 to 5%), making it impossible to sustain the same level of pensions; fiscal support for private pension plans managed by banks and insurance companies, and restriction of occupational pension schemes jointly managed by unions and employers (and financed by social contributions); reforms of the social allowance system based on a workfare profile, at zero cost.

Two key issues that are central to this agenda, and have either been implemented or are underway[18], configure the shift in resource regime.

First, the planned reduction in compulsory social contributions will redefine resources: it is argued that employees will pay lower contributions but receive a higher direct wage, which they can then use to acquire goods and access new, but differentiated, employment and citizens rights. The state and the social partners will have less control over these monetary flows, which are to be channelled through private actors (private pension funds, insurance companies, training and education agencies, job centres, possibly with some fiscal support). A residual social protection system will remain to support the working poor and the other categories of the workforce characterised by low wages, discontinuous careers, job insecurity, and the lack of savings. The tax reform and the announced reduction of pension contributions amount to a programmed collapse of public expenditures and benefit provisions. Whereas the previous government sought to reduce the total wage by financing a part of social contributions for some categories of workers through taxation, the new right-wing government intends to cut social contributions directly and to lower state income from general taxation. Property-based rights and selective universalism will be the main features of the planned resource regime, with a marked reinforcement of the shifts towards increased means-testing, tutelary allowance, deferred

---

18 In its second year of power, the government had progressed somewhat with regard to the deregulation of work and fiscal reform. The final design of the taxation profile has not yet been implemented, but should be operative by the end of the legislature; there was some marginal tax cut on low income compensated by deep cuts in local welfare provision.

wage, pre-financed wage and employee savings implemented by the *Ulivo* government.

Secondly, a new political process is being used to implement this agenda. It involves a "chaotic strategy" which mixes direct government action and a new social dialogue based on the inclusion of some unions and the exclusion of others: cooperating unions are being offered participation in the management of some systems (training, unemployment benefits) whereas a conflictual stance is being maintained with others. Social pacts that vary according to circumstance and new social conflicts are the emerging features of this strategy. But the scenario is not stable. At first, the government sought to ignore growing opposition and protests and to introduce a number of the measures outlined above. This led to a mobilisation of three million people in Rome in March 2002, the largest demonstration in the history of the country; and in April, to a general strike called by all the unions (with an estimated participation rate of 80%). Then, the government changed its strategy and promoted a social pact -*Patto per l'Italia*- that was signed by the less representative unions[19] (CISL and UIL) but was contested by the powerful CGIL and several autonomous unions. A number of regional strikes were held in the spring of the same year, and a second general strike the following autumn, which was as successful as the first. The number of wage disputes at the sectoral level increased, and the unions that had not signed the new pact began to call for wage increases above the programmed rate of inflation. Those participating in the pact, on the other hand, are experiencing growing difficulties as the government proves unable to meet its commitments due to financial difficulties.

It is difficult to tell what the outcome of this conflictual situation will be. The unions, together with the new social movements that have arisen (around education, justice, health, the media, the environment, gender and migrant issues, peace) represent crucial actors in the social and political arena. The generalisation of conflicts reveals the difficulty in consolidating and institutionalising the emerging resource regimes.

C. The United Kingdom: increasing separation of welfare and unionism

The neo-liberal restructuring undertaken in the UK during the 1980s and 1990s led to a weakening or even break up of the links between employment, industrial relations and social rights.

---

[19] CISL (*Confederazione Italiana Sindacati Lavoratori* – Italian Union of Workers' Unions) and UIL (*Unione Italiana del Lavoro* – Italian Labour Union).

The attempts to retrench the welfare state led to a reconfiguration of the regime of resources and social rights that had emerged in the post-war period. The system of social protection developed from the 1940s to the 1970s had come to feature many traits of citizenship-based and employment-based rights, although it remained somewhat hybrid due to the model of industrial relations and the limited role and influence of the labour movement in welfare.

For the UK, the limited scope of (direct) trade union influence over the regime of resources and social rights is striking. The trade unions had no direct say over National Insurance or the pensions system (SERPS). Responsibility for the Social Security systems lies with the state departments and (most importantly) under the financial control of the Treasury. The unions mainly had leverage over the Labour Party, and were thus dependent on the latter's electoral success. Nevertheless, up until 1979, they gained some degree of influence through their participation in a number of institutions – such as the Manpower Services Commission (MSC, organising Vocational Education and Training in the UK) or the Wages Councils (which set minimum wages in a number of sectors). These were part of the rather flawed attempt to construct a corporatist system of economic management in the UK. It should be noted that at the times when major decisions concerning the construction of the welfare state were due (in 1911 or 1945) the unions refused to participate and explicitly rejected any form of responsibility over resource flows (Finlayson, 1994). The traditional focus of collective bargaining on pay, pay systems, benefits and the regulation of working time permitted the unions to gain a considerable degree of influence in the social construction of employment. After 1945, collective bargaining was encouraged by the state, who refrained from direct intervention. But this meant that the unions did not win a foothold in macro-economic policy-making and welfare apparatuses. As soon as the strategy of the state changed the weakness of the unions became apparent.

Where collective bargaining still exists today, it is mainly concerned with direct wages and wage savings (occupational pensions). The growing degree of decentralisation in industrial relations has increased the diversity of connections between direct wages and the socialisation of resources via wage savings. At the same time the centralised power of the state/treasury over the welfare system has grown.

1. Welfare developments

It would be a mistake to underestimate the socialised aspects of the British welfare system before the 1970s. Although it was originally based on the Beveridgean principle of flat-rate benefits for flat-rate contributions, aspects of a more "continental" nature were introduced subsequently. In 1975, flat-rate contributions were replaced by an earnings-related contributory system, making unemployment benefits and sickness pay earnings-related and enabling the introduction of SERPS (State Earnings Related Pensions Scheme).

The incoming Labour government of 1974 wanted to secure and extend universal coverage, which meant the introduction of universal non-contributory benefits (for children and the disabled). These welfare strategies were accompanied by a corporatist strategy of channelling industrial conflicts. Labour proposed a so-called "Social Contract" – which basically aimed at wage moderation in the crisis-prone 1970s – to the rather militant trade union movement of the time. By restraining wage demands in exchange for social and economic policies, the unions were to some degree able to strengthen their role and that of collective bargaining. Nevertheless, the essential features of the Beveridgean system remained intact, and the Treasury kept central control over the resource flows in the welfare state. Notwithstanding their mobilising capacities and subsequent radicalisation throughout the 1970s, the unions' strategic remit remained more or less limited to collective bargaining around such issues as pay, pay systems, and job demarcation.

In 1978 the "Social Contract" broke down because the unions and the left wing of the Labour party rejected the government's request for a further year of wage restraint. A wave of strikes in the public services – the Winter of Discontent – followed. In the general election of 1979 the Conservative Party under Margaret Thatcher came to power.

2. Neo-liberalism and welfare policies

One of the most important goals of the successive Thatcher governments was the reduction of public spending and the containment of the welfare state, which was seen as a crucial impediment to entrepreneurialism and the flexible functioning of the labour markets (that is, a downwards adjustment of wages).

The retrenchment of the welfare state has to be understood as a re-configuration of the British regime of resources and social rights. The aim was to weaken or even dismantle the institutional links between time in and out of employment, between industrial relations and social rights.

Elements of this reconfiguration revolve around the replacement of the indexation of benefits to wages by an indexation to RPI (Retail Price Index), the abolition of the earnings-relation of unemployment and sickness benefits and the swing towards means-tested benefits financed out of taxes. Combined with high unemployment and the restructuring of the labour markets, these measures led to a considerable increase in inequalities. The gap between wages and benefits increased, and most benefits are now paid at a flat rate. The expansion of means testing represents one of the key strategies to break the link between the financing of in- and out-of-work situations. In 1985 the government proposed to abolish SERPS, but met with strong resistance. Nevertheless a major reform was implemented to make the scheme less "generous", while the possibility to opt out of SERPS and take up Personal Private Pensions was introduced and encouraged through tax allowances.

Thus, entitlements are no longer based on employment and wage levels but on "need". Social security is now far less concerned with living standard maintenance and (citizenship or employment-based) participation in society than with preventing individuals from falling into absolute poverty. The rationale is that welfare benefits should not act as a "disincentive" to work. Time out of work – defined by social rights to certain resources – has been progressively delegitimised.

3. Neo-liberalism and the trade unions

The changes in the regime of resources and social rights outlined above are linked, among other things, to an attack on the bargaining power and the influence of the trade unions. The 1980s and 1990s saw a major shake-up of the traditional system of industrial relations and collective bargaining. Some commentators (Clark, 1996; Beardwell, 1996) even speak of the creation of "New Industrial Relations".

For neo-liberals, the strength of the trade union movement represented a fundamental reason for the UK's poor performance and decline in the post-war period. Institutional support for collective bargaining and corporatist arrangements was progressively withdrawn and tough legal regulation of trade union organisation, behaviour and practices was rolled forward. The legislative attack aimed at regulating and curbing union activities with regard to collective bargaining and industrial action, and successfully eroded the power base of the unions. The laws focussed on the regulation of trade union membership (to outlaw closed shops), trade union governance and operations (to "give the unions back to their members"), and industrial action (to outlaw secondary picketing and to limit, control and regulate strikes).

The strategies of "de-collectivisation", "fragmentation" and "individualisation of industrial relations" are clearly underpinned by the changes in the welfare system. On the one hand the neo-liberal reforms of the welfare state broke the institutionalised links between (direct) wages and rights over resources. On the other hand the attack on the unions clearly served to change employment conditions at company level and aimed at an individualisation of wage relations. This led to the removal of collective mechanisms for determining terms and conditions of employment (pay, working time). The attack on instituted links between (direct) wages and welfare rights and on collective bargaining over employment conditions created a highly segmented and polarised labour market, based on long working hours, a huge wage spread, high numbers of working poor and people on low income, and a large share of so-called atypical forms of employment (Gregg and Wadsworth, 1999).

This resulted in the longest period of decline ever experienced by the British trade unions. After reaching a peak in 1979, union membership decreased by more than 40%, dropping from 13.3 million to between 7 and 8 million by the late 1990s. Similarly, a remarkable decrease was reported in the number of industrial stoppages and working days lost. This was especially true for the 1990s, which saw the lowest strike figures ever recorded.

These changes reflect not only the hostile policies implemented by the Conservative government throughout this period, but also sectoral changes in the economy such as persistent high rates of unemployment, a decline of manufacturing and parallel increases in the services sector, the growth of atypical and precarious forms of employment and the feminisation of the labour force. All these dynamics created severe problems for the traditional labour movement organisations.

However, not all sectors were affected in the same way. The most remarkable feature is the apparent difference in union density between private and public workplaces (19% and 61% respectively), and between manufacturing (30%) and utilities (60%, water, mining, etc.) on the one hand and private sector services (often below 15%) on the other (Milward *et al.*, 1999).

In the 1990s, due to the continuing weakness of the unions, union representation for collective bargaining purposes was derecognised at numerous workplaces. This enabled management to obtain far-reaching flexibility, individualised employment conditions and non-strike agreements.

Industrial relations in the public sector, which are somewhat different, demonstrated a remarkable stability. The Conservative government showed a particular hostility towards the public sector unions (Edwards *et al.*, 1998: p. 35). However, despite the important changes that affected industrial relations in this sector – most notably privatisation, Compulsory Competitive Tendering, the creation of internal markets and decentralisation – the unions were comparatively successful in defending their position (Bailey, 1996).

The reaction of the unions

After a number of decisive defeats, the trade union movement was forced to drop its initial strategies of non-cooperation and non-compliance with the Thatcher government's legislative changes and to adopt a strategy of "New Realism". The "relaunch" of the TUC in 1994 acknowledged the death of the traditionally voluntarist system of the UK. The union re-thought its positions, notably its hostility towards legal regulation of employment relations and statutory employment rights especially in relation to workplace representation and minimum standard setting (minimum wage, working time).

The TUC also modified its initially hostile position on the EU. It began to support fuller integration and the implementation of the Social Charter as well as the Social Chapter of the Maastricht Treaty – which the Conservative government had opted out of. Furthermore, many unions dropped their traditionally adversarial stance towards management and tried to develop a "social partnership" approach at government and employer peak body level as well as at corporate/workplace level.

4. New developments

The situation has changed somewhat since the Labour government replaced the Conservatives in 1997. While Labour had ruled out a repeal of the neo-liberal legislation on industrial relations, it promised to implement a statutory minimum wage, legislation on union recognition and the ratification of a number of European directives (on working time, consultation, part-time work). These were all issues the unions had energetically campaigned for.

These more favourable conditions – together with a sustained economic boom in the late 1990s – put an end to the decline of the unions and of the level of industrial action, and the trend was slowly reversed. In the 1999 Employment Relations Act, a statutory procedure for trade union recognition was introduced which obliged employers to recognise trade unions for collective bargaining purposes if the majority of the workforce was in favour. These measures were not, however, presented as a means to strengthen union power but rather as a question of "fairness". The Labour government has sought to avoid any reminiscence of the conflictual 1970s, offering instead an ideology of a "social partnership" between unions and employers at the company level. This strategy does not aim to resolve conflicts over employment conditions and wages by changing economic structures and power relations, but by promoting a fuller cooperation between employers and employees with a view to increasing economic productivity and safeguarding competitiveness.

There have also been some changes in the field of welfare (Ainsley, 2001). In contrast to the Conservative governments, New Labour does not simply want to break the instituted links between wages and welfare rights in order to retrench public spending. Rather, it has sought to reconstruct resource flows and social rights in such a way as to revive the work ethic and increase labour market attachment through a number of new institutional features which critics summarise as "workfare" – that is, the coupling of welfare entitlements to increasingly more stringent work requirements.

Thus under the heading "Welfare to Work", the main programmes are geared to making employment (based on individualised employment conditions) the only accepted form of integration into society. These measures – such as the creation of in-work benefits (the Working Family Tax Credit) and the New Deal Programmes for the long-term unemployed – are closely linked to the implementation of a National Minimum Wage designed to "make work pay", and contribute to the transformation of resource regimes (see Chapter 2).

Though the unions have regained some influence over social policies through their – albeit shaky – affiliation to the Labour Party (Ludlam, 2001) and their participation in commissions that devise these policies, the political character of wage conflict has clearly been sidelined in favour of national competitiveness and a rhetoric of social inclusion.

Conclusion

The analysis of these three societal dynamics highlights historical differences as to the role and influence of unions in resource regimes. Beyond the transformations of the productive systems, which we have not discussed here, the long-term trends shown in our case studies are a decrease in union membership and the search for new ways of ensuring legitimacy in a context of growing unemployment and flexible work. However, there were differentiated changes in the power unions exercise over the definition and management of rights over resources during the past two decades. Three transversal elements contributed to these transformations: changes in the origin of the resources linking the wage and social protection; changes in the instituted bargaining processes; and the impact of employment policies on the modes of financing these resources, on the conditions of entitlement and on the nature of the provisions.

We have seen that the nature of the resources has changed in different ways depending on the country. In France, the growth in the share of tax-financed social protection has served to erode the socialised wage and the power of the unions over the definition and management of resources; their power with respect to wage bargaining has been modified by the weakening of the *ordre public social* and changes in the rules of representativity. In Italy, the nature of their power has changed: they gained a say in questions concerning taxation, even if this was partly lost when the process of *concertazione* came to an end. In the UK, where social protection is largely based on taxation traditionally defined through the intermediary of the Labour Party, the unions have maintained a role in wage bargaining and the management of occupational pension funds; the more distant relationship with New Labour, however, has entailed a loss of influence over the definition of the resources derived from taxation, while the individualisation of the employment relation jeopardises their power to bargain over wages.

Changes in the unions' spheres of action have also led to changes in the nature of their power over rights over resources. In France, decentralisation of collective bargaining has reduced the generality of the rules governing rights over resources, while the rising influence of a structured programme devised by the employers and the reforms to the social protection system have served to restrict union power over the management of social protection. In Italy, the process of *concertazione* opened up new spaces of action for the unions, but in a context of a growth in tax-financing on one hand, and of employee savings on the other. In the UK, the Employment Relations Act introduced at the end of the 1990s gave the unions back their legitimacy to negotiate at firm level, whereas, despite the relative increase in wages (in particular through the introduction of a minimum wage), they have even less leverage over the national social protection system.

The question of employment has marked all these changes, and particularly the modalities of the relations between government, employers and unions. In the UK, the focus has shifted from maintaining a standard of living to preventing poverty, and, more recently, to "welfare to work" policies. In Italy, the national interest in meeting the Maastricht criteria prevailed; here, the unions contributed to creating a dual labour market with a divide between the core salariat and flexible employment. In France, employment policies provoked a decline of the wage in favour of taxation. This shows the extent to which unemployment and threats to delocalise weighed on negotiations over resources, both for the wage and for social protection.

In conclusion, it can be seen that government reform programmes played a major role in redefining the unions' scope for action, and therefore, the nature of their power over resources. In France and Italy, recent governments have aimed at dividing the unions, favouring those with whom they could rapidly reach agreement in order to push through their reforms; this leads the major unions like the CGIL and the CGT to radicalise their opposition. At the same time, the unions distanced themselves from their base, opening the way for new social movements and a potentially explosive social situation. Moreover, in all three countries, the effective or possible political intermediaries have changed and other actors now participate in political deliberations over resources, in particular concerning social protection: the question of parliamentary debate on these matters could be an interesting field of study in a context of declining social democracy. Finally, the impact of the construction of the EU has had differential effects in the three countries. Whereas in Italy, integration into EMU was, to a large extent, the source of the transformations observed here, in France it had a less direct impact on bargaining processes, and in the UK, European directives provided a basis for the unions to gain influence over employees' rights. It would be of interest to examine how the distribution of competencies between the EU and the nation-state in the fields of employment, the wage and social protection progressively serves to introduce an additional level for action and to change the nature of union powers at national level.

References

Accornero, A. and Carrieri, M. (1997), "Relazioni industriali nella storia politica europea", *Stato e Mercato* No.50, Il Mulino, Bologna.

Ainsley, C. (2001), "New Labour and Welfare", in Ludlam, S. and Smith, M.J., *New Labour in Government*, Houndmills, Basingstoke, Hampshire and London, MacMillan Press, pp. 202-218.

Audric, S. and Forgeot, G. (1999), "Le développement du travail à temps partiel". In *Données sociales. La Société française. Statistique publique*, INSEE, Paris, pp. 177-181

Barrat, O., Yacubovitch, C. and Maurice, J. (2002), "Évolution de la négociation collective des salaires en France", in Pochet, P. (dir.), *Politique salariale dans la zone euro*, P.I.E.-Peter Lang, pp. 277–304.

Banca D'Italia (2000), *Relazione del Governatore*, Roma.

Beardwell, I. (ed.) (1996), *Contemporary Industrial Relations. A critical analysis*. Oxford, Oxford University Press.

Bloch-London, C. and Boisard, P. (1999) "L'aménagement et la réduction du temps de travail", in *Données sociales, La société française, Statistique publique*, INSEE, Paris, pp. 207 –214.

Bohm, F. (1999), "Les 35 heures, la loi Aubry et ses enjeux", in Mouriaux, R. (dir.), *L'Année Sociale*, Paris, éditions de l'Atelier, pp. 109-128.

Clark, I. (1996) "The State and New Industrial Relations", in Beardwell, I. (ed.), *Contemporary Industrial Relations. A critical analysis*, Oxford, Oxford University Press, pp. 37-65.

Concialdi P. and Ponthieux S. (1999), "Les bas salaires en France depuis le début des années quatre-vingt et quelques éléments de comparaison avec les États-Unis", in *Données sociales, La société française, Statistique publique*, INSEE, Paris, pp. 162-168.

Crouch, C. (1999), "Employment, Industrial Relations and Social Policy: New Life in an Old Connection", *Social Policy and Administration*, Vol. 33, No.4, pp. 437-457.

Ebbinghaus, B. (2001), *"Reform Blockage or Self Regulation. The Ambiguous Role of Social Partnership in European Welfare States"*. Max Planck Institute for the Study of Societies, Cologne, Germany.

Ebbinghaus, B. (2002) "Trade unions' changing role: membership erosion, organisational reform, and social partnership in Europe" EU Paper Series, The European Union Center, University of Wisconsin – Madison.

Ebbinghaus, B. and Visser, J. (1998), "When Institutions matter: Union growth and decline in Western Europe", Mannheimer Zentrum für Europäische Sozialforschung, Working Papers.

Edwards, P., Hall, M., Hyman, R., Marginson, P., Sisson, K., Waddington, J. and Wichester, D. (1998), "Great Britain: From partial collectivism to neo-liberalism to where?" in Ferner, A., Hyman, R. (eds), *Changing industrial relations in Europe*, Massachusett, Blackwells, pp. 1-54.

Esping-Andersen, G. (1992), "The emerging realignment between Labour Movements and Welfare States", in Regini, M. (ed.), *The Future of Labour Movements*. London/Thousand Oaks/New Dehli, Sage, pp. 133-149.

Fajertag, G. and Pochet, P. (eds) (2000), *Social Pacts in Europe – New Dynamics*, European Trade Union Institute, Brussels.

Finlayson, G. (1994), *Citizen State and Social Welfare in Britain: 1830-1990*, Oxford, Oxford University Press.

Freyssinet, J. and Seifert, H. (2001), *Negotiating collective agreements on employment and competitiveness*, EIRO, Luxembourg, Office for Official Publications of the European Communities.

Friot, B. (1999), *Et la cotisation créera l'emploi*. Paris, La Dispute.

Evandrou M., Glennerster, H., Hills, J. and Evans J. (eds) (1998), *The State of Welfare. The Economics of Social Spending*, Oxford-New York, Oxford University Press.

Gregg, P. and Wadsworth, J. (1999), *The State of Working Britain*, Manchester University Press, Manchester.

Hassel, A. and Ebbinghaus, B. (2000), "From Means to Ends: Linking Wage Moderation and Social Policy Reform" in Fajertag, G., Pochet, Ph. (eds),

Social Pacts in Europe – New Dynamics, European Trade Union Institute, Brussels, pp. 61-84.

Higelé, J.P. (2002), "Histoire de la négociation Unedic 1999-2001", GREE, Université Nancy 2.

Institut des Sciences du Travail (2000), "Negotiating Employment – Compared Forms of Employment Regulation in Europe", UCL, Louvain-la-Neuve, Dossier No.19.

Jefferys, S. (2003) *Liberté, Égalité and Fraternité at Work; Changing French Employment Relations and Management*, Palgrave Macmillan, Basingstoke, New-York.

Jefferys, S. and Contrepois S. (2000), "Wage Determination and the French State", IIRA, 6th European Congress.

Jobert, A. (2000), *Les espaces de la négociation collective, branches et territoires*, Octares, Paris.

Kasten, G. and Soskice, D. (1999), *Europäische Beschäftigungspolitik – Möglichkeiten und Grenzen*, Marburg, Schüren.

Kauppinen, T. (ed.) (1998), "The impact of EMU on Industrial Relations in European Union", *Finnish Labour Relations Association*, Publication No.9, Helsinki.

Labbé, D. (1998), "La syndicalisation en France depuis 1945", in *Un demi-siècle de syndicalisme en France et dans l'Est*, Nancy, PUN, pp. 21-28.

Léonard, E. (2001), "Industrial Relations and the regulation of employment in Europe", *European Journal of Industrial Relations*, Vol. 7, No.1, pp. 27-47.

Ludlam, S. (2001), "New Labour and the Unions: the End of the Contentious Alliance", in Ludlam, S, Smith, M.J., *New Labour in Government*, Houndmills/Basingstoke/Hampshire and London, MacMillan Press, pp. 111-129.

Martin, A. (1999), "Wage Bargaining under EMU: Europeanization, Re-Nationalization or Americanization", DWP 99.01.03.

Mermet, E. (2001), *Wage Formation in Europe*. European Trade Union Institute, Brussels.

Millward, N., Forth, J. and Bryson, A. (1999), "Changes in employment relations, 1980-1998", in Cully, M., Woodland, S., O'Reilly, A., Dix, G., *Britain at Work. As depicted by the 1998 Workplace Employee Relations Survey*. London and New York, Routledge, pp. 216-250.

Pochet, P. and Fajertag, G. (2000), "A new era for Social Pacts in Europe", in Fajertag, G., and Pochet, Ph. (eds), *Social Pacts in Europe – New Dynamics*, European Trade Union Institute, Brussels, pp. 9-40.

Radaelli, C. (2000), Logiques de pouvoirs et récits dans les politiques publiques de l'Union Européenne, *Revue Française de Science Politique*, Vol. 50, 2/2000.

Radé, C. (2003),"SMIC et réduction du temps de travail : la fin du cauchemar", *Droit Social*, No.1, janvier, pp. 18-24.

Scharpf, F.W. (2001), "Employment and the Welfare State. A Continental Dilemma", In Ebbinghaus, B. and Manow, Ph. (eds), 2001, *Comparing Welfare Capitalism. Social Policy and Political Economy in Europe, Japan and in the USA*, London/New York, Routledge, pp. 270-283.

Schulten, T. (2001), "A European Solidaristic Wage Policy – Conceptual reflections on a Europeanisation of trade union wage policy", DWP 2001.01.01.

Sisson, K. and Artiles, M. (2000), *Handling Restructuring. Collective Agreements on Employment and Competitiveness*, EIRO, Luxembourg, Office for Official Publications of the European Communities.

Traxler, F. (2000a), "National Pacts and Wage Regulation in Europe: A Comparative Analysis", in Fajertag, G. Pochet, Ph. (eds), *Social Pacts in Europe – New Dynamics*, European Trade Union Institute, Brussels, pp. 401-418.

Traxler, F. (2000b), "Nationale Pakte im internationalen Vergleich", in *WSI Mitteilungen* Vol. 53/No.7, pp. 411-418.

Volovitch, P. (2001), "L'évolution des ressources de la protection sociale", in *Revue de l'IRES*, No.37, 2001/3, pp. 3-29.

Waddington, J. and Hoffmann, R. (eds) (2001), *Zwischen Kontinuität und Modernisierung; gewerkschaftliche Herausforderungen in Europa*, Münster, Westfälisches Dampfboot.

Zagelmeyer, S. (2000), *Innovative Agreements on Employment and Competitiveness in the European Union and Norway*, EIRO, Luxembourg, Office for Official Publications of the European Communities.

CHAPTER 6

The European Union.
Reorganising Resources:
Employment, Pensions and the Wage

Corinne GOBIN, Gaël CORON and Anne DUFRESNE

Introduction[1]

The natural approach to the question of how value is translated into financial resources and how these resources are institutionalised and distributed amongst the population, and thereby create specific social relations, would be to turn to a comparative study of national socio-economic systems. And yet, although the state still provides the reference framework for measuring the different resource flows produced by work, a key factor has changed the situation: the member states of the European Union (EU) have agreed to construct a new economic space that "absorbs" the old national socio-economic spaces by imposing compliance with an ever increasing battery of legal and political constraints. We are thus seeing the development of a European political system that is made up of Community institutions *and* national institutions with new roles and new loyalties and which, for the moment, still co-exist with each state's old references and roles. There is consequently a pressing need for a comprehensive study of the interplay between national dynamics – and their remaining spheres of autonomy – and this new integrated political system. Much remains to be done in this area, in particular with regard to the relations between types of resources, rights, political systems, and the content of socio-political decision-making. But before tackling that task in our future studies, we would like first to examine here the EU's specific modes of functioning, noting that, for the moment, they reflect political logics and representations that have

[1] We would like to thank Jean-Claude Deroubaix, Sylvie Regnault and Pierre Wathelet for their useful comments.

shifted away from the model of representative and redistributive democracy of the post-1945 period.

The first part of this chapter will thus examine the political and legal foundations of the EU and how these have shaped the approach to the hierarchisation of values introduced through the law and the status of socio-political deliberation in this specific political space. A specific system of "structural" constraints weighs on the EU actors and implicitly obstructs a clear expression of the redistributive conflict. We have chosen to explain this system using its own terms before examining its influence on the distribution of wealth and more precisely, on social protection. The second part then addresses the question of the impact of the EU on the overall re-organisation of resource flows introduced by EMU (and the new "stability" requirements). Since research on this topic within the network is still in the early stages, we have not attempted a comprehensive analysis but will limit our discussion to three particular cases which serve to illustrate the major dynamics in this field: 1) EU employment policy, since it contributes to a far-reaching restructuration of the labour market and thus of the wage relation, is an essential point of entry to this analysis: Community discourse has placed the topic of job creation at the centre of a vast undertaking to reform the whole range of monetary transfer systems (wages, social contributions, savings, taxation); 2) a discussion of the EU approach to the organisation of the supplementary pensions "market" highlights the efforts deployed – from drafting an ad hoc directive to case law decisions confronting social protection with competition law – to legitimate and thus encourage the development of funded pension schemes via the wide dissemination of the three "pillars" schema; 3) the initiatives to co-ordinate collective bargaining at EU level raise the question of the actual or potential autonomy of union actors to protect wages or weigh on their orientation within EMU, given that collective bargaining still plays a key role in the distribution and redistribution of wage-related resources. Each case study illustrates a particular configuration of the relations between Community actors. In the sphere of employment, the Commission is in a position to propose a cognitive model that will influence the representations and positions adopted by the other actors. It shares this capacity with the Court of Justice in the case of supplementary pensions[2]. Finally, the situation of EU-level unionism illustrates the difficul-

---

[2]   Different levels of analysis are applied to the Commission in the sections on employment and supplementary pensions. For the latter, the author (Gaël Coron) found it important to "disaggregate" the Commission and to approach this actor at the level of the Directorate-General. He wished to emphasise the fact that, even before the question of social protection had been raised as an overall issue at EU level, the most

ties facing political actors seeking to propose an alternative model, based for example on the defence of wages at transnational level.

I. The status of norms[3] and socio-political deliberation in the EU

The European Union, which was founded by an agreement between states forged on the classical model of diplomatic negotiations, bases the legitimacy of its action on the Treaty of Rome (1957, revised in 1986, 1992, 1997 and 2000). Its forerunner the ECSC, which had been constructed in a context of democratic concessions linked to the "cold war", had been endowed with a political character (notably the weight accorded to parliament and the unions). But this was toned down in favour of a technocratic conception of the management of the *res publica* when the EEC was created in 1958 (Gobin, 1997). For the EEC did not draw on the model of the national democratic state: its references were international organisations which are effectively run by diplomats and experts (that is, in both cases, "technicians").

When the Treaty of Rome was negotiated, the idea that World War II was the result of the destabilising effect of the political passions of the masses (communism *vs.* fascism) was prevalent among various conservative clubs with influence in international circles. Their ideal was thus to replace the governing of people by an administration of things – that is, by the joint management of the member states through the harmonious development of trade. Trade was seen as a "technical" activity existing outside of ideological passions and "naturally" linking populations whose activities would develop all the more harmoniously if the EEC could function in symbiosis with economic experts. This techno-

---

strongly neo-liberal component of the Commission had already prepared the ground by imposing a metaphor (the three pillars) which promotes putting pension schemes on the market. In the section on employment on the other hand, Corinne Gobin did not find the break-down between pro-market departments (Ecofin) and social policy departments (ex-DG 5) necessary since the subordination of employment to economic policy guidelines is directly expressed in the Treaty. The social affairs branch has attempted to correct this orientation, but not only do their correctives remain minor in face of the dominant dynamic described in this section, but precisely due to this implicit hierarchisation of values, this branch has assimilated an alienated vision of the social sphere (seen as geared to improving production). For an interesting analysis of this confrontation between departments over the issue of retirement schemes, see Math (2001).

3   By this mean any form of act produced by the EU political authorities that is binding for one or all the member states (and their populations), whether this act be legally binding in the strict sense, or politically or morally binding.

cratic dynamic has had an enduring impact in that it has depoliticised the processes involved in the production of norms. The tendency to present Community norms as technical instruments rather than political constructs has served to reduce the role played by institutional processes of deliberation and collective conflict in their production, thereby marginalising the parliament and collective bargaining.

A. Construction of the EU: a juridical order prevails over the socio-political

The EU space was created by and for experts, in particular market experts for the construction of the common market and experts on Community law. The specialists in this new sub-discipline of international law played a significant role in the building of the EU structure. Thanks to EU Court rulings, the two key characteristics at the basis of Community law – its direct effect and its primacy over national law – have fulfilled the ideal of the submission of political power to a juridical construction and have created the image of a community based on a legal order rather than on a political contract. This idealistic vision, however, obscures the fact that law is subject to its own internal conflicts between different conceptions and finalities, notably between social law and the dominant formal legal categories of civil and commercial law. That is, between what may be termed "social-historicised" law and "self-referring" law.

Max Weber (1986) constructed models for these two opposing visions, which he called "rational-material law" and "rational-formal law". In the latter, the superior norms only confer the authorisation to create other norms, and law as it has been created by case law and legal doctrine is imagined to enjoy a wide measure of independence from political decisions and the social world. Weber argues that rational-formal law gained power along with the development of the capitalist economy, in a mutually enriching process (law supplying the instruments necessary to the circulation and accumulation of capital: cheques, bills of exchange, and such like). In rational-material law, norms are conceived as being subordinated to one another in terms of the societal hierarchy of values (political, ethical). While this law does not deny a certain measure of independence of legal thought, it is seen as being a receptor of social and political facts.

Weber, in his time, noted a trend towards the re-materialisation of law through the advances of labour law. However, in the past twenty years, the formal rationality of law has been reinforced, notably by the rising power of EU law. The theoretical basis of this EU law draws on the work of Kelsen[4] (1953), which has partially supplanted political theory and endows jurists with considerable power:

> La tentative de Kelsen pour fonder une théorie pure du droit n'est que la limite ultra-conséquente de l'effort de tout le corps des juristes pour construire un corps de doctrine et de règles totalement indépendant des contraintes et des pressions sociales et trouvant en lui-même son propre fondement. (Bourdieu 1986)[5]

Labour law disrupted this legal formalism in two ways. First, it compelled legal recognition of collective social phenomena: strikes do not constitute a breach of the employment contract; and collective agreements cannot be interpreted according to the rules of civil law. Second, it re-introduced a material principle in the hierarchisation of norms: this is what French law recognises as a social public order, in which an inferior law (in the Kelsinian sense) can "derogate" from a superior law if it is more favourable to the employee. This principle of a social public order is at the heart of the construction of the continental model of social protection based on the socialised wage.

The tense balance existing at national level between these two legal rationalities has been altered by the rising force of EU law and its primacy over national laws. As established in the case of Costa *vs.* ENEL[6], "The law stemming from the Treaty, an independent source of law, [can]not, because of its special and original nature, be overridden by domestic legal provisions, however framed, without being deprived of its character as Community law and without the legal basis of the Community itself being called into question".

The European Court of Justice expressly applied this reasoning to the provisions of national constitutions: "The validity of a Community act or its effect within a member State cannot be affected by [...] either

---

[4]   Very briefly, Kelsen proposes a construction of law in which the validity of a norm depends solely on its compliance with the formal criteria and procedures necessary to its conception and adoption. This creates a pyramidal hierarchy of laws, the inferior laws submitting to the principles of the higher laws, the supreme law being the constitution. The EU, drawing on this Kelsinian model, has added another level to the top of the pyramid: Community law.

[5]   Kelsen's attempt to found a pure theory of law is no more than the ultraconsequent limit of the efforts of the entire body of jurists to construct a corpus of doctrine and rules totally independent of social constraints and pressure and providing itself with its own basis.

[6]   Case of 15 July 1964: Costa *vs.* ENEL, 6/64.

the fundamental rights as formulated in that State's constitution or the principles of a national constitutional structure"[7].

The power of the EU today, as covered by the agreement of its members, is such that it can openly apply this rule of the supremacy of EU procedures over the constitutional functioning of the member states[8]. The next stage will be the drafting of a "European Constitution": the political stakes here will concern the place and the status of a legal order capable of thwarting the hegemony of the market. For it should be noted that the predominant logic of Community law gives priority to competition law and the implementation of economic freedoms.

The European system is thus based on a legal formalism that organises and legitimates the market order and reduces the political to a role of merely accompanying this order. It is a system that varies according to circumstance: it is structured on a strong principle of a hierarchy of norms (for a norm that is favourable to or does not threaten the general dynamics of free competition) and on a principle of subsidiarity (when a Community law might interfere with such competition). This opens up a wide avenue for case law and thus to the weight of experts and to a balance of power imposed by employers and financial forces.

In a framework such as this, the place left to the emergence of European social law has always been extremely ambiguous, and all the more so since the implementation of the single market in 1985. This explains the fact that the Community corpus of legal rules in the social field remains so "thin". The first social directives were only adopted in 1975, prompted by the post-1968 context of social protest and the beginning of the economic difficulties linked to the "recession". Indeed, Community social law has often been motivated primarily by the concern to ensure equal conditions of competition between firms within the Common Market, even if this has sometimes resulted in the introduction of transnational rights favourable to employees.

The subordination of social law to neo-liberal values has been reinforced since the Single European Act of 1986: by the introduction of a notion of "minimum norms" for legislation in the social field (limited to the presentation of framework principles and often reduced to the smallest common denominator existing between the member states); and by a clear order of priority, for these rules must not hinder the expansion

---

[7] Case of 17 December 1970: Internationale Handelsgesellschaft, 11/70.

[8] See the Luxembourg European Council decision of November 1997 to make the "Employment" chapter of the Treaty of Amsterdam directly applicable, without waiting for this new Treaty to be ratified by the national parliaments.

of small and medium-sized companies (Single European Act, 1986) or the competitiveness of firms (Treaty of the European Union, 1992).

The ambiguous approach to the social field is also expressed in the quasi-systematic referral to national legal definitions of the concepts used in social directives, and the wide margin allowed for exemptions. The vagueness created induces – *de facto* – highly variable results with regard to national-level implementation depending on the balance of power between socio-professional organisations and on the role played by social legislation in the national tradition. Thus, while some directives have permitted improvements in certain employee rights, mainly in the UK (enhanced rights for part-time or fixed-term contract workers; regulation of working time), the general trend in the EU has been to restrict the impact of rights that could tilt the capital-labour conflict in favour of the world of work.

B. Governance, and the decline of socio-political confrontation

The current model of "governance" defines political power as a vast network uniting public and private bodies in a partnership around common values (free market, growth and employment, competitiveness of firms, social cohesion). This political model tends to reduce the separation between the three traditional powers (executive, legislative and judicial), as well as between private and public actors, and to drain opposition forces of their substance (it is difficult to both participate in a network and oppose it) (Gobin, 2002). The consensus required by the partnership mode also favours the replacement of legal texts by what are referred to as "soft laws" – specifically in the social field – that have a vague status and are not legally binding (Charvin, 2002).

The network model of decision-making serves to give "theoretical coherence" to a political system that is characterised by an extraordinary institutional dispersion for the production of norms:

- The Commission initiates the legislative process and has control over parliamentary amendments and the suggestions from the various consultative bodies whether the latter are directly part of the internal order provided for in the Treaty (Social and Economic Committee, Committee of the Regions) or not;
- Parliament has been co-legislator for the past ten years, and the revisions of the Treaty have given it increased powers (to propose amendments, or in the case of disagreement, to veto the final version of a decision emanating from the Council)
- The Council of Ministers adopts the common policy decisions that will be written up in final regulatory texts

- The European Council establishes the broad guidelines that set the frame for what will be possible
- The Court of Justice gives flesh to the content of the laws via extensive jurisprudence
- The COREPER[9] prepares and *de facto* adopts the vast majority of decisions that are subsequently endorsed by the Council of Ministers
- The European Central Bank defines the socio-economic guidelines necessary to maintaining the stability of the euro.
- Social representatives may sign framework collective agreements that can be moulded into directives.

While these mechanisms are fairly easily identifiable, a multitude of other actors also influence the preparation of decisions: through the countless ad hoc consultative and expert committees, the more informal consultative bodies (such as the Forum for Civil Dialogue), and the numerous behind-the-scenes contacts with private sector lobbies. Powers and responsibilities are blurred (who decides where and who is responsible for what), and the dividing line that had progressively been constructed at national level between private interests and the public interest has become fuzzy and uncertain.

The Commission's White Paper on Governance (July 2001) calls for legally binding norms to be limited to the "strict minimum necessary". This restraint on the legislative ambitions of the EU has been the rule in the social sphere since the 1993 Green Paper on social policy.

The Treaty of Amsterdam, it is true, broadened the scope of parliament by opening up the co-decision procedure to new social issues[10]. But, at the same time, it also instituted a Community work method, subsequently baptised the "open method of co-ordination" (OMC), that effectively reduces the role of parliament to that of consultant. This was denounced by the European Parliament:

---

[9] The Permanent Representatives Committee, comprised of diplomatic delegations seconded by each member state.

[10] However, the Parliament's role in the co-decision procedure is being reduced: the Commission and the Council are pressing for the introduction of an accelerated adoption procedure for laws concerning financial services (some laws would be adopted by the Commission alone) (see European Council, 2001). The trend is thus to open the way for self-regulatory practices (by the financial actors alone) or co-regulation (Commission and financial actors) (see Lamfalussy, 2001).

[The Parliament] calls on the Commission and Council to ensure that the open coordination process incorporates democratic elements, so that the assessment and solutions are not confined to the thinking of technical experts working behind closed doors; points out that to solve these problems and respect European integration will mean involving Parliament and public opinion in such processes. (European Parliament, 2002: p. 9)

The method is based on the definition of common guidelines reached through an adjustment between the positions of the Commission, the Council and the member states; it uses a benchmarking procedure to assesses national "good practice" and greatly increases the inter-penetration between national-level and EU-level administrative work. A growing number of social policy issues are being withdrawn from the legislative process for management via the OMC. In addition to employment (Amsterdam) and social exclusion (Lisbon), this has been the case for pensions (Göteborg) and is to be extended to other fields such as education and training, the environment, and health care.

The extent to which European norms are legally binding can thus serve as an indicator of the system's values. On the one hand, binding laws, which can be invoked before any national court of justice by anyone under European jurisdiction, settle infringements of competition law and oblige member states to comply with the principles of economic freedom. On the other hand, policies aimed at reducing poverty and unemployment or regulating the employment relation are channelled through administrative processes for safeguarding social cohesion, where collective social rights become less a matter of law than of "business ethics".

The OMC destabilises democratic dynamics in more ways than one. In addition to marginalising the legislative role of European and national parliaments alike, it promotes the generalisation of benchmarking practices that could potentially lead to "de-historicised" societies with no political memory and thus no democratic expression of conflict. The result would be the adoption of a single mode of operation in the name of an "efficiency" measured in terms of the satisfactory functioning of the market and the maintenance of a minimum safety net for social cohesion. Furthermore, this method renders the decision-making process more opaque. The EU procedure of recommendations based on reports from member states introduces a cyclic administrative process. It becomes impossible to tell who recommends what to whom and who ultimately decides, since it is the heads of state and government in the European Council that adopt the guidelines they have set for themselves. The method also promotes the idea that consultation of a multitude of

actors (the OMC[11] solicits an increasing mix of social and civil dialogue) can usefully replace the old, more confrontational methods of
deliberation in which the parliament and the trade unions symbolically
represented the people.

European-level trade union actors are thus placed in a dynamic of
dialogue (based on consensus) rather than of bargaining (based on
compromise) and their opportunities for expression have been segmented according to the categories of public action or EU law. This
tends to depoliticise their action, which is now reduced to that of one of
many interest or expert groups (Gobin, 2000). The EU order, based as it
is on a Treaty that expressly excludes the recognition of the right to
transnational union strikes from its sphere of competence, undermines
the role of social conflict as a driving force for social change. "Economic and monetary union has helped to create a more cooperative
industrial relations climate based on shared macro-economic objectives.
The sharp drop in the number of labour disputes illustrates this change"
(CEC, 2000: p. 2).

The European Monetary Union (EMU), which represents a veritable
change in political regime (characterised by a kind of "constitutionalisa-
tion" of capitalism) has thus led to a profound restructuring of the
meaning of political power, of the content of rights and the instruments
founding, guaranteeing and implementing these rights, as well as of the
relations between socio-political and socio-economic actors. "Yet,
Economic and Monetary Union implies an important regime change that
entails additional responsibilities for all major policy actors in making it
a success" (CEC, 2001b: p. 5).

II. The EU: a new framework for the distribution of resources

With the Treaty of Maastricht, the question of the allocation of resources was directly attached to the problematic of competition and free
trade: "The Member States and the Community shall act in accordance
with the principle of an open market economy with free competition,
favouring an efficient allocation of resources [...]" (TEU, article 98).

The focus on controlling national budgetary policies (the core of the
new common economic and monetary policy) allows the EU to indirectly tackle the member states' overall system of resources. State

---

[11] See de la Porte and Pochet (2002), for the first general work analysing the OMC,
which they presented in a more favourable light. See also Pochet and Goetschy
(2000) on the European Employment Strategy in particular.

budgets are funded by tax revenues and directly or indirectly have a close relationship with monetary transfer systems for social security benefits. State fiscal systems have already been submitted to indirect pressure since 1 July 1990 when the internal market was opened up to the free movement of capital (Council of the European Communities, 1988) despite the failure to reach a compromise on fiscal harmonisation. This has placed national systems in a situation of "competitive taxation", particularly with regard to corporate tax rates.

The difficulty in reaching an agreement[12] on Community legislation regarding the issue of resources would appear to leave member states a wide margin of control over this politically highly sensitive field. However, the absence of harmonisation allows the EU to intervene ever more strongly in this area, but indirectly, under the guise of monitoring the efficient management of the capital, goods and services market.

The change in regime brought about by EMU has involved the Union in a vast operation of redefining and adjusting national resource allocation systems in order to integrate them into a unified financial order dominated by market mechanisms. But the European political system cannot progress at the same rate in all the member states since each national system is structured around distinct national and transnational actors and has a specific institutional history.

We will now examine the effects of this restructuring of meaning in three key fields: employment policy, retirement pension policy, and the search for a common trade union policy around the definition of a "wage norm" or "wage standard".

A. Social policy: supporting employment as the mainspring of competitiveness[13]

During the last two decades of the 20th century, "job creation" emerged as a major focus in Western European government programmes and discourse. It came to be imposed as the key component of social policy, and progressively replaced the conflict and debate over the

---

[12] Taxation, social security and social protection are still classified as areas requiring unanimous vote in the Council. Legislating on pay is expressly excluded from the EU sphere of competence.

[13] This section is based on the annual employment reports (1989-2001); the BEPGs (Broad Economic Policy Guidelines) (1993-2001); the 1993 White Paper on Competitiveness, Growth and Employment; Employment Guidelines (1998-2001) and Council Recommendations to Member States on Implementation of Employment Policy (1999-2001); as well as the Presidential conclusions to the European Council summit meetings (1991-2002).

redistribution of wealth. With the 1997 European Employment Strategy (EES), the central focus on this theme at EU level has implied an overall reconfiguration of social policy around employment.

The need for a Community-level approach to employment has long been debated. It should be recalled that throughout the 1970s, Euro-Trade Unions attempted to promote the idea of a Keynesian model of political responsibility at Community level with regard to employment, but met with little success.

During the 1980s, with the neo-liberal plan for the Single European Market in 1985, two different conceptions of "job creation" were adopted by Community authorities. On the one hand, it was seen as the near-spontaneous consequence of the development of the European internal market. This led to the 1988 "Cecchini report"[14] which announced the automatic creation of 5 million jobs. On the other hand, job creation was advocated as a medium for establishing a pact between the social actors and the public authorities in order to gain support for the new European project. The idea was developed in 1985 by Jaques Delors as part of the social dialogue process, but a general political agreement on the question was not reached at the time. However, the preparatory work undertaken to this end by the Commission opened the way for the idea that came to the fore during the 1990s that an EU employment policy could be developed.

1. Employment: economic policy or social policy?

The European Commission progressively developed an employment policy via its annual employment reports starting in 1989. The first four reports (1989-1992) served to establish the "concepts" (such as "target populations", "ageing of the population", "source of jobs", "active measures", "employment rate", "social exclusion", "long-term unemployment"), and to present what were perceived as the "problems" and their "solutions". This laid the foundations for a "theorising" of the question of employment in the White Paper on Growth, Competitiveness and Employment presented by Delors in 1993 (CEC, 1993). The paper included an employment programme which was first "tested" by the member states in a "multilateral surveillance" process decided on by the European Council in Essen in December 1994, and then transformed into a common interest policy by the Treaty of Amsterdam and the 1997 Luxembourg Summit for Employment.

---

[14] Experts' report under the direction of P. Cecchini, senior official, Internal Market and Industrial Affairs DG.

In what has become the dominant system of thinking, employment is viewed above all as a "factor of production" for the competitiveness of firms, and the population between 15 and 64 years of age as human capital to be mobilised. The notion of "employment rate" has replaced former references to the unemployment rate and the working population. The idea is to follow the examples of Japan and the US and significantly increase the number of people in the labour market by transforming all the "hidden and invisible unemployed" – that is, the non-workers – into workers. As a result, the reform of resource transfer systems became geared to providing employment incentives not only for the unemployed but also for the non-working population.

The overall objectives defined at the Lisbon summit were to raise the employment rate from 62% to 70% by 2010. An intermediary goal, of 67% by 2005, was set in Stockholm, as well as two specific goals: to increase the female employment rate from 52% to 57% by 2005 and then to 60%; and to increase the "participation rate" of workers aged 55 to 64 to 50% by 2010 by curtailing support for early retirement and implementing partial retirement arrangements. The European summit in Barcelona added the objective of raising the effective average retirement age by 5 years for 2010.

The view of employment as the mainspring of competitiveness has given rise to two important shifts in meaning:

- Employment policy has become labour market policy and thus, *in fine*, a policy to adapt labour to the market; this explains the strong linkages appearing in European policy documents between employment policy, the pursuit of wage restraint, increasing wage disparities, and greater flexibility of working conditions and working time.

- With employment as the focus of the EU social agenda, all the other components of social policy have been geared to supporting employment, and have thus also become "factors of production".

In response to the demands from the unions and certain political actors to give EMU more social "balance", the EU adopted a smokescreen solution which presented the social and economic spheres as "complementary" rather than "contradictory". But, in fact, the social sphere was totally transformed, primarily into a means to maintain the "broad macroeconomic balance" and secondarily, into a "factor of social cohesion", that is, a safety net to avoid what are considered to be dangerous social tensions. This balance was also supposed to be achieved through a policy promoting the quality of work by establishing a set of "indicators on quality in work" that were approved by the Laeken European Council (December 2001). In the end, the process boiled down to reviewing some thirty fairly traditional statistics, some of which have a rather strange relationship to the notion of "quality in work"[15]. In themselves, they have little meaning if they are not part of an overall policy to define a direction for employment that would clearly diverge from the current neo-liberal trend. But, as the European Commission declared, "Strengthening the quality dimension does not imply any new processes, or even a radically new approach to policy, at European level"[16].

A lexicometric[17] analysis of the French version of the Broad Economic Policy Guidelines (BEPGs) (1993-2001) reveals the extent to which *travail* and *emploi* have been transformed into economic management tools: *marché, emploi, travail* and *croissance*, in that order, top the list of the most frequently used terms, *travail* being attached to *marché* and *emploi* to *croissance* in the majority of cases.

Historically, the 19th century saw the "invention of the social sphere" (Donzelot, 1984): social and political struggles for democracy led to the introduction of statutory social rights which permitted the progressive decommodification of employment relations. Conversely, the "absorption" of the social into the economic sphere has direct repercussions on the content of social rights and on their position as the basis of society.

Have we not reached a turning point where the very notion of "social rights" has been completely transformed? We seem to have moved from a political form of organisation where certain instruments were developed as a basis for ensuring rights (such as social security systems), to a system in which these same instruments seem essentially to be geared to serving market policies and would only subsidiarily form a basis for rights; these rights, furthermore, are being "de-universalised" to adapt to diversified markets.

The activation of social expenditure on employment advocated at EU level has, in certain national contexts, led to benefit entitlement becom-

---

[15] Such as statistics on "working days lost in industrial disputes", the "proportion of workers with a financial interest/participation in the firms where they are employed", or the "proportion of workers with basic or higher levels of digital literacy".

[16] Communication on "Employment and social policies: a framework for investing in quality", European Commission, COM(2001) 313 final: 16, 20 June 2001.

[17] The results of the lexicometric analysis of the English-language version were not available at the time of going to press. The study of this and other languages is in progress. For a presentation of lexicometry, see Lebart and Salem (1994).

ing conditional (unemployment or minimum income benefits provided in exchange for mandatory training or labour market "integration").

Moreover, the concern of the EU to redefine fundamental rights (as in the Charter of Fundamental Rights) by distancing itself from existing international texts (such as the European Convention on Human Rights or The Social Charter of the Council of Europe) can also be seen as an indication of the will to "adjust" these rights to logic of the single market (see de Bodt, 2001, Gobin, 2003)[18].

2. *Employment: mobilising resources for a competitive economy*

Once employment was established as the key feature on the EU "social" agenda, it became the system of reference for all the other elements of social policy. Educational and training policies, as well as social protection, had to become part of "employment systems":

> [...] it is important to bring as much empirical evidence to bear in order to improve understanding of the way labour markets function and how employment systems – more broadly defined to encompass influences such as education and training and social protection – operate to create jobs and provide work and income for people. (CEC, 1994: p. 8)

The definition of social protection as a component of employment systems has enhanced the legitimacy of the EU to deal with the relationship between different resource flows – but as an element of economic policy, and not as a political question of "how to redistribute wealth".

In the Commission's view, financing social security benefits through compulsory social contributions and/or taxation is unfavourable to competitiveness and thus to employment since it weighs on the "cost" of labour:

> A distinguishing feature of the European economies is the high level of social protection provided through the State or State-supported systems. The financing of extensive social welfare systems has become an increasing matter of concern as regards the possible consequence for competitiveness and the process of job creation. (CEC, 1994: p. 16)

---

[18] For example, certain fundamental rights gained through the wage conflict, such as "equal pay for equal work" or the explicit right to a replacement income for unemployed or retired workers, do not appear in the EU Charter. For a more general analysis of the status of the declaration of rights in modern societies, see Fauré (1997).

In line with this viewpoint, the recommendations[19] addressed by the EU to the member states seek to ensure that available public resources (taxation and social contributions) will be used as "incentives" to support competitive systems of employment. The objective is thus to reform the overall body of transfer systems in that direction.[20]

It may be noted that in the wording of the EU texts, the notion of taxation encompasses all the systems of mandatory contributions financing social protection, regardless of their nature. Thus social contributions and taxation are systematically linked together. The lexicometric analysis of the French version of the Broad Economic Policy Guidelines (BEPGs, 1993-2001) shows that *cotisations* is associated with taxation 10 of the 12 times it appears. The frequent use of the phrase *systèmes de prélèvements et de prestations* should also be emphasised: the linking of social benefits with "deductions" turns them into a simple accounting factor that can be adjusted, and their definition as a right fades away.

The boundaries between the notions of tax-funded subsidies, social security benefits and wages become porous, and this permits to combine them or to substitute one for the other:

> Improving the prospects of labour market entry for the least competitive by restructuring national government income support schemes in ways which enable income from work to be topped up with income from social security by developing integrated taxation and income support systems with appropriate safeguards. (CEC, 1993: chapter 8.8.c)

This non-determination between categories of resources facilitates the disconnection between work and direct remuneration by the employer. The good old saying "all work deserves a wage" is being replaced by "all work deserves something".

Since 1993, the general proposal has been for an overall reduction of taxation on labour and of social contributions[21]. This reduction is to be greater in the case of "low skill" workers. In addition, a distinction is being made between "national solidarity" expenditure (family benefits, old-age, severe illness, long-term unemployment) for which social

---

[19] These recommendations have been included since 1993 in the BEPGs "paving the way" for EMU, and since 1998, in the guidelines for employment that must be compatible with the content of the BEPGs.

[20] The last reform of the European Social Fund is also part of the plan to promote the new European Employment Strategy, see the EC Regulation 1784/1999, 12 July 1999.

[21] In the 1993 White Paper, the Commission estimated that 40% of Community GDP was "channelled" through statutory charges, compared to 30% for Japan and the US.

contributions could be replaced by taxation, and "contributory" benefits (retirement pensions) for which: "[…] it is for each Member State to determine the respective proportions of compulsory and voluntary contributions to be paid under insurance schemes or savings arrangements" (CEC, 1993: chapter 9.3.b).

Conditionalities such as accepting and/or finding a job, are increasingly attached to benefits, and this has involved a revision of their duration, their rules of application and conditions of entitlement (CEC, 2001b).

Nonetheless, these changes are deemed insufficient, and it has been deplored that "There has been little progress in reforming tax-benefit systems to make work pay" (CEC, 2000: p. 13). In other words, the EU has announced that the bulk of the reforms of transfer systems is yet to come.

B. Pensions: developing a funded second pillar

1. The Commission's enduring goal

The Commission's Directorate General for the Internal Market (MARKT DG, formerly DG 15) has, since the 1990s, repeatedly expressed the desire to see the introduction of regulations designed for the pension funds industry that manages occupational pension schemes in a small number of the member states. This concern stems from their wish to round off the single capital market, which cannot effectively be considered as such until it includes the capital managed by these funds. One of the Commission's goals is thus to favour the expansion of this sector by limiting the restrictions on pension investments and thereby creating the opportunity for increased investment returns (freedom to acquire more foreign assets, more shares, and such like).

Despite their numerous semantic precautions, the proposals envisaged were not limited to organising the free movement of capital between the funds and the managers of their reserves. They touched on the politically more sensitive issue of the freedom to provide services, that is, the possibility for a pension fund to offer its services to residents of another member state in the name of free competition between pension institutions. This, however, necessarily means envisaging the possibility of a conflict between Community competition law and national provisions for compulsory affiliation to a pension scheme (whether set by law or by collective agreement). And that is a domain in which the Commission also has to take account of the conceptual framework set by the Court of Justice[22].

In the case of basic pension schemes, the Court of Justice ruling in the Pistre and Poucet case[23] explicitly rejected the possibility of challenging the "monopoly" involved in compulsory affiliation to a social security fund. The Court ruled that the funds managing basic pension schemes for the self-employed were not private companies and thus were not subject to Community competition regulations.

Case law on the supplementary schemes is far more difficult to grasp. Nonetheless, it appears after the 1999 Albany International case ruling[24] that if a collective agreement provides for compulsory affiliation to a pension fund which "pursues a social objective", this is consistent with Community law inasmuch as the hindrance of competition is necessary to achieving the goal of solidarity.

The initial proposals were thus significantly modified as case law evolved. The Council's reactions also compelled the Commission to scale down its plans. A preliminary document drafted in 1990 (9 October) had envisaged guaranteeing three major freedoms:

1. The freedom for fund managers to select the asset manager of their choice;

2. Freedom of investment of pension fund assets, in order to limit restrictions such as the currency matching requirement which requires a certain proportion of the assets providing interest to be in the same currency as that paid to the beneficiary.

3. The freedom to join a pension fund in another country. That is, the possibility for an employee or an employer to choose a pension fund in another member state, first for migrant workers and then for employees of multinationals. (Although the Commission has always claimed that this would not call into question national provisions for compulsory affiliation, it is difficult to lend credence to this assertion).

However, the first directive proposal of 1991 (CEC, 1991) was more limited in scope. It only included the first two freedoms since the Commission anticipated meeting with opposition on the third. The insurance

---

[22] The Commission is however able to present its views before the Court via the submissions of its legal department during each of the proceedings. Their arguments are then frequently taken up by the court (Sweet et Caporaso, 1998).

[23] ECJ, 17 February 1993, Poucet and Pistre, C-159/91 and C-160/91.

[24] ECJ, 21 September 1999, Albany International, C-67/96.

companies' representatives were displeased with the proposal because it did not include a section on liabilities (the obligations imposed on pension institutions and their investment policies). They claimed to be more qualified to play a role in the future private pension system on the grounds that they offered more substantial financial guarantees.

This first attempt to pass legislation was thwarted by the Council in 1993 due to opposition from several countries. France in particular wanted to avoid unfair competition for her national insurance companies, to maintain a high currency matching rate in order to sustain the French franc, and to protect compulsory affiliation to the pay-as-you-go supplementary schemes (AGIRC and ARRCO) over the long-term.

This failure prompted the Commission to present the text in the form of a Communication including strong binding components. But a joint case brought by France and Spain led the Court of Justice to annul the act on the grounds that the Commission had over-stepped its functions.

The Commission then launched a broad consultation of the member states and economic actors (following the 1997 Green Paper on supplementary pensions) before presenting further proposals.

A new directive proposal, which was more likely to achieve consensus, was presented in October 2000, and resulted in the Council adopting a common position in May 2002. Certain structural factors, such as the introduction of the euro, had served in the interim to reduce the antagonisms at the origin of the previous failures. Above all, the insurance companies had realised that they should seize the opportunity to position themselves on the occupational pension market that was in the process of being Europeanised, and their representatives succeeded in imposing their point of view during the parliamentary debates. The financial institutions managing occupational pension plans are now no longer under obligation to restrict their activities to this field exclusively. A private insurance company need only draw up a separate balance sheet for the assets and liabilities concerning the management of an occupational pension plan in order to enter the market. In exchange for this, the pension funds obtained a compromise that tended to restrict prudential requirements.

The unions and other European actors defending a social vision of occupational pensions (favouring defined-benefit schemes and their bipartite management) had limited institutional access to the debate, since the defenders of the directive argued that it was of a strictly economic nature focused on extending the free movement of capital.

2. Defining social security and the three pillars of wisdom

It has not been an easy matter for the Commission to promote the market for funded supplementary pension plans. The major problem has been how to advocate the need for a single market and define it when many countries do not even have such a market, and the vast majority of assets are held by Dutch, Danish or British institutions. The goal of achieving a single market has necessitated establishing the conceptual tools that will legitimate it and lend credence to the idea that advanced-funding is the natural way to finance employment-linked schemes. To put it clearly, defining the role of private initiatives entails giving a restrictive definition of pay-as-you-go systems. But the succession of EU documents addressing the field in relation to diverse social policy issues has made it difficult to establish a single definition of social security or social protection. This role has thus been played by the Court of Justice, whose rulings have delimited the field of application of the texts concerned[25] – and thereby, the respective spheres of the market and of social protection.

The Commission's solution to these difficulties was to follow the example of the World Bank, and to promote a single analytical framework that restructures the question of the future financing of pensions and corresponds to its goals to reduce the role of pay-as-you-go and expand that of funded schemes (Bonnoli and Pallier, 2000; Math, 2001). This framework – the segmentation of social protection into three pillars – was disseminated in the majority of the Commission's documents: expert reports, Committee on Economic Policy reports (drafted by the Economic and Financial DG), the directive proposals described above, and the conclusions filed before the Court of Justice[26].

The 1990 draft document expresses this position fairly clearly. First, it is asserted that pensions can be financed through three different sources (the three pillars): social security schemes, employment-related supplementary schemes, and personal retirement plans. While acknowledging the difficulties in using these distinctions, the Commission argued that they exist "in theory" all over Europe, and could thus serve as a basis for defining the field of application of the future text:

---

[25] The documents concern, in particular, the coordination of social security schemes, governed by Regulation 1408/71; the application of the principle of equal pay for men and women since the benefits linked to an employment relation are considered as part of the pay packet; and the question of the delimitation of competition law.

[26] Sweet and Caporoso (1998) have shown how important these documents are for "predicting" the subsequent rulings of the Court of Justice.

Keeping these precautions in mind, the present document will deal with the second pillar and in particular, financial institutions other than private insurance firms which provide private employment-linked retirement benefits to individuals or groups, even if these pension schemes partially or fully replace benefits which would otherwise be provided by social security bodies. (CEC, 1990)

The case of France – where the pay-as-you-go supplementary pension schemes AGIRC and ARRCO play an important role – is of particular interest, for it highlights the semantic shift that has taken place. For the Commission not only defines the pillars on the basis of type of scheme. It also asserts their "natural" modes of financing, claiming that the second pillar, defined by its link to the employment relation, is generally managed by funded systems. The pillar-based distinction thus becomes as normative as it is descriptive:

> Pay-as-you-go systems imply compulsory affiliation and a social contract between the contributors (between the active population and the beneficiaries). Practically all the social security systems in the Community are financed in this way. Recourse to this system for private pensions is essentially limited to France [...]. The compulsory nature of affiliation is a major obstacle to achieving the third objective (cross-border affiliation). However, it remains crucial for the long-term stability of a pay-as-you-go scheme and it would be unreasonable to require the suppression of this obligation. It is thus proposed to exclude pay-as-you-go schemes from the field of application of the proposal. In fact, these schemes will be considered more as an extension of the social security system than as a component of the second pillar (occupational pensions). (CEC, 1990)

During the 1990s, this categorisation progressively came to be accepted by the French supplementary schemes, which are now almost unanimously considered as belonging to the first pillar. However, their inclusion in this category was achieved not only by recourse to binding legal norms, but also through an interplay between strategy anticipation, cognitive connections and personal career-building

C. Wage policy: an issue for trade unions at European level?

The co-ordination of collective bargaining over wages is an issue that is not addressed in Community documents. These, moreover, rarely use the term "wage policy": the preferred phrase is "wage development". This is not a neutral expression, and its use shows that wage restraint has come to be accepted by all the European actors.

1. Is the ETUC the guardian of wage restraint?

In its monthly bulletins, the European Central Bank informs the "so-cial partners" of the level of wage development that will be tolerated for the maintenance of monetary stability (Dufresne, 2000b). Furthermore, the Bank has insisted that "careful monitoring of wage development and the availability of reliable data at frequent intervals is essential"[27]. Recommendations to reduce the wage bill have a long history at Community level (the Ortoli Commission aligned with UNICE positions as early as 1975). Thus, the Commission recently noted with pleasure that "although the situation in the labour market is improving and the unemployment rate is decreasing, wage growth has remained moderate in recent years and should continue to do so for the next two years" (CEC, 2001c). It selectively used two structural arguments to justify this position on wage restraint in 2001: labour market flexibility and reductions in social security contributions. In addition, the Commission called upon the social actors to adopt what it calls "responsible" strategies and to increase their co-operation in order to ensure the continuation of this trend.

The Commission thus envisaged social dialogue as a means to achieve a convergence of interests between the "social partners", and one of the important roles of this process is to ensure wage restraint. As a result, social dialogue has little substance: both the European Trade Union Conference (ETUC) and the European Industry Federations (EIFs) appear to be dependent on the Commission's agenda, and their presence to essentially serve to promote Community policies. Two further – major – institutional obstacles to the Europeanisation of collective bargaining should also be noted. First, the Social Agreement signed in Maastricht, which has been included in the Treaty since Amsterdam, explicitly excludes wages from EC legislative competence. And second, trade union co-ordination initiatives have been handicapped by the lack of an interlocutor on the employers' side: the employers' representatives, however well-organised (and this is not always the case at sectoral level) have, to date, refused to negotiate or even to discuss the subject of wages.

---

[27] ECB, Monthly Bulletin, February 2001.

2. Is the autonomy of the ETUC the key to achieving a co-ordinated wage policy?

Does this conception of wage restraint allow for a rethink of the role of wages in the euro zone economy? And if so, what scope would the trade unions have for action within the European institutional complex? It can be observed today that trade-union initiatives are being developed outside of the tight institutional network of the EU. It is possible that the more the unions allow themselves to adopt a position other than that of wage restraint[28], the greater their chances of asserting their independence.

The ETUC is thus faced with transnational initiatives at both cross-sectoral and sectoral levels (the latter will not be examined here, see Dufresne, 2000a, 2000b, 2001 and 2002). This raises the question of how these different initiatives interconnect and who will be responsible for what.

a) Cross-industry orchestration and sectoral responsibility

At its 9th Congress in Helsinki in1999, the ETUC adopted a resolution explaining its role "to impulse the co-ordination necessary to guarantee the overall coherence of the demands of the European trade union movement and to support in every way possible the European Industry Federations in their initiatives" (ETUC, 1999a). Although certain national confederations are seeking to regain power through the ETUC Collective Bargaining Co-ordinating Committee (CBCC), it is in fact the European Industry Federations that have "primary responsibility for European co-ordination of collective bargaining". That is why it is deemed necessary "to devise appropriate policies and structures in each federation" and "to strengthen and/or establish social dialogue in every sector of the economy" (ETUC, 1999b). However, it is still too soon to have a clear picture of the roles the ETUC and the other union organisations will adopt in the co-ordination process.

b) Cross-border activity: An alternative, or a step on the way to Community action?

In addition to the industrial (sectoral and cross-sectoral) interconnections at EU level, the co-ordination dynamic also needs to take into consideration the interplay between the Community, national and cross-border levels.

---

[28] The ETUC agreed to wage restraint after having accepted the principle of EMU.

The cross-border Doorn Initiative[29] and the various sectoral co-operation agreements are all in essence transnational. However, a number of trade unions (especially from southern countries) expressed their disapproval of the regional nature of the Doorn initiative, on the grounds that it could risk fragmenting and weakening the union movement and the ETUC. The third meeting of the Doorn Group was thus opened up to ETUC representatives, and members repeatedly asserted that their Group represented "a step towards European co-operation on collective bargaining". Nonetheless, cross-border co-operation – a novel and dynamic development – appears more realistic in the immediate term, given the smaller number of participants and their geographical – and often cultural – proximity (which explains their sometimes long-standing historical ties). It is not yet known whether the Doorn Group will open up to other countries or whether other regional initiatives will be organised along the same lines. But, "if such cross-border agreements continue to be signed, the question will be how to co-ordinate them with Community initiatives" (Delbar and Walthéry, 2000). What would be the role of the ETUC or EIFs in these three- or four- country processes? There could conceivably be some competition between a Community trade union structure (set up by European actors) and a transnational structure (with direct inter-union co-operation bypassing Europe) – which is why the EIFs and the ETUC often seek to head these co-operation agreements. This raises the important question of the possible forms of Europeanisation and the legitimacy of the European players.

3. Content of wage co-ordination: what is meant by wages?

In a political and economic environment marked by strong wage restrictions (which have lasted for over twenty-five years), the various wage co-ordination initiatives are all working on developing a joint position on wages that could be translated into a "wage norm" or "standard". Is this a rationalisation of constraints and/or the will to regain greater autonomy in order to renew pressure with regard to wages, or at least to avoid unions accepting competitive wage dumping in order to protect "national" employment? Although the attempts to establish a wage norm have not yet produced a result that can be used in national

---

[29] After the Belgian government adopted its 'law on competitiveness' in 1996, the two major unions (the CSC and the FGTB) were obliged to systematically compare Belgian wage levels with those of their country's three main trading partners (Germany, France and the Netherlands). They thus took the initiative, in 1997, of bringing together their German and Dutch counterparts, along with their main sectoral unions. They agreed to meet annually and to establish a contact group which was subsequently dubbed the "Doorn Group".

negotiations, the meetings of the various co-ordinating bodies have enabled trade unions to consolidate their strategies and to provide a partial response to the emergence of new questions concerning the notion of pay.

a. "Extended" wages: Bargaining on qualitative aspects

The aim of the wage norm is to defend employees' purchasing power against inflation, or even boost it where possible by means of a "fair" distribution of productivity gains between capital and labour. It nonetheless leaves national federations fully autonomous as regards the utilisation of the available distribution margin. Part of this margin can thus be allocated to employment, reductions in working time, training, early retirement, or any other forms of solidarity, depending on the country. Trade-offs between wage progression and what are presented as other "more qualitative" aspects of employment are thus beginning to appear in collective agreements. As Jean Lapeyre, Deputy Secretary of the ETUC explains, "if a European social model existed, qualitative aspects could be a factor in correcting the curves, as compared with the American curves" (CBCC, 1999).

The focus on "qualitative aspects", however, not only raises technical problems because of quantification difficulties. It also raises political problems, since it clouds the fundamental issue of who should pay for social rights. Calling collective social rights that are rooted in work and the wage "qualitative aspects" can be dangerous: it could depoliticise the question of the content and status of these rights, which could then easily be turned into negotiable "aspects" tied to the local labour market situation (which is what the Commission is pressing the unions to do); and this would serve to further "de-universalise" collective social rights.

b. "Diluted" wages: New forms of pay

The notion of the wage is not only being extended to qualitative aspects, it is also being "diluted". Rather than focussing on the wage in the strict sense of the term, pay bargaining is constantly being diluted in discussions on new, additional and increasingly individualised forms of income; these range from profit-sharing to other types of bonuses such as stock-options and top-up pensions (Van het Kaar and Grünel, 2001). The definition of the wage has thus become fuzzy. This issue, like the more traditional question of the articulation between collective bargaining and social protection, taxation and minimum wage, is now at the forefront of trade union thinking. This redefinition of wages and their limits are part and parcel of the ongoing co-ordination process.

4. From technical obstacles to political will?

These union initiatives all serve to exchange information on which to base appraisal of the outcomes of individual national bargaining rounds. The norm is thus used only as an *ex-post* monitoring tool. It has been explained that for the moment, this is why "there is no evidence of an effective move towards co-ordinating actual bargaining topics" (Dufour and Hege, 1999); all that is involved is exchanging information and lists of claims. But is there not a way to turn the wage norm into an *ex-ante* tool for raising claims and defending employees' rights at national level?

Structure (social actors), substance (wage formation) and objectives (socio-political agendas) are intrinsically linked in the history of national wage policies. Sociological analysis makes it possible to comprehend the micro-economic "wage relation", the creation of a balance of power between the actors who determine wages. At European level, on the other hand, there is currently a tendency to define substance before structure, that is, to define a technical and macro-economic "wage norm" without having constructed a sufficiently solid multi-level trade union player to defend them. That is why the development of a co-ordinated collective bargaining policy is accompanied by the establish-ment of Community institutions that serve as forums for mutual observa-tion by the trade union organisations involved in the process and in a phase of learning about their different systems. The question is, what structures will be capable (in terms of political clout) of defending a plan to redistribute wealth in order to prevent the macro-economic wage relation (restraint enforced by the economic sphere since the beginning of the 1980s) from continuing to weaken wage relations in each of the member states?

In the continental states in particular, wages are determined and de-fined in a political process at national level (whether sectoral or cross-sectoral). Could one imagine deliberations on a different scale? If so, what form of policy-making community would need to be constructed at European level, predicated on the right to a wage, rather than on "put-ting employment first", which is the *leitmotiv* of Community jargon?

Conclusion

The primary aim of this chapter has been to show that the political system of the EU has come to play a predominant role in the current redefinitions affecting the entire range of national systems for the collec-tion and transfer of resources. Thanks to the Community policy on budgetary control introduced in the Treaty of Maastricht and re-iterated with force in the 1997 Stability and Growth Pact, the EU has progressively become a single political system – formed by Community and member state apparatuses – that gives impetus to policies leading to the far-reaching reform of national systems of distribution of resources. Employment serves as the vector for the transfer of the logics of financial accumulation – as the priority logic – towards all the fields related to social protection.

The European Commission and the Court of Justice are key actors in the elaboration of these reforms. These institutions have defined a cognitive framework in which the economic sphere is approached via the entry points of competition policies and the consolidation of the internal market: this includes completing the capital market, which in turn shapes the treatment of social questions. EMU is thus the tool for achieving a "change of regime" which, thanks to a network metaphor serving to merge "political society" and "civil society" and to blur the boundary between private interests and the collective interest, is leading to a revision of the role assigned to socio-political institutions.

Our future research will look more closely at the interplay between national and Community systems and the room for manoeuvre that remains thanks to the principle of subsidiarity, the verdict of national elections, and the weight of national socio-political and institutional histories. Keeping in mind, of course, that the progress towards a single system of free trade will always allow for an adaptation to marginal variations.

Our second aim, as a corrective to this preliminary overall approach, was to show that despite the strong system of constraints produced through the political system of the EU, the multiplication of institutionalised actors coupled with the multiplication of procedures for producing EU norms allows the institutional actors a certain – albeit limited – margin of freedom. For instance, the Court of Justice, through rulings that establish a distinction between the sphere of competition law and the sphere of social protection, offers a finer reading than that produced by the Commission (although to what extent can this effectively protect social law, given the hegemony of free market logics?).

Another example is offered by Euro-Trade Unionism. The decision-making framework of the system of Community constraints (which includes the social dialogue procedures) does not permit the union actor to weigh on the choice of political direction. At sectoral level in particular, social dialogue more often than not serves to produce joint demands addressed to the EU – which can be likened to a particular form of lobbying – rather than reciprocal commitments between the social interlocutors within their direct fields of responsibility (such as working time, health/security, or training). However, the Europeanisation of both political and economic relations resulting from EMU has made it crucial for the social movements to occupy the transnational spaces existing between the national and supranational levels and which are not directly subjected to political constraints. It is within this space that the unions are attempting to develop a more offensive strategy (are we seeing a rediscovery of autonomous internationalism?).

Ultimately, one of the keys to the successful development of co-operation between trade unions will be the confidence that each of the national organisations has in its transnational or supranational authority (Secretariat of the Doorn Group, EIF or ETUC). It is the creation of a strong inter-union fabric that will convince national organisations to partially relinquish their sovereignty in favour of a European mandate for supranational or transnational bodies. This would then lend strength to the idea of a joint programme pursued by European trade unionism as a whole, and perhaps make it possible to move beyond mere declarations of principle that are rarely applied.

References

Bourdieu, P. (1986), "La force du droit. Éléments pour une sociologie du champ juridique", *Les Actes de la Recherche en sciences sociales*, No.64, Minuit, Paris, pp. 3-19.

CBCC (1999), Statement of meeting of the Collective Bargaining Co-ordinating Committee, 3-4 November 1999.

Cecchini, P. (1988) (col. Catinat, M. et Jacquemin, A.), *1992. Le défi. Nouvelles données économiques de l'Europe sans frontières*, Flammarion, Paris.

CEC (1990), L'achèvement du marché intérieur dans le domaine des retraites privées, 9 October 1990.

CEC (1991), Proposal for a Council directive relating to the freedom of management and investment of funds held by institutions for retirement provision, COM (91) 301 final of 21 October 1991.

CEC (1993), *Growth, Competitiveness, Employment. The Challenges and Ways forward into the 21st Century, White Paper*, Office for Official Publications of the European Communities, Luxembourg.

CEC (1994), *Employment in Europe – 1994*, Office for Official Publications of the European Communities, Luxembourg.

CEC (1989 à 2001), *Employment in Europe* (Annual Report), Office for Official Publications of the European Communities, Luxembourg.

CEC (2000), *Industrial Relations in Europe – 2000*, Office for Official Publications of the European Communities, Luxembourg.

CEC (2001a), "European Governance: A White Paper", COM (2001) 428 of 25 July 2001.

CEC (2001b), Commission Recommendation for the 2001 Broad Guidelines of the Economic Policies of the Member States and the Community, COM (2001) 224 final of 25 April 2001.

CEC (2001c), Prévisions printemps 2001 pour 2001-2002, European Economy, Supplément A, Perspectives économiques, No.3-4, mars-avril 2001.

Charvin, R. (2002), "Régulation juridique et mondialisation néo-libérale. Droit 'mou', droit 'flou' et non-droit", *Actualité et Droit international*, January 2002.

Council of the European Communities (1988), Council Directive 88/361/EEC of 24 June 1988 for the implementation of Article 67 of the Treaty, OJ L 178 of 8 July 1988, pp. 0005-0018.

Council of the Ministers of the EU (1993 à 2001), Les Grandes orientations de politique économique.

Council of the Ministers of the EU (1999 à 2001), Recommandation du Conseil adressée aux États membres concernant la mise en œuvre des politiques de l'emploi.

European Council (2001), Résolution relative à une régulation plus efficace des marchés des valeurs mobilières dans l'UE, Stockholm Summit, March 2001.

European Council (1991 à 2002), European Council, Presidency Conclusions.

de Bodt, R. (2001), *Les Quinze contre les droits de l'Homme?*, Luc Pire, Brussels.

de la Porte, C. and Pochet, P. (2002), *Building Social Europe through the Open Method of Co-ordination*, P.I.E.-Peter Lang, Brussels.

Delbar, C. and Walthéry, P. (2000), "Belgian, Dutch and German Construction Unions Sign Co-operation Agreement", Eironline, Sept.

Donzelot, J. (1984), *L'invention du social. Essai sur le déclin des passions politiques*, Fayard, Paris.

Doorn Initiative (1998), "The Doorn Declaration", Joint Declaration adopted by the Belgian, Dutch, German and Luxembourg trade unions, Doorn, 5 September 1998.

Dufour, C. and Hege, A. (1999), "Quelle coordination syndicale des négociations en Europe?", *Chronique Internationale de l'IRES*, No.60, pp. 108-117.

Dufresne, A. (2000a), "La BCE, un acteur politique ?", *L'année sociale 2000*, Institut de sociologie de l'ULB, Brussels, January 2000.

Dufresne, A. (2000b), "L'état des négociations collectives au plan européen dans les secteurs du textile et de l'habillement – Étude sur trois pays", in Ministère français des Affaires sociales, du Travail et de la Solidarité (ed.),

La négociation en 1999, Tome III : Les dossiers, éditions législatives et Ministère français des Affaires sociales, du Travail et de la Solidarité, Paris.

Dufresne, A. (2001), "Le chantier de la coordination syndicale : l'état des négociations collectives au plan européen dans le secteur de la construction – Étude sur trois pays", in Ministère français des Affaires sociales, du Travail et de la Solidarité (ed.), *La négociation en 2000*, les dossiers, éditions législatives et Ministère français des Affaires sociales, du Travail et de la Solidarité, Paris, pp. 20-45.

Dufresne, A. (2002), "L'état des négociations collectives au plan européen dans le secteur du graphisme", in Ministère français des Affaires sociales, du Travail et de la Solidarité (ed.), *La négociation en 2001*, Tome I : La tendance, les dossiers, éditions législatives et Ministère français des Affaires sociales, du Travail et de la Solidarité, Paris, pp. 223-244.

ETUC (1999a), "Towards a European System of Industrial Relations", Resolution adopted by the IXth Statutory Congress of the European Trade Union Confederation, Helsinki, 29 June-2 July 1999.

ETUC (1999b), Comité de coordination des négociations collectives, Décision du Comité exécutif du 16 septembre 1999.

ETUC (2000), "ETUC Recommendation on the co-ordination of collective bargaining", adopted by the ETUC Executive Committee, 13-14 December 2000.

European Parliament (2002), Report on the Commission communication "Supporting national strategies for safe and sustainable pensions through an integrated approach", Rapporteur: Carlo Fatuzzo, Report A5-0071/2002, 27 February 2002.

Fauré, C. (1997), *Ce que déclarer des droits veut dire : histoires*, Presses universitaires de France, Paris.

Gobin, C. (1997), *L'Europe syndicale*, Labor, Brussels.

Gobin, C. (2000), "Union européenne et dévaluation du contre-pouvoir syndical", in Fouquet, A., Rehfeldt, U. and Le Roux, S. (eds.), *Le syndicalisme dans la mondialisation*, Éd. de l'atelier, Paris, pp. 137-147.

Gobin, C. (2002), "De l'Union européenne à... l'Européanisation des mouvements sociaux ?", *Revue internationale de politique comparée*, Vol. 9, No.1, pp. 119-138.

Gobin, C. (2003), "La Charte européenne des droits fondamentaux : vers une régression des droits démocratiques au sein de l'Union Européenne", in Béroud S. and Mouriaux R. (eds.), *L'Année sociale 2002*, Éd. Syllepse, Paris.

Kelsen, H. (1953, 1988), *Théorie pure du droit* (adaptée de l'allemand par H. Thévenaz), Éd. de la Baconnière, Neuchâtel.

Lamfalussy (2001), Final report of the Committee of WiseMen on Securities Markets Regulation, Brussels, 15 February.

Lebart, L. and Salem, A. (1994), *Statistique textuelle*, Dunod, Paris.

Math, A. (2001), "Réforme des retraites et concurrence.Une analyse des rôles et stratégies des acteurs au niveau communautaire", Working paper No.01.04, IRES, Noisy-le-Grand.

Pochet, P. and Goetschy, J. (2000), "La politique européenne de l'emploi: réflexions sur les nouveautés de 1999 et leur impact pour la Belgique", *Revue belge de sécurité sociale*, No.1, March 2000, pp. 69-86.

Sweet, A.S. and Caporoso, J.A. (1998), "La Cour européenne et l'intégration", *Revue française de science politique*, Vol. 48, No.2, pp. 195-244.

Van het Kaar, R. and Grünell, M. (2001), "Variable Pay in Europe", Eironline (http://www.eiro.eurofound.ie/2001/04/Study/TN0104201S.html), April 2001.

Weber, M. (1986), *Sociologie du droit*, PUF, Paris, French translation.

CONCLUSION

Whither Social Rights and Societal Resources?

Willibrord DE GRAAF and Bernadette CLASQUIN

The two main objectives at the start of this project were to provide a specific theoretical framework to analyse changes in employees' resources and associated social rights, and to investigate the different spheres in which these rights are constructed. The book represents a first attempt to test the fruitfulness and robustness of this framework. It is a risky undertaking because it is based on work in progress, and as such, cannot claim to offer an extensive discussion of other theoretical approaches. In that sense, as explained in the Introduction, it seeks more to provide a challenging agenda than a firmly proven case. Furthermore it is the result of a collective endeavour, and is to be seen as reflecting the gradual and ongoing construction of a common understanding between different researchers. Although what the authors collectively share has been an interest in the link between employment, the wage and social protection, there was no initial agreement at an epistemological or theoretical level when our work began. The diversity of academic and political histories of individuals in their countries plays a decisive role in the exchange of positions and arguments. The extensive dialogue undertaken to grasp the theoretical and practical presuppositions underpinning the reasoning of the different groups has, despite some continuing disagreements, served to enhance the effort to cooperate. It has become clear that our view on the importance of the complexities of the relation between resources and rights offers a promising start for analysing developments in employment and social protection at national level and in the European Union as a whole. We see our framework as a relevant tool for analysing the formation of what is called a social Europe.

In this conclusion, we will summarise the arguments presented in the preceding chapters in order to examine the major aspects currently under debate within the group and which we consider to be of general interest. This naturally leads us to address some of the limitations of the

193

present work, and finally, to highlight the perspectives it opens up for future research as well as for the national and international debate.

I. Accomplishments and the questions raised

A conceptual framework and analytical categories

Centring the analysis on the link between the resource flows channelled through the wage and social rights (Chapter 1) opens up two broad avenues for research that have to varying degrees been developed in the different chapters. These are

- mobilising research fields that are traditionally separated according to disciplinary divides in order to understand the impact of the dynamics of employment, the wage and social protection on rights over resources,
- introducing new analytical categories.

This framework first opens new perspectives for analyses of the labour market: the concept of the work-welfare nexus proposed in Chapter 2 permits a fresh approach to the issues of the segmentation of employment and of the link between public policies, organisation of the labour market and dynamics of inclusion/exclusion. Then, in Chapter 3, it serves to problematise public action in a new way: the analysis of changes in the origin of resources permits to characterise different figures of the worker based on the nature of their rights. Policies of fiscal support for low-income populations and low-wage workers change the orientation of state action (tutelary state), and serve to construct the benefit-recipient worker. In symmetrical fashion, employee savings and the pre-financed wage develop the figure of the property-owning worker. In proposing "resource regimes" as a central category, this chapter opens up important avenues for international comparisons. Chapter 4 introduces the debate on competencies, and outlines a framework for analysing the link between training, job, wage and social rights that are often separated into two poles: education or training and employment, or level of education and wage; it points to the further question of the more or less collective attributes of wage-earners that, depending on the country, underpin the formation of wage hierarchies. Chapter 5 establishes the linkage between the field of industrial relations and that of social protection studies; it raises the question of wage conflict in terms of the construction of rights over resources and opens up perspectives for the analysis of the actors, institutional forms, and on a more overall level, the power relations shaping the dynamics of change in the spheres of the wage and social rights. In addressing the

European level, Chapter 6 enriches this point of view by introducing the debate on the relationship between the production of norms, employment, wage and social rights; it questions several aspects of the EU, in terms of the political and legal construction of the Union and industrial relations, that are usually analysed separately.

The various spheres identified here (labour market, public policy, wage hierarchies and industrial relations) represent a first step in our attempt to reveal the societal logics underpinning the construction/ deconstruction of rights to resources. This objective has entailed an in-depth reflection on the conceptual approach to comparative analysis which we hope will contribute to the crucial academic debate on the topic of undertaken by such authors as Lallement and Spurk (2003). The perspective we have adopted warrants further explanation in that it has led us to propose an alternative to the dominant approach.

The question of typologies

A major difficulty facing any comparative study is that of defining the common features on which to base an analysis of national differences. Although it is frequent practice in European comparisons to form clusters like Beveridgean or Bismarckian regimes, or Anglo-Saxon versus continental systems with a special place for the Nordic countries, or social-democratic, liberal and corporatist states – in the end this proves somewhat infertile because these are highly "idealised" constructions in the Weberian sense. The difficulty with comparisons is that they can easily produce the pitfall of implicit value judgements on the qualities of one or another system. The typologies cited seek to characterise national models, whereas the framework we propose permits to study the effects of the specific linkages between wage-related resources, rights and provisions in relation to questions of administration, exclusion and power. It does not presuppose any "just" linkage but provides a means of analysis of the processes of differentiation between resource regimes, in terms of dynamic flows of societal wealth. As both convergent and divergent transformations can be observed in different European countries, a typological approach makes these changes difficult to understand. Thus, rather than adopt a classificatory approach that slots national cases into pre-ordained boxes, we are interested in exploring dynamic processes of a more transversal nature in order to understand the processes of construction of resource regimes and social rights in each national space. We are seeking to analyse not the dominant form of resource regimes but the coexistence of different types of regimes within different societal configurations and the tensions and interactions between them. Furthermore, by adopting this dynamic approach to resource regimes and social rights, we can more easily interpret each country's specific modalities of absorbing changes occurring at the European Union level, and interactions between national and European processes. The explicit normative assumption is that it is possible to promote debate about what is constructed as rights within the dynamic of the wage conflict.

The process involved in constructing this conceptual framework has led to a heightened awareness within the network of the thorny issue of language.

The discussion of key concepts presented in the section titled "Questions of terminology" highlights the debates inherent in the construction of a common ground in an international group whose representations and research environments are marked by national origins. What, on the surface, may appear to be simply problems of translation, point in fact to a more complicated issue: words are not innocent vehicles of meaning but are rooted in discourses about what is to be seen as the world. These discourses are inspired by specific histories and practices and thus, beyond questions of systems of meaning, must be perceived as "worldviews". A worldview is an epistemological, theoretical and practical perspective on what the world looks like and how we can know it and act in it. When this is acknowledged, it becomes possible to articulate differences and to analyse the ways in which they can contribute to the elaboration of the framework. The process of stepping back from national realities required for an international comparison has brought to the fore two key questions that remain under debate.

Social rights and the total reproduction of labour

Thus far, the network has chosen to centre its analysis on the social rights linked to employment, this being considered the dominant form of the recognition of work in our societies. However, the question of social rights must be seen as part of the broader question of the dynamic of the reproduction of labour. How can general rights to education, housing, infrastructures, sport or culture be taken into account? These social provisions are financed by income tax, whether deducted at source or not, and depending on the country are more or less directly linked to the wage. This question also relates to the nature of the political framework and raises the question of the link between wage and income. It is striking that in all of our countries, major changes are occurring across the whole range of social provisions, but these tend to be treated piecemeal, without an overall assessment of the changing nature of social rights over societal resources. Such general provisions have their role in the differential reproduction of social hierarchies and as such impact on access to the labour market and its related systems of social protection. Our framework does not exclude these kinds of general provisions, but the linkage between them and those rights more directly linked to employment needs to be established if the total social reproduction of labour is to be taken into account.

The articulation between analytical levels within the comparative framework

Although at present our analysis remains at the macro level, mainly national or European, we are aware that resources, social rights and their linkages are also constructed elsewhere, in particular at the company level. In classical accounts it is the wage (employees) and capital (employers) that confront each other, with the state playing the role of third party as a mediator, intervener and/or accomplice of capital, depending on the theory. Our framework distances itself from this picture by accepting that some rights may be more influenced by social partners and others by the parliamentary-political system – or by other groups of actors[1] whose role needs to be more clearly identified – without any a priori judgement as to the rightfulness of these divisions of arenas. But at the national level there is much more at stake than the relative distribution of power between public and corporatist institutions, and we need to take account of the increasingly fragmented nature of wage bargaining and the growth of company-based agreements (some of which bypass the unions). Furthermore it is important to break down the aggregate levels of analysis and to examine the regional and local spheres of policy-making. What may also be missed is the interplay between European and national social actors; as far as our studies show, this is mostly not a simple bottom-up or top-down movement, but a very complex effort to coordinate policies, and, to a certain extent as shown in Chapter 6, takes place in diverse spaces. It is thus important to analyse the articulation between the national and European levels as a first step, and then to integrate the local and regional levels and multinationals.

II. Limitations and paths to be explored

The three issues discussed below are considered as essential to the further development of our analytical framework. They are situated at different levels, and question the spheres chosen for the examination of

---

[1] Such as lobbies and private insurance companies, on the one hand, and social movements on the other.

the societal logics underpinning the construction of rights over re-sources.

Work/non-work and employment/non-employment

Two paths remain to be explored which would help expand the way in which the work-employment relationship has been approached thus far. These are related to the question of gender and to how resources serve to construct social units for which the links between social rights and citizenship rights are not clear.

In choosing the links between wage, rights and provisions as our main axis, we adopt a strong social-historical perspective on the con-struction of social protection and propose to look at the struggles over the nature and extension of the wage as a resource for reproduction. Chapter 1 shows how this permits to analyse the formation of new social groups differentiated by access to rights and provisions, and points out the gender dimension. However, we stated that "our focus on the wage and resource flows recentres the analysis on an economic institution and the institutional forms organising the resource flows". European coun-tries have developed different historical patterns of women's participa-tion in the labour market, but they have the common starting point of the model of the male breadwinner. Thus we need to extend our analysis to the gendered nature of the linkage between deductions and resources, together with an analysis of the development of forms of part-time work and new labour markets in the field of care and services. One of the main problems with welfare regime reforms is that they both promote equal opportunities for women by stimulating their participation in the labour market, and force them back into the social realm of respon-sibility for care by diminishing the access to welfare resources. As Mairhuber (1998) has observed in a study of the Italian case,

> [...] the so-called 'welfare state crisis' additionally reinforces the impor-tance of the 'family' (that is women) in providing unpaid care and satisfying the individual needs of children, older people and the disabled. At the same time women are especially affected by cuts in social expenditure, which leads to a policy of rationing individual (female) social rights and abolishing or at least reducing the few existing supports for unpaid care work.

Beyond the division between paid and unpaid work, it may even be useful to take another look, as Glucksmann (1995) has done, at the division of labour between the household economy and the market economy. She introduces the concept of the "total social organisation of labour" which she defines as "a conceptual device to refer to the manner by which all the labour in a particular society is divided up between and allocated to different structures, institutions and activities". This line of questioning opens the way for a fruitful criticism of our theoretical framework, and would no doubt contribute to broadening its basis.

This concept could also be applied to other forms of work that are not included in the sphere of employment, such as informal work, which is more or less widespread depending on the country. Work that is not registered as formal employment and that is thus fully or partially excluded from the formal wage or from taxation, leads to the formation of specific sub-groups with differing degrees of entitlement to social provisions.

Another of our limitations concerns the position of migrants insofar as they are economically active in our societies (Morris, 2002; Geddes, 2003). Since the 1960s, enormous flows of labour force have been imported, and the streams of refugees arriving over the last two decades have merely contributed to the manifest formation of a new under-class. A special group of migrants concerns those with an illegal status: they are sometimes used, sometimes deported, and spheres of informal economy have been developed around them. Not enough is known about the ways in which the existing welfare regimes deal with the effects of the presence of these legal and illegal groups. The question of the relationship, in terms of the law, between social rights and citizenship rights could also be investigated. But given our approach, we need to specifically examine the ways in which differential access to labour markets, hence different relations to wage flows and social rights articulated by employment, construct differences in social rights over societal resources for both ethnic groups and migrant labour.

Social groups defined by rights to resources

Another question to be addressed is whether the focus on the wage as the channel of resource flows offers the possibility to analyse the construction of rights in a broader and more sociologically effective way. Of particular interest is the issue of the institutional forms of the linkages developed in different countries and the possible clusters or patterns of social units they give rise to, given the central focus on rights over resources. In this book the "subsidised worker" has come to the fore as one such new social category: although in principle such workers are not excluded from social protection rights, their limited and conditioned access to the labour market may result in systematically lower entitlements compared to regular workers. This category, however, combines various groups with more or less distinct characteristics, such as the long-term unemployed, chronic psychiatric patients, low-skilled young people, or re-entering women, that are affected to differing degrees by labour market regulations. The identification of these groups would lead us to clarify the question of the relation between social rights and the mode of job distribution according to skills .

The need to develop statistical and empirical studies

The analytical framework proposed here is not yet sufficiently backed up by empirical material. Although we present some comparisons between countries (mostly in Chapter 3), we now need to confront these with statistical data on resource flows and to develop qualitative field studies: these will enable us to expand or modify our framework both with regard to the identification of the spheres in which societal logics are constructed and with regard to the overall architecture of the reasoning developed to examine the links between resources and social rights. This process will entail a re-examination, and probably a modification of the analytical categories used thus far.

III. Research perspectives

Nonetheless, beyond its current limitations and the necessary criticisms it may generate, the analytical framework provides a valuable basis for developing future lines of enquiry. A research project seeking to apply this framework to pension reforms and the growth of subsidised employment in nine European countries is now underway[2]. There are several complementary fields of investigation, however, that can be explored, and we have chosen to present three of these here. They concern three different levels and would permit both to go more deeply into the question of societal spheres, and to test the relevance of approaching the employment-wage-social protection triptych via the analysis of resources and social rights.

Workers' resources and corporate strategies

Differences between countries reflect specific institutional arrangements, but how are these articulated with company strategies concerning employment, the wage and social protection? Given "globalisation", this is an essential level of analysis which could be examined at the European level in a comparison of several multinationals in different countries. The notion of the work-welfare nexus developed in Chapter 2 could provide a basis for a more precise elaboration of comparative hypotheses regarding both the role of social protection expenditures in

---

[2]   "Employees' Resources and Social Rights in Europe" (RESORE). For more information and the website address, see the Introduction to this volume.

the modes of labour cost determination and their influence on job distribution and volume.

Changes in workers' representations

In a completely different, more clearly sociological direction, a comparative study could be undertaken of the changes in workers' representations of their rights over resources, given reform trends. This investigation would concern both the "high-skilled" segment of the workforce whose forms of remuneration are being diversified, and the "less skilled" – or categorised as unskilled by statistical offices – whose social rights are changing in nature. This line of research would address the question of European citizenship together with that of work-related resources, and could bring to light important elements for the construction of a social Europe. The role of the media in the formation of new representations of employment, the wage and social rights could also be investigated.

Problems of comparison at the European level

This third perspective is directed towards European strategies for social scientific and multi-disciplinary research into work and employment. The different chapters in this book have highlighted the multiple interactions between EU and national levels in such areas as labour markets, policy frameworks, the production of industrial relations norms, or their impact on wage hierarchies and consequently social hierarchies. Furthermore, the category of resource regimes proposed in Chapter 3, while particularly pertinent to the analysis of national configurations, also permits to draw out transversal trends. This does not mean losing sight of the national level, for this would be overlooking what Lallement (2003) calls *l'historisme*, that is, embedding the analysis in a past/present relationship. It means the comparison between national spaces must first take account of societal configurations, in order to then take more firmly into account the interactions between the various levels of construction and determination of the problems examined. We thus propose to include the study of national spaces in a more transversal analysis of systems, or regimes in the case of our problematic, which permit to capture more clearly the intersection and the articulation between the different levels that construct and give meaning to a measure, a fiscal reform, the strategies of companies or social actors, statistical categories, and many more. Whether the aim is to produce results concerning a particular country or the European Union, it now seems necessary, at least for the problems that concern us, to find ways to take account of the interweaving of levels, processes and forms across a more global space whose economic, political and social construction is impacting ever more directly on the daily lives of its populations.

These suggestions are far from exhaustive, but they can be useful for the debate between the actors involved in the construction of Europe.

IV. Continuing the debate in Europe

Europe is our given horizon of analysis. It is the social, cultural, political and legal sphere within we conduct our comparisons. Its political architecture, the citizenship arising from work, and the combination between full employment, market and social protection are at the heart of the questions launched in this book.

A new societal configuration

The EU is thus one of the social actors influencing the linkages between resources and rights. It sometimes appears as a primary actor and at other times as a background player, depending on the focus of the analysis and the evolution of the distribution of competencies. It is undeniable that European legislation and regulation has become more dominant in the last two decades. But at the same time each country has developed its own course in relation to these measures: histories and institutions do not suddenly disappear when new arrangements are established, for they have their own continuity or weight over time. Even if, as we have shown, European institutions have considerable weight in the decisions that are made, wage conflict takes specific forms in the oppositions between the various European bodies, and other collective actors intervene. It is important to identify these actors in order to highlight the interaction between their respective powers to influence decisions on resources and social rights at different levels. This field still needs to be investigated, but the question of the distribution of competencies and the scope for political action opens new perspectives for debate.

Work and social citizenship

It is important to note that since the summits of 1994 (Essen) and 1997 (Luxembourg), the EU member states have been encouraged to strive for full employment and to reduce dependency on provisions and benefits. This focus also appeared indirectly in the agreement to impose budgetary discipline: national deficits were seen as resulting from over-generous welfare regimes. The goal of full employment is thus formulated in terms of the financial sustainability of welfare regimes, and now, in addition to the unemployed, is targeted at young people, women and older people. In this context it is important to examine the different paths chosen for national activation policies and to relate these to the existing systems of wage bargaining and types of labour market policies. Our analysis of rights over resources has focussed on a comparison between countries and on the influence of European measures on the construction of the institution of the wage. But a study of the dynamics at work in the interplay between the nation states and the EU may help to highlight the different forms of social citizenship that have been constructed through the specific arrangements and field forces existing within the nation states. Analysing the dynamics in this way may shed more light on the intended and unintended consequences of European regulations and permit a better evaluation of perspectives for improving the social dimension of Europe.

The EU and employment

The dominant discourse on employment as the key tool for both economic growth and social cohesion has contradictory implications in the context of a competitive market. On the one hand, increasing the number of persons employed could be favourable for both workers and living standards. But, on the other hand, employment policies frequently seek to promote job growth through the reduction of labour costs – and thus lead to a reduction of wages and social contributions. This situation is not new but seems to have taken other forms with the individualisation of wages, which implies that wages and contributions are more vulnerable to the private regulation of social protection. In following this path, the EU is promoting a social model which seeks to transform the tension between collective rights and resources on the one hand and the optimalisation of economic growth on the other, and to tip the balance in favour of the latter. However, the point is not to analyse the dominant developments as "just going in one direction" but to see what kinds of dynamics and contradictions they produce. Similarly, it is important to look at how the EU has intervened in the employment relation by regulating working time, by providing for worker mobility without loss of social rights or by stipulating equal treatment for men and women. Such measures acknowledge the necessity for a greater degree of regulation than a strict neo-liberal agenda would prescribe. At the same time it is essential to look into the precise field of application of these regulations in order to analyse what contradictory effects they may have and for whom.

Opening out the debate on social rights over societal resources

But of course, neither Europe nor the nation states within it (increasing in number), are insulated from global changes in technologies, markets, demographics, and international divisions of labour. The whole thrust of our approach is to bring to the fore the dynamic relations between economic change as reflected through the wage and employment, and social rights. We need to look towards new ways of understanding societal resources and their development, new vehicles for expanding social rights, and new ways of political understanding and mobilisation. It might seem strange that we see taxation, social insurance, pension systems, as so central to this major political question. But basing the big political questions concerning the nature of social rights over societal resources on the nitty-gritty economic and financial institutions of our contemporary societies, enables us to think afresh at modalities by which social rights are constructed, and the real dynamics of change. Too often, piecemeal changes, or a multitude of disparate policy reforms, obscure the big picture, and fragment the significant issues. The comparative and cooperative way of developing these questions is a way forward to thinking more systemically both about how societal resources are constituted and how rights over them are constructed.

References

Geddes, A. (2003), *The Politics of Migration and Immigration in Europe*, London, Sage.

Glucksmann, M. (1995), "Gender and the 'Total Social Organization of Labour'", *Gender, Work and Organisation*, 2:2, pp. 63-75

Lallement, M. and Spurk, J. (eds.) (2003), *Stratégies de la comparaison internationale*, Éditions du CNRS, Paris, France.

Mairhuber, I. (1998), "The gendered family dimensions of the Italian welfare state", paper written for the workshop *Family and Family Policies in Southern Europe*, Università degli studi di Torino, November 20-21.

Morris, L. (2002), *Managing Migration: Civic Stratification and Migrants' Rights*, London, New York, Routledge.

Contributors

Roland Atzmüller

Researcher in political sciences, *Forschungs und Beratungstelle Arbeitswelt* – FORBA Institute, Vienna, Austria. He is currently finishing his Ph.D on his main area of interest, the development of states, industrial relations and politics. In 1998 and 1999, he was a graduate student and researcher at the University of Manchester Institute for Science and Technology (UMIST) and worked with the *Centre for Research in Innovation and Competition*. He joined the "Social Construction of Employment" network in 1999.

Bernadette Clasquin

Sociologist, researcher in the team *Emploi et Politiques Sociales – Groupe de Recherche sur l'Éducation et l'Emploi, EPS/GREE – CNRS*, Université Nancy 2, France. She works on industrial relations, wage and social protection, and has been co-coordinator of the network since 1997.

Gaël Coron

Political scientist, Ph.D student in sociology, member of the *EPS/GREE-CNRS*, Université Nancy 2, France. His research interest concerns the European Community legal framework and jurisprudence on social protection issues. He joined the network in 2001.

Anne Dufresne

Socio-economist, researcher in European studies and industrial relations at the *Observatoire Social Européen*, Brussels, Belgium. She is preparing her Ph.D jointly at the Université de Paris X-Nanterre, France, and Université Libre de Bruxelles (ULB), where she is member of the *Groupe de Recherche sur les Acteurs Institutionnels et leurs Discours* (GRAID). She works on macro-economic issues related to EMU, European social dialogue and collective bargaining coordination (at cross-sectoral and sectoral level). She joined the network in 2001.

Enrico Fravega

Sociologist, contract researcher, *Dipartimento di Scienze Anthropologiche* (DiSa), Università di Genova, Italy. He works on employment and welfare, immigration, cultural processes and methodology. He joined the network in 1999.

Bernard Friot

Economist and sociologist, Professor of Sociology at the University of Paris X-Nanterre, France, member of the *Travail et Mobilités*-CNRS research group. Formerly at EPS/GREE – CNRS, Université Nancy 2, and the network's *scientist in charge* since 1997. Special fields: employment, the wage and social protection.

Corinne Gobin

Researcher in political science, Fonds National de la Recherche Scientifique, Université Libre de Bruxelles (ULB), Belgium. She is co-director of the *Groupe de Recherche sur les Acteurs Institutionnels et leurs Discours* (GRAID) at the ULB Institute of Sociology. She works on EU political power issues and especially on the history of European Trade Unionism, using in particular discourse analyses. She joined the network in 2001.

Willibrord de Graaf

Psychologist and sociologist, senior teacher and senior researcher at the Department of General Social Science, Utrecht University, the Netherlands. His research interests deal with youth unemployment, drug addiction, homelessness, and the constitution of identity in changing social developments. He is a member of the *Dynamics of Inclusion and Exclusion* group, and has been involved in the network since 2000.

Mark Harvey

Political economist, senior researcher fellow at the ESRC *Centre for Research in Innovation and Competition* (CRIC), University of Manchester, United Kingdom. His research work is concerned with Instituted Economic Process, comparative research in markets, institutions, regulatory systems and employment relations. He joined the network in 1998.

Robert Maier

Psychologist and sociologist, Professor, Department of General Social Science, Utrecht University, the Netherlands, and member of the group *Dynamics of Inclusion and Exclusion.* Research fields: social theory of debate and forms of exclusion (citizenship, education), in a European framework. He joined the network in 2000.

Nathalie Moncel

Labour economist, has just started working at the *Centre d'Études de l'Emploi* (CEE) Noisy-le-Grand, France. She spent two years as Marie Curie research fellow at the *CRIC*, University of Manchester, and then at the *European Work and Employment research Centre* (EWERC), Manchester School of Management (UMIST), Britain, after obtaining her Ph.D at EPS/GREE – CNRS, Université Nancy 2. She studies the relation between employment and social protection and has been network co-coordinator since 1997.

Luca Queirolo Palmas

Sociologist, researcher, *Dipartimento di Scienze Anthropologiche* (DiSa), Università di Genova, Italy. In 1996, he had a fellowship at EPS/GREE – CNRS. His research interests are labour and social protection transformations, immigration, education and inequalities. He joined the network in 1997, firstly as a member of the *Istituto di Recerche Economiche e Sociali (IRES)*, Torino, Italy, and then as a member of DiSa.

Coralie Perez

Labour economist, researcher at the *Centre d'Études et de Recherche sur les Qualifications* (Céreq), France. Her research interests are in labour economics and international comparisons; and skills and labour markets in the advanced countries. Previously at EPS/GREE – CNRS, she participated in the network from 1997 to 2001.

Margarida Ruivo

Economist, researcher, *Centro de Estudos de Economia Industrial, do Trabalho e da Empresa* (CETE), and lecturer, Faculty of Economics, Porto, Portugal. Her research interests are labour economics, part-time work, working time and gender and local approaches to employment. She joined the network in 1997.

Merle Shore

Translator (French to English). She has a Ph.D in English from the University of Paris VII, and has specialised in translating social science research. She has been working with the network since 2002 and participated in the preparatory workshops for the present book.

Joan Miquel Verd Pericas

Lecturer in sociology, Universitat Autónoma of Barcelona, Spain. member of the *Grup d'estudis Sociológics sobre la Vida Quotidiana i el Treball* (QUIT). His special fields of research are the analysis of discourse and practice in the field of employment and training and social network analysis. He worked with the EPS/GREE – CNRS, Nancy, in 2001 while preparing his Ph.D. He joined the network in 1997.

"Work & Society"

The series "Work & Society" analyses the development of employment and social policies, as well as the strategies of the different social actors, both at national and European levels. It puts forward a multi-disciplinary approach – political, sociological, economic, legal and historical – in a bid for dialogue and complementarity.
The series is not confined to the social field *stricto sensu*, but also aims to illustrate the indirect social impacts of economic and monetary policies. It endeavours to clarify social developments, from a comparative and a historical perspective, thus portraying the process of convergence and divergence in the diverse national societal contexts. The manner in which European integration impacts on employment and social policies constitutes the backbone of the analyses.

Series Editor: Philippe POCHET, Director of the Observatoire Social Européen (Brussels) and Digest Editor of the Journal of European Social Policy.

Series Titles

N° 43– *Wage and Welfare. New Perspectives on Employment and Social Rights in Europe*, Bernadette CLASQUIN, Nathalie MONCEL, Mark HARVEY & Bernard FRIOT (eds.) (2004), 208 p., ISBN 90-5201-214-8

N° 42– *Job Insecurity and Union Membership. European Unions in the Wake of Flexible Production* (provisional title), Magnus SVERKE (ed.) (forthcoming), ISBN 90-5201-202-4

N° 41– *L'aide au conditionnel. La contrepartie dans les mesures envers les personnes sans emploi en Europe et en Amérique du Nord*, Pascale DUFOUR, Gérard BOISMENU & Alain NOËL (2003) en coéd. avec les PUM, 248 p., ISBN 90-5201-198-2

N°40– *Protection sociale et fédéralisme*, Bruno THÉRET (2002) en coéd. avec les PUM, 2002, 495 p., ISBN 90-5201-107-9.

No.39– *The Impact of EU Law on Health Care Systems*, Martin MCKEE, Elias MOSSIALOS & Rita BAETEN (eds.) (2002, 2nd printing 2003), 314 p., ISBN 90-5201-106-0.

No.38– *EU Law and the Social Character of Health Care*, Elias MOSSIALOS & Martin MCKEE (2002, 2nd printing 2004), 259 p., ISBN 90-5201-110-9.

No.37– *Wage Policy in the Eurozone*, Philippe POCHET (ed.), Observatoire social européen, 2002, 286 p., ISBN 90-5201-101-X.

N°36– *Politique salariale dans la zone euro*, Philippe POCHET (dir.), Observatoire social européen, 2002, 308 p., ISBN 90-5201-100-1.

No.35– *Regulating Health and Safety Management in the European Union. A Study of the Dynamics of Change*, David WALTERS (ed.), SALTSA, 2002, 346 p., ISBN 90-5201-998-3.

No.34– *Building Social Europe through the Open Method of Co-ordination*, Caroline DE LA PORTE & Philippe POCHET (eds.), SALTSA – Observatoire social européen, 2002, 311 p., ISBN 90-5201-984-3.

N°33– *Des marchés du travail équitables ?*, Christian BESSY, François EYMARD-DUVERNAY, Guillemette DE LARQUIER & Emmanuelle MARCHAL (dir.), Centre d'Études de l'Emploi, 2001, 308 p., ISBN 90-5201-960-6.

No.32– *Trade Unions in Europe: Meeting the Challenge*, Deborah FOSTER & Peter SCOTT (eds.), 2003, 200 p., ISBN 90-5201-959-2.

No.31– *Health and Safety in Small Enterprises. European Strategies for Managing Improvement*, David WALTERS, SALTSA, 2001, 404 p., ISBN 90-5201-952-5.

No.30– *Europe – One Labour Market?*, Lars MAGNUSSON & Jan OTTOSSON (eds.), SALTSA, 2002, 306 p., ISBN 90-5201-949-5.

No.29– *From the Werner Plan to the EMU. In Search of a Political Economy for Europe*, Lars MAGNUSSON & Bo STRÅTH (eds.), SALTSA, 2001, 526 p., ISBN 90-5201-948-7.

N°28– *Discriminations et marché du travail. Liberté et égalité dans les rapports d'emploi*, Olivier DE SCHUTTER, 2001, 234 p., ISBN 90-5201-941-X.

No.27– *At Your Service? Comparative Perspectives on Employment and Labour Relations in the European Private Sector Services*, Jon Erik DØLVIK (ed.), SALTSA, 2001, 556 p., ISBN 90-5201-940-1.

N°26– *La nouvelle dynamique des pactes sociaux*, Giuseppe FAJERTAG & Philippe POCHET (dir.), Observatoire social européen – European Trade Union Institute, 2001, 436 p., ISBN 90-5201-927-4.

No.25– *After Full Employment. European Discourses on Work and Flexibility*, Bo STRÅTH (ed.), 2000, 302 p., ISBN 90-5201-925-8.

N°24– *L'Europe syndicale au quotidien. La représentation des salariés dans les entreprises en France, Allemagne, Grande-Bretagne et Italie*, Christian DUFOUR et Adelheid HEGE, IRES, 2002, 256 p., ISBN 90-5201-918-5.

N°23– *Union monétaire et négociations collectives en Europe*, Philippe POCHET (ed.), SALTSA – Observatoire social européen, 1999, 284 p., ISBN 90-5201-916-9.

No.22– *Monetary Union and Collective Bargaining in Europe*, Philippe POCHET (ed.), SALTSA – Observatoire social européen, 1999, 284 p., ISBN 90-5201-915-0.

No.21– *The Regulation of Working Time in the European Union (Gender Approach) – La réglementation du temps de travail en Europe (Perspective selon le genre)*, Yota KRAVARITOU (ed.), European University Institute, 1999, 504 p., ISBN 90-5201-903-7.

N°20– *Wégimont ou le château des relations humaines. Une expérience de formation psychosociologique à la gestion*, Marcel BOLLE DE BAL, 1998, 353 p., ISBN 90-5201-811-1.

P.I.E.-Peter Lang – The website

Discover the general website of the Peter Lang publishing group:

www.peterlang.net

You will find

- an online bookshop of currently about 21,000 titles from the entire publishing group, which allows quick and easy ordering
- all books published since 1992
- an overview of our journals and series
- contact forms for new authors and customers
- information about the activities of each publishing house

Come and browse! We look forward to your visit!